The Education of Laura Bridgman

Ernest Freeberg

The Education of
Laura Bridgman

*First Deaf and Blind Person
to Learn Language*

Harvard University Press
Cambridge, Massachusetts, and London, England · 2001

Copyright © 2001 by the President and Fellows of Harvard College
All rights reserved
Printed in the United States of America

Library of Congress Cataloging-in-Publication Data

Freeberg, Ernest.
  The education of Laura Bridgman : first deaf and blind person to learn
language / Ernest Freeberg.
      p. cm.
Includes bibliographical references and index.
ISBN 0-674-00589-9
    1. Bridgman, Laura Dewey, 1829–1889.   2. Blind-deaf women—United
States—Biography.   3. Blind-deaf women—Education—United States.
I. Title.

HV1624.B7 F74 2001
362.4'1'092—dc21   00-054219
[B]

Contents

To Lauren

The Education of Laura Bridgman

1. Samuel Gridley Howe's education of Laura Bridgman was considered by many of his peers to be one of the greatest humanitarian acts of the nineteenth century. *(Courtesy of Perkins School for the Blind, Watertown, Massachusetts)*

Introduction

In 1851 a "Great Exhibition" was held in London. There, under the dome of the Crystal Palace, each nation displayed its finest contributions to nineteenth-century civilization. Many Americans were mortified to learn, however, that their own offerings to this pageant were a dismal failure. The American exhibit, which included a model of Niagara Falls, some false teeth, and a large collection of pasteboard eagles, had "fallen so far short of expectation as to excite ridicule." Some citizens of the young republic were stung by this blow to the nation's self-esteem.[1]

The editor of the *Boston Evening Transcript* offered a solution. There was one thing his countrymen could send to London which was sure to attract an even larger crowd than the one lining up for a peek at the "Great Diamond"—one product of "American art" which would surpass "the looms of England, the delicate fabrics of France, and all the products of Germany." This great accomplishment of American culture was Laura Bridgman, a humble young woman from a farming village in New Hampshire. In 1837, when Laura was seven years old, she had entered Boston's Perkins Institution for the Blind. There, under the guidance of the institution's director, Dr. Samuel Gridley Howe, she had become the first deaf and blind person ever to learn to communicate through language.[2]

No European treasure, this editor proclaimed, could teach the exhibition's visitors "a higher or better lesson of humanity" than Laura Bridgman. America might not be able to compete with its Old World ancestors in a "contest of show and parade," but the republic had its own new and priceless "art" to offer the world, the transformative power of Christian philanthropy and enlightened democratic education. Laura Bridgman was a perfect symbol of her society's commitment to educate and respect *all* of its members, no matter how humble their station.[3]

In the fourteen years between Laura's first words and the opening of London's Great Exhibition, the story of her accomplishment had been retold countless times, in newspapers, literary and theological journals, children's books, and most often in writings and speeches by Dr. Howe him-self. Fascinated by this tale of intellectual resurrection, tourists flocked to the Perkins school to take a look for themselves. Each Saturday hundreds jammed into the school's exhibition hall to see Laura read, write, and talk with a manual alphabet. Many clamored for a souvenir—an autograph or a piece of knitting—made by Laura's own hand. By mid-century, Howe boasted that his student had become one of the most famous women in the world, second only to Queen Victoria.

A century and a half after Laura signed her first words, we can still share in the curiosity which so many nineteenth-century Americans felt when they first heard her story. For us, no less than for them, the thought of ex-periencing such a double handicap evokes mingled emotions of dread, sympathy, and fascination. Just as they had done for her contemporaries, Laura's handicaps force us to reflect about what life might be like sealed off from all sight and sound. Perhaps even more inconceivable, Laura's early years make us wonder about what human consciousness could be like without language.

Contemplating the depth of Laura's predicament, we can appreciate the joy that so many antebellum Americans felt when Howe announced that the isolation experienced by the deaf and blind could, in large measure, be overcome. Though the story of Helen Keller has made this discovery com-monplace today, we may still recover some of the wonder felt by Laura's peers when they first learned that a person whose sensory experience of the world was so radically different from their own was still fully human, that her mind could be enlivened and her isolation conquered by the mys-terious power of language.

Though we share this common ground of interest and sympathy with our nineteenth-century predecessors, still this does not seem a sufficient explanation for the intense interest which her case aroused in the 1830s and 40s—the scientific and theological debates, the throngs of tourists, and the countless newspaper and magazine accounts. Why were these early Victorians, on both sides of the Atlantic, so fascinated, so moved by her story? What did her breakthrough into language, and her subsequent edu-cation, *mean* to them? This book is an attempt to answer that question by showing how relevant Howe's famous experiment with Laura Bridg-man was to the wider theological, intellectual, and social controversies of their day.

One plausible explanation for the public's fascination with Laura Bridg-man might simply be that the child was a curiosity, a freak of nature who captured the attention of a society that was hungry for spectacle. Her story did coincide with a seminal period in the development of American popular culture, a time when entrepreneurs like P.T. Barnum were first learning how to make money by satisfying the public's demand for novelty. As urban centers grew in the antebellum period, more middle- and working-class Americans enjoyed the financial means and the leisure time to read popular scientific magazines, attend lectures, visit museums, and buy tickets to public exhibitions. Inspired by democratic ideals and an expanding educational system, many were ready to spend money to satisfy their curiosity—especially when this could be justified as a respectable and edifying experience. From this perspective, the public's fascination with Laura Bridgman might well be classified with their desire to see Barnum's exotic but "scientific" curiosities, such as Tom Thumb and the FeeJee mermaid.

Further evidence for this view might be drawn from Howe's role as an energetic publicist of his own work with Laura Bridgman. No less than Barnum, Howe mastered the art of manipulating the public's interest in her story, capitalizing on their concern in order to advance both his career and his institution. Recognizing that Howe was an ambitious man who built a career on his own kindness helps us to understand what motivated him to attempt to become the first person to ever successfully teach a deaf-blind person. But such an explanation is ultimately insufficient. For Howe, Laura Bridgman was much more than a celebrity to be exploited. He was deeply concerned about her welfare and came to look upon her as his own adopted daughter. As we shall see, Howe learned to play a complex and sometimes contradictory role as both a publicist and a humanitarian.

Just as important as Howe's concern for the child's welfare was his conviction that her double handicap provided him with an unprecedented chance to conduct a profound psychological "experiment." As he explained to his readers around the world, Laura's calamitous state of sensory deprivation had sealed her off from almost all environmental influence. Whatever thoughts and feelings came out of her once she began to communicate, he reasoned, could only be understood as an expression of *pure* human nature. In short, he believed that Laura's deafness and blindness had not made her a bizarre exception to the human condition but rather had transformed her into a prototype, an example of the innate potential of all children.

From this perspective, Howe's interest in Laura Bridgman finds precedent in a series of similar experiments with handicapped children, most notably the work done by the French educator Jean-Marc Itard with Victor, the "Wild Boy of Averyron." In 1800 Victor was captured in the woods near a village in southern France. Estimated to be about twelve years old, the boy was found naked and mute, apparently having lived as a "savage" in the woods for many years, presumably after being abandoned by his parents. Mingling humanitarian compassion with scientific ambition, Itard seized this opportunity to explore what he took to be a rare example of "natural man," a person who had grown almost to adulthood with a mind untouched by civilization. Itard hoped that, by teaching Victor to communicate, he would reveal new insights into the origin of language and the relative importance of nature and culture in human development. Though Victor clearly benefited from his education and humane treatment, he never learned to speak or write, and Itard eventually abandoned the project to pursue the education of the deaf. Though inconclusive, his experiment with the "wild boy" was widely discussed and admired.[4]

Other eighteenth- and nineteenth-century intellectuals shared Itard's fascination with those unusual cases when the human mind seemed in some way "broken." Just as Newton had discovered the nature of light only by "breaking" it into its component parts with a prism, those searching for a scientific understanding of human nature hoped that the study of people with damaged nervous systems might offer a chance to analyze processes of the human brain that were too fast and subtle to be observed in "normal" people. In Howe's day, the deaf, the blind, and other "wild" children all became the subject of intense scrutiny and lively debate.

As a result, the scientific community was fully prepared to accept Howe's claim that, by observing the gradual development of a deaf-blind child's mind, he might glean insights into the fundamental forces that shape human nature. Intellectuals on both sides of the Atlantic were eager to peer over Howe's shoulder as his experiment with Laura progressed, joining him in the search for answers to age-old questions about the role that the senses play in the formation of the human mind.

Historians of antebellum reform have often noted that liberal reformers such as Howe were inspired by an "optimistic" or "romantic" theory of human nature, a generalization that obscures the complexity of the reformers' ideas on the subject. As Howe's investigation into Laura Bridgman's mind and soul reveals, "human nature" was not a single, neatly packaged concept in the antebellum period but a complex set of interrelated questions about the nature and origin of language, the relationship between mind and body, the meaning of gender differences, the source of conscience, and the ultimate reliability of religious knowledge. Searching for answers to these questions, Howe drew on traditional philosophical and theological concepts, but also from new ideas generated by the fledgling sciences of psychology, linguistics, sociology, and heredity.

At a time when these human sciences were increasingly respected but still quite naive in their methods, many accepted Howe's claim to be a fair and dispassionate observer of Laura's case. But his science was never far removed from his social goals. Howe was a Unitarian and a Conscience Whig, an active supporter of a wide array of liberal causes, including Horace Mann's common school reforms, Dorothea Dix's campaign to build asylums for the insane, and efforts to improve the criminal justice system by creating new penitentiaries. Howe's interpretation of Laura Bridgman, then, must be understood not as an objective psychological experiment but as an attempt to vindicate ideas about human development, education, and discipline which were at the foundation of the liberals' program of social reform.

Howe was particularly eager to use Laura's story as a way to combat orthodox Calvinism and to help overturn the traditional classroom practices of rigid order and rote learning which he felt were a natural outgrowth of Calvin's pessimistic view of human nature. Howe turned Laura's education into a showcase of "moral discipline," a new form of correction that liberal reformers were trying to establish in penitentiaries and public schools. These quite public attacks on Calvinism, along with some controversial speculations about Laura's religious intuitions, outraged many orthodox leaders, igniting very public struggle over the meaning of Howe's experiment and the fate of Laura Bridgman's soul.

It is natural to wonder what Laura Bridgman thought of this controversy about the true meaning of her experience. Surprisingly, she was never asked. Both Howe and his critics assumed that she could never understand the issues involved and would only be shocked and confused to learn that so many people were scrutinizing her every word and deed. Though such a view seems paternalistic in the worst sense of the word, judging from Laura's writings later in her life, this assumption seems to have been correct. She did become remarkably fluent, developing a wide range of friendships and maintaining a large correspondence. But she never developed the ability to think very deeply or abstractly. It seems unlikely that she would have been able to reflect on the philosophical implications of her own sensory deprivation or join in the complex theological debate between Howe and his Calvinist adversaries.

Because Laura never entered into this discussion, it would be possible to write a history of her education that was not really about her at all, but only explored the way she was used by others, like a pawn on a cultural battlefield that she never even knew existed. Undeniably, the deaf and blind girl who appeared in Howe's scientific reports and Charles Dickens's travelogue and in dozens of scientific reports and children's morality tales was not an historical being, a flesh and blood child, but a literary artifact.

Yet the "real" Laura Bridgman did play a central role in the outcome of Howe's experiment. For a time, Howe enjoyed complete power to interpret Laura's story for the public. Likewise, he had an enormous and lasting influence on her personality. To a great extent, he succeeded in molding his student into the kind of person he expected her to be. But in the end Laura emerged with a will of her own, and psychological needs of her own, which overpowered Howe's effort to shape her into the incarnation of his ideals. Ultimately, it was not the orthodox conservatives' criticism but Laura Bridgman's free will—one might even say her "perversity"—which destroyed Howe's famous experiment.

After his original ideas about human nature were shattered by his inability to mold Laura as he wished, Howe cast about for a new theory. His disillusionment with Laura ultimately led him to conclude that her mind and soul had been damaged when her senses had been destroyed. By the 1850s, as Laura emerged into adulthood, her education complete, Howe arrived at a new paradigm. Human character, he announced, was determined by "bodily organization." Without abandoning his faith in the value of education, he urged reformers to take the long-range view, seeking gradual social progress through attention to the natural laws of health and the control of heredity. In this way, Howe's experience with Laura Bridgman—his grand hopes and his subsequent disillusionment—reflects a broader transition in nineteenth-century reformers' ideas about human nature, from romantic optimism toward biological determinism.

Perhaps it was this disillusionment which led Howe to veto the *Evening Transcript* editor's suggestion to send Laura to London in 1851, to shore up the American exhibit in the Crystal Palace. Howe had convinced many around the world that Laura Bridgman represented one of the most profound psychological discoveries of the nineteenth century. Yet, as she reached adulthood, he had become deeply ambivalent about what his own experiment had revealed about human nature.

Chapter 1

In Quest of His Prize

In 1831, as New England entered its period of romantic flowering, Samuel Gridley Howe struck many Bostonians as their city's very own Byronic hero. Howe had just returned from seven years in the fabled land of Greece, where he had answered a call from his favorite poet Lord Byron to enlisted in the cause of the Greek Revolution. For over four centuries Greece had been controlled by the Ottoman Empire. When Greek patriots declared independence from their Turkish rulers in 1821, many Anglo-American intellectuals understood the conflict as an epic struggle between freedom and tyranny, Christianity and the Sultan's "strange and barbarous faith." Byron beckoned other young romantics to follow him to this "land of honourable death."[1]

Americans responded enthusiastically to what Thomas Jefferson called the "holy cause" of the Greeks. In many communities in the Northeast, "Philhellene" societies were formed, raising donations of arms, money, and supplies for the rebels. Edward Everett, the editor of the *North American Review*, praised these efforts, describing them as a chance for Western Christendom to repay its debt to those people "whose ancestors fill so important a place in the history of the world and of the human mind." In 1823 Everett urged that even more might be done, suggesting that some young American men—"in their private capacity"—should volunteer for this "glorious work of emancipation."[2]

Samuel Gridley Howe, twenty-three years old, was one of only a handful of Americans willing to risk his life for the cause. Howe had just graduated from Harvard's medical school in 1824 and had already decided that a conventional medical practice in Boston could never give full scope to his ambitions or his appetite for adventure. Over the objections of his father, he sailed for Greece, where he spent seven years as a commissioned surgeon in the patriots' bedraggled army. There he shared in the hardships of the soldiers' life, experiencing "the sharp gnawing of *real* hunger," going for months "without eating other flesh than mountain snails and roasted wasps."[3]

Howe, like Byron, was disillusioned by the Greeks at close range, finding them to be morally depraved, "ignorant, selfish, & thievish." And, in the eyes of this rational Boston Unitarian, their ancient peasant religion was no better than idolatry. Though their land was considered the ancestral cradle of democracy, Howe concluded that democratic self-government for the Greeks was out of the question. By 1827 they had succeeded in driving the Turks from their country, but only one out of twenty Greek men was literate, and, in Howe's estimation, their entire culture had been misshapen by centuries of Islamic tyranny.[4]

Yet Howe's idealism was only dampened, not extinguished, by this first-hand experience of brutality, selfishness, and incompetence perpetrated by both sides in the conflict. Finding some admirable traits in the Greek people, he concluded that their national character was not innately and hopelessly corrupt. Once the bad influence of Turkish rule was removed, he reasoned, the Greeks could be trained in those moral virtues which were a prerequisite for republican government. In an early rehearsal of the ideals that he would espouse for the rest of his life, Howe concluded that the firm hand of educational reform was a necessary first step before the people could be trusted to govern themselves wisely.[5]

Turning his energies from medical aid to relief work, Howe developed a plan to teach those democratic virtues, a grand scheme born out of the Greeks' desperate need and the young New Englander's boundless self-confidence. As the war neared conclusion, Howe returned briefly to the United States to raise funds and supplies for the thousands of Greeks who had lost their homes during the conflict. Reasoning that a simple handout would undermine their initiative, he searched for a way to use relief aid that would cultivate habits of responsibility, hard work, and cooperation. To this end, he organized refugees in Corinth into a massive public works project. In a grand gesture symbolic of Howe's exuberant Yankee Protestantism, he supervised seven hundred Greeks in the excavation of massive stone blocks from a ruined "Temple of Venus," converting the ancient pagan shrine into a stone wharf that restored the local harbor to usefulness. He then created an agricultural colony which he alternately called Colombia and Washingtonia, a community he presided over as "governor, legislator, clerk, constable, & everything but patriarch." In recognition of Howe's steadfast service to his nation's cause, the King of Greece awarded him the honorary title of Chevalier of the Order of St. Savior.[6]

In 1831 Howe returned to his native Boston, where his friends kept the memory of his Greek exploits alive by nicknaming him "Chev." At the age of thirty he was a local celebrity, the returning hero of an exotic war, and by many accounts "the handsomest man" in Boston. As one woman later

2. Howe in his early thirties, painted by Jane Stuart, daughter of Gilbert Stuart. *(Courtesy of Perkins School for the Blind, Watertown, Massachusetts)*

recalled, when he "rode down Beacon Street on his black horse, with the crimson embroidered saddle-cloth, all the girls ran to their windows to look after him." Friends assured him that he could quickly convert his local notoriety into a lucrative medical practice. But in a letter to a friend, Howe declared that "the glare of gold has no charms for me, and if I find that I cannot in this country fill a more useful sphere than getting a large practice and making a large fortune, why, futurity is to me a blank without charm." The young hero was unwilling merely to bask in the glow of past deeds and unable to accept the prospect that his future held a calling less adventuresome and less worthy of the public's "gratitude and affection."[7]

As Howe's biographer Dr. Harold Schwartz has pointed out, his great ambitions in this period were balanced by strong self-doubts. "This country," Howe confided to his journal, "is too well supplied with men of talent and experience and ambition for those of my moderate pretentions [sic] and mediocratic [sic] talents, to hope to make much of a figure or do much good." Without success, he looked for work as the editor of a Whig journal in New York, then as the director of a "negro colony" in Liberia. He supported himself by dabbling in journalism but worried that, with the meager income that writing afforded him, his prospects for marriage were grim. "Not that I am old physically," he told a friend, "but I feel old and time-worn within."[8]

But Howe's self-doubts were quickly dispelled when a group of philanthropists asked him to accept the directorship of Boston's new asylum for the blind, the first of its kind in America.[9] In 1829 the Massachusetts legislature had granted a committee of concerned citizens a charter for the school and had promised to pay the tuition of thirty students. However, for the next two years the project languished. According to a story that may be only Howe family legend, Dr. John Fisher, the school's strongest advocate, was walking down Boylston Street one day in 1831 with two of the school's other trustees, discussing ways to revive their plans. By chance they ran into Fisher's old Harvard classmate Samuel Gridley Howe. "Here is Howe!" Fisher told his companions, "the very man we have been looking for all this time." In a process which one historian has described as "something very much like a conversion experience," Howe immediately accepted the challenge and entered upon a new life as a committed reformer. Undaunted by the fact that he was now the head of an institution that lacked a building, students, teachers and secure funds, he set sail for Europe in order to spend several months observing the latest innovations in education for the blind.[10]

At that time the Old World was at least fifty years ahead of the New in the development of educational facilities for the blind. Europe's interest in the subject may be traced back to the speculations on blindness produced by the philosophes of the French Enlightenment. In a widely read essay entitled *Letter on the Blind,* Diderot profiled the remarkable accomplishments of several blind contemporaries, including Nicholas Saunderson, the Cambridge mathematician and philosopher. Diderot was particularly fascinated by the insights which the experience of blindness might provide into Locke's sensationalist theory of mind. He urged philosophers to explore the psychological experience of blindness as a way of finally resolving "the difficulties which make the theory of vision and of the senses so intricate and so confused."[11]

Thirty-five years later, Diderot's essay inspired another Frenchman, Valentin de Haüy, to combine philosophical interest in blindness with more humanitarian concern. Like Diderot, Haüy was impressed by the remarkable accomplishments of a few blind citizens. But Haüy was also appalled by the degrading beggary to which so many of the rest were reduced. In 1784 he founded The National Institution for Young Blind Children in Paris, the first such institution in the world. Hoping his students could learn to earn a more dignified livelihood, Haüy's school combined academic and vocational training, the latter organized in craft workshops. He placed particular emphasis on the cultivation of musical talent, since a number of blind people had distinguished themselves in that field in the past. Haüy also began the first efforts to develop a system for teaching reading and writing to the blind, through raised letters.[12]

Since that time, most European countries had followed Haüy's lead. England's School for the Indigent Blind was founded in Liverpool in 1791. The Scots followed soon after, and by 1820 there were similar institutions, of varying size and quality, from Dublin to St. Petersburg. Howe's tour of European institutions concentrated on those in the British Isles, Paris, and Germany. He returned to America convinced that his unbiased mind and "native ingenuity" would allow him to easily surpass the Old World's efforts. American schools for the blind, he reported that year in the *North American Review,* should "avoid the dangerous error of copying every thing from the European schools."[13]

Howe felt that, out of an illiberal respect for tradition, European schools had improved little since the days of the "benevolent and enthusiastic Haüy." Experimenting with ways to create more suitable teaching materials for the blind, Howe soon developed a cheaper and more effective method of producing the embossed maps used to teach geography. And, perhaps dearest to his heart, he created a new "Boston" or "Howe" style of raised-letter printing that accelerated the printing process while reducing the cost and bulk of books for the blind.[14]

But Howe's criticisms of Old World institutions and his hopes for American improvement went far deeper. He was disturbed to learn that, even in the best European schools, fewer than one in twenty graduates were "enabled to gain their own livelihood." Upon graduation, the rest either returned to the streets as beggars or, in the more progressive cities, became lifelong residents in the newly created asylums for the indigent. In either case, thought Howe, they suffered a fate worse than blindness itself—

the humiliation of dependence. In Europe, Howe charged, the blind were "not taught to rely with confidence upon their own resources, to believe themselves possessed of the means of filling useful and active spheres in society." Instead, they were treated as "mere objects of pity," an attitude which became a self-fulfilling prophecy.[15]

In the first of dozens of public statements on the problems of the physically handicapped, Howe sounded a theme he would return to many times throughout his life. Society, he argued, is bound by a "sacred and fundamental law" to help those who cannot provide for themselves. But, as his efforts to found a colony in Greece had shown, the only truly benevolent form of assistance is that which allows the afflicted ultimately to escape dependency through the application of their own talents. Too often, Howe warned, good intentions were misguided: "the hand of charity has wounded, while it soothed the sufferer." An effective reform effort, he thought, must never stigmatize its recipients as members of a distinct and dependent "class" nor rob them of the initiative that would allow them to make their way in life as self-reliant individuals. In fact, the young doctor argued, the very act of providing one's own living is essential to mental and physical well-being, since the process gives healthful exercise to the full range of mental and physical powers. The blind were more often physically sick and mentally inferior than sighted people, he reasoned, simply because they had been pitied and sheltered and were too rarely given the chance to exercise their limbs, develop their hidden talents, and earn their own livings.[16]

While the European schools also tried to teach their pupils to earn a living, Howe claimed they had so often failed because they had treated the blind as a single, separate class of people, rather than as individuals with distinctive talents and needs. The Parisians taught all their pupils to play music, for example, regardless of their ability to carry a tune. The French school also spent too much time, in Howe's opinion, giving every student intellectual training in fields such as "polite literature," paying little regard to each child's individual abilities or likely station in life after leaving the school. The result was an education which was all "parade and show," a training in "surprising but useless things" which impressed visitors to the school but did not give the students the preparation they needed to become self-reliant citizens.[17]

If the French erred by emphasizing esoteric intellectual feats, the English, Howe believed, made the opposite mistake, giving all students rudimentary manual skills and allowing capable intellects to remain undeveloped. For Howe, the great advance of the nineteenth century, the insight which made the age more humane than any in the past, was the fact that "never has more attention been paid to individual man than now." As soon as blind people were treated as individuals with distinctive talents to be cultivated, rather than as members of a single dependent class, they would be able to take a place as equal participants in society, enjoying full access to any profession for which the absence of sight was no insurmountable barrier.[18]

Following European precedent, Howe expected that many of his pupils would become church organists or choirmasters. The less intelligent would work in handicrafts; the boys might learn to sew mattresses and weave mats, while the girls learned to knit, do needlework, and perform domestic chores. The career possibilities of blind girls were limited more by their sex than by their handicap; but Howe believed that the most talented blind boys might soon advance into other areas which "a blind man can fill equally as well as a seeing person." A young blind man with intellectual talents, he speculated, might well go on to "gain collegiate honors," becoming "an elegant and accomplished scholar." Howe added that, "I know not why they should not make first rate councillors, and think it is possible that they might fill the pulpit both ably and usefully." By treating each blind student as an individual, Howe predicted, American educators would be more successful in teaching them to earn their own livings. But more importantly, they would help the blind to erase the stigma of dependency and segregation that had always isolated them from society, robbing them of their full humanity.[19]

Howe's early faith that the blind were capable of integrating into society, and deserving of every opportunity to do so, still wins him the respect of advocates for the blind today.[20] But it is worth noting that in 1833, as he began his work as an educator, his expectations were guided by untested social ideals rather than by actual experience with blind people and the obstacles they would face beyond the walls of Perkins. Entranced by what he called "the sun of science high in the ascendant," Howe saw no limits to what philanthropy was about to accomplish now that "the blaze of education [was] pouring upon every class of men." In the early 1830s these "sacred laws" of science and education which he confidently invoked were actually mere hypotheses—guidelines for a social experiment that was only just beginning.[21]

Laura Bridgman was born on December 21, 1829, the third daughter of Daniel and Harmony Bridgman, prosperous farmers in the Connecticut Valley town of Hanover, New Hampshire. Laura had been a sickly child during her infancy, subject to convulsions until the age of eighteen months. Her health seemed to recover then, and her mother later remembered her as a happy and "more than commonly bright" child. By her second birthday she had already learned some of her letters, spoke in sentences, and "was rather more forward in talking than the generality of children at that age."[22]

A month later, Laura was stricken with scarlet fever. "I was attacked," she wrote later, "by horrible sores on my face, neck & back." The fever killed her two older sisters, and for a week Laura's mother was sure that "almost every hour would be [Laura's] last." "The disease was evidently seated in the head," Harmony Bridgman recalled, "and her eyes became badly swollen and just closed together." After ten days, the local doctor examined the young girl's eyes and reported to her mother that they were "spoilt." Within a few weeks, the Bridgmans realized that their daughter's sense of hearing had also been destroyed. Over time they also found that the fever had almost completely obliterated the child's sense of taste and smell. Facing the death of two children, and this devastation of her last surviving child, Harmony Bridgman later wrote that "my feelings would be more easily conceived than expressed."[23]

For five months light caused acute pain in Laura's eye, and she was kept in a darkened room. Extremely feeble and scarcely able to walk, she remained confined to her bed for two years after her illness. When she was five her health seemed to recover. She still retained a slight ability to sense light in one eye, though this was lost when she punctured her eyeball by walking into a spindle projecting from her mother's spinning wheel. At the age of five, Laura began to orient herself to a sightless and soundless world, one that she could know only through the single, relatively inarticulate sense of touch.[24]

❧ As soon as Howe returned from Europe in the summer of 1832, he began searching for his own pupils. Some he recruited off the street corners of Boston; others he located by sending letters of inquiry to selectmen in surrounding towns. A few came from poor families, but most were the children of artisans and moderately successful farmers. Hoping to begin his experiment with the best possible prospects, Howe accepted only students who were young, and showed some intellectual talent and a desire to be educated. Once he had located a half dozen promising recruits, he began holding classes temporarily at his father's house.[25]

With the help of two teachers he had hired in Europe, both of whom were blind, Howe and his students made rapid progress. However, within six months the state's initial appropriation was exhausted. To keep the school open, he had to turn to a fund-raising technique that he would successfully apply dozens of times, in dozens of states, for years to come. He organized a public exhibition of his students, at Boston's Masonic Temple. At Howe's invitation, the governor and most legislative leaders attended, along with those whom one Boston paper described as "a large portion of the learning, taste, and fashion of the city." What they saw moved and amazed them; more than one reporter suggested that the exhibition was "one of the most delightful and gratifying spectacles we ever beheld."[26]

Following a formula that Howe would use again and again, the program began with music, a choral work performed "with much taste and feeling" by the blind scholars. They sang a hymn "written on purpose for this occasion," one which assured a curious audience that their handicap had not left them bitter, that their physical calamity had not dampened their hope and gratitude toward their God:

> Thou, at whose word Creation rose
> In all its bright array;
> Though for our eyes no radiance glows,
> No living waters play;—
>
> We waft the music of our hearts
> In gratitude to thee;
> For all the beams thy love imparts
> Our minds can clearly see!

Following the hymn, one of the boys recited a poem with a similar theme, a piece that compared the blind boy's situation "to that of a singing bird, which has always lived in a cage, and does not pine for the liberty he never enjoyed." The only aspect of his fate that had made him sensible of the "bitterness of his lot" was the lack of an education; now that the Perkins school offered him "the privilege of instruction," he told his audience that he would be "as happy as any other little boy." The poem played artfully on the deepest sympathies of the crowd, and reportedly "drew tears from many of the spectators of both sexes." As importantly, the hymn and the poem reassured the audience that the blind were not a class apart, permanently alienated and embittered by their loss.[27]

Howe then presented a lecture on the art of educating the blind which was "listened to with profound attention." Society has a sacred obligation, he told his audience, to provide all of its children with a common school education. The blind boys and girls on the stage before them, Howe insisted, should no more be considered the recipients of public charity than any other child who attended any other publicly supported school. While the cost of education for the blind was greater, Howe declared that his students were simply laying claim to a democratic birthright, a social obligation more fundamental than any financial consideration.

Underscoring his point that blind children were capable of succeeding in "all the common branches of education," Howe interspersed his talk with a variety of student demonstrations: they read Scripture from raised letter books, correctly pointed out state boundaries on a relief map, and "enumerated large numbers, by passing their hands over metallic types." Illustrating his claim that the blind should not be coddled and pitied but challenged to become self-reliant, he sent one blind boy on an errand, asking him to leave the temple by himself and walk to the Perkins School to retrieve a book. "With a triumphant expression of success" the student returned to the exhibition hall, book in hand, "in as short a time as a seeing boy would have done." After a demonstration of the mats and baskets that the children were learning to make, the exhibition closed with several more vocal numbers. Howe's demonstration evoked sympathy for the young students, and admiration for his pedagogical talents. Legislators were evidently as moved by this exhibition as the reporters were and quickly approved an annual appropriation of $6,000, enough to support twenty students.[28]

"We are gratified to learn that this novel exhibition is to be repeated," one reporter at the Boston exhibition added. Indeed, Howe and his students gave hundreds of such performances over the next two decades, appealing for funds and raising public concern about the educational needs of blind people. Within a month of his first Boston exhibition, for example, he brought his pupils to the Salem Lyceum, earning the institution $150 from the proceeds. He then toured other large towns in Massachusetts and found that at each exhibition "a general interest in the welfare of the Institution was excited." Looking beyond Massachusetts' borders, he brought his students before the legislatures of Connecticut, New Hampshire, and Vermont, winning from each state an annual appropriation to send its blind children to the Boston school.[29]

With his first round of public exhibitions, Howe won not only the financial support of New England's lawmakers but also the admiration of Boston's elite society. The charismatic young philanthropist soon turned his new institution into one of Boston's favorite charities. Colonel Thomas

Perkins, a wealthy merchant, donated his Pearl Street mansion as the school's first permanent residence, an act of generosity which the trustees acknowledged by changing the school's name to the Perkins Institution. At the same time, "ladies'" groups from surrounding towns competed to raise the most money for the new cause. While the wealthy members of society took the lead in raising funds, interest in the charity was widespread. As Edward Everett Hale later recalled, "The whole town of Boston, from the stevedore on the wharf to John P. Cushing, the great Canton merchant . . . was interested . . . in this new Institution for the Blind."[30]

As an adult, Laura Bridgman had no memory of the sights or sounds she had experienced before her illness. Accordingly, most of her recollections from her childhood were tactile. She remembered the feel of grass under her bare feet, the swing of her small rocking chair set up by the kitchen hearth, and "many cozy reposes in a rocking cradle." She was fascinated by the moving parts of the family clock and her mother's loom, and the comforting feel of flannel and silk. Though her sense of taste had been nearly destroyed, foods provided another important tactile sensation; she was "extremely fond of new boiled maple syrup," a diet that her mother balanced with "an abundance of very new milk."

Not all of Laura's tactile memories were pleasant. Years later, she still remembered the dread she felt at the touch of her mother's old fur-lined trunk. Unable to see it, she was convinced that the trunk was actually a live animal, and she "disliked to touch it." Sparks from the fireplace burned her; barnyard animals collided with her. And she found that she "hated to approach the dead" after running her hands over some "killed animals" that her father had brought into the kitchen.[31]

In an interesting premonition of her future education, she also recalled the feel of her own special tin plate, "the border embossed in letters as an alphabet."[32] But the letters were meaningless, and the rudimentary knowledge of spoken language which she had acquired before her illness was lost, never to return. For a year after her fever subsided she had continued to speak but, lacking the sense of hearing, this facility dwindled away by her third year. The last word her mother heard her say was "book." She was now forced to learn to communicate with her family through gestures, a crude language of pantomime. "I made signs for my Mother for food and drink," she recalled, "but it was difficult for her to understand the reality of things whatever I wanted. She was very anxious to satisfy my little hungry mouth."[33]

In this new and difficult learning process Laura was greatly assisted by her own temperament. From these earliest days she displayed a good-natured spirit and insatiable curiosity which characterized her personality for the rest of her life. As soon as she was able, she insisted on helping her mother in every possible way, quickly learning to sew, knit, braid, and do simple household chores. One visitor to the Bridgman farmhouse in these years was amazed to find the young girl ironing muslin, pounding mustard with a mortar and pestle, churning butter, washing potatoes, and setting the table: "All this she did voluntarily." Another visitor observed that Laura was "uneasy when out of employment, and if allowed would attempt to do most kinds of work in the house which she finds others doing." Though she had no toys to play with—her mother, she later complained, "had not the knowledge of dolls"—she turned one of her father's boots into a make-shift doll and lavished attention on it. "I rocked and played with it, and kissed and fed it—many times."[34]

The young girl's isolation during these years was eased by the fond attention of an elderly bachelor from the neighborhood, Asa Tenny, a man described by his neighbors as "an eccentric in every sense of the word tho' by no means a 'fool.'" Tenny would visit the Bridgman farmhouse for days, even weeks, at a time, devoting many hours of attention to the child.[35] "He would contrive many ways of amusing my little self," Laura later recalled, "& took me in his arms out doors for hours." Tenny greeted the girl by stroking his finger on her cheek, sparking immediate recognition. The unusual pair went on long walks in the surrounding fields, he sometimes carrying her on his shoulders or swinging her in his arms. Together they gathered eggs in the hen house, picked and ate wild berries, and threw rocks into a nearby stream, an activity that delighted Laura despite the fact that she could neither see nor hear the splash. Bereft of sight, sound, and smell, she was hungry for the physical sensations afforded by these walks with the old man. And cut off from the normal channels of conversation, she eagerly embraced his companionship and silent communion. "When I wished to play with him," Laura remembered, "I made signs to try to make him comprehend what I meant by the signs. He would kindly attend to my deficiencies." After Tenny's death years later, Laura wrote, "I loved him as a father."[36]

Within a few years of his first exhibition of the blind at the Masonic Temple, Howe no longer needed to tour his students through the lyceums and town halls of Massachusetts. Instead, a growing number of tourists flocked to Perkins to witness the new philanthropy in action. For the next twenty years, his school put on regular Saturday afternoon performances, often to overflowing crowds. Howe also worked to spread the gospel of education for the blind beyond New England, taking his best blind students on exhibition tours through the South and Midwest.

By many accounts, Howe was not a particularly effective public speaker, but he understood that the blind children themselves held the key to the public's heart and purse strings. "There is no such powerful appeal to be made as can be made by the appearance and appeal of blind children," he assured a friend of the blind in Kentucky. "With such children as I could select, I would . . . carry the hearts of your legislators by storm and get a bill through both branches before the members could have time to wipe the tears away from their eyes." Likewise, he told a South Carolinian that he did not have "the slightest doubt" that he could "carry the feelings of your legislature entirely away with the subject." Howe quickly added that his confidence was not based on "any peculiar power" of his own. Rather, "the very absence of eloquence gives additional effect to the irresistible appeal that the blind children make themselves."[37]

Although Howe learned to skillfully manipulate public sympathy for the blind through these exhibitions, he was ambivalent about the process and adopted it only as a necessary expedient. In the early 1850s, when schools for the blind were more firmly established around the country, he gladly ended the practice at Perkins. Public exhibitions only encouraged the "lower" motivations for study, he believed, the "parade, and tinsel, and glitter, and noise" of public praise, rather than the love of knowledge for its own sake. He also confessed that these exhibitions pandered to his own baser motivations, flattering the educator's "self-interest or self-esteem."[38]

As Howe's concern about his own "self-interest" suggests, he groped to define a vague line that divided his private ambitions from his public purpose. From the start, he understood that his job as champion of the blind demanded just such an elegant balance between aggressive self-promotion and the strict appearance of complete selflessness. In this difficult task he seems to have succeeded enormously well and was viewed by his many admirers as the absolute incarnation of his ideals, a man whose dedication to his calling was unsullied by the prospect of monetary reward, or even by the less tangible reward of public acclaim. Charles Sumner spoke for many of his contemporaries when he described Howe as "the soul of disinterestedness," his character purged of "all considerations of *self*."[39]

Historians of the antebellum period have been more skeptical. Over the last few decades, they have probed the psyches of Howe and his fellow reformers, trying to explain what motivated these men and women to devote their lives to helping those less fortunate than themselves. Why, they ask, did these men and women feel an urgent need to build institutions for those who were deaf, blind, insane, or indigent; why did they attempt to reform everything from the American diet to the prison system, and champion the cause of slaves? Few scholars have accepted the notion that these moral crusaders were inspired by a simple and unadulterated impulse of Christian charity.

Some historians have characterized the New England reformers as a declining rural elite who used moral crusades as a way to reassert their leadership and ease the status anxiety they experienced when challenged by a rising class of industrialists and entrepreneurs in Jacksonian America.[40] Howe was certainly critical of the hectic pace, the "calculating self-interest" and economic ambition he saw around him in the 1830s. Yet this explanation does not match his family background and social standing very well. While the Howe family was proud to trace its ancestry back to the earliest years of colonial settlement, Howe's father, Joseph, was not a member of the old New England aristocracy. Far from being an educated, landed Puritan, he was liberal in religion and a self-made entrepreneur who manufactured cordage along the Charles River waterfront.[41]

In addition, Joseph Howe was an ardent Jeffersonian Democrat, a "radical republican" whose political allegiances placed him well outside the circle of Boston's Federalist elite. His business went bankrupt, in fact, because he had too generously extended a line of credit to the Democratic federal government during the War of 1812. As a result of these losses, during Howe's adolescent years his family suffered straitened economic circumstances. But Joseph Howe had not lost his ambition. He sacrificed to send Samuel, whom he judged to be the most able of his three sons, to Brown University and then to Harvard Medical School, hoping to see him move up into a stable position in Boston's professional class.[42]

Adopting his father's Democratic sympathies in the capitol of Federalism, Howe grew up an iconoclast. Indeed, his classmates at Boston Latin once kicked him down the school's stairs, "clawing and fighting all the way," for refusing to renounce his allegiance to the Jeffersonian party. Howe switched parties as a young adult, becoming a lifelong Whig. But he proudly retained what he called his father's "republican prejudices" and became one of the Conscience Whigs who took pleasure in denouncing his society's bastions of old wealth and clerical privilege. The year that he took up the cause of education for the blind, Howe told a friend that he was driven by "a desire to attack the Powers that be, Powers I think from my soul have disgraced the country." While Howe disliked the economic scrambling of ambitious newcomers, he never idealized New England's conservative elite as a legitimate alternative.[43]

In recent years, social historians have depicted reformers like Howe as members of the middle class who were troubled less by the challenges from ambitious entrepreneurs than by the antisocial rumblings of immigrants, the working classes, and poor people.[44] While often acknowledging that Howe and his colleagues were sincerely motivated by humanitarian concerns, these historians conclude that they were primarily inspired by worries about social "disorder." In this view, reformers created a variety of new institutions in this period—common schools, prisons, asylums, orphanages, and workhouses—to cope with a perceived rise in crime, immorality, poverty, labor unrest, and civic corruption that accompanied the nation's first experience with industrialization and urbanization. Summing up this line of thinking, one historian suggests that antebellum institutions may have provided a sanctuary for some of their residents but that their overall effect was "downright insidious." Under the guise of instilling "the conventional virtues," reformers used their institutions "against the interests of particular classes and ethnic groups."[45]

Guided by this assumption that reformers were motivated by a fear of working-class unrest, these historians have focused on those institutions which were designed to deal with the most dangerous, disruptive, and potentially class-conscious groups—particularly criminals and poor people. While the new prisons, reform schools, and poorhouses developed in this period were certainly an important part of the antebellum reform movement, these same reformers were also building institutions to serve very different, and much less threatening, populations. We are more likely to sympathize with the reformers' motives if we remember that, along with their efforts to control dangerous criminals and parasitic paupers, these men and women tried to apply some of the same methods to help the blind, the deaf, the mentally handicapped, orphans, and other groups who posed no conceivable threat to the social order in general, or to middle-class interests in particular.

In fact, reformers often found that their first task was to alert the public to a problem that they feared was largely unnoticed. Howe, for example, felt that blind people suffered from a kind of social invisibility because they were so often confined in private homes. Out of public view, their actual numbers and human needs were too easily ignored by the rest of society.[46]

The historian John L. Thomas offers an alternative, and in Howe's case more fitting, view of the motivations of New England reformers, one which suggests that the fear of social disorder was balanced by an even stronger faith in the possibility of progress. Thomas argues that, immediately following the Revolution, reform movements were organized by conservative ministers who hoped to contain democratic excesses by promoting piety and orderliness. He suggests, however, that this reform impulse was transformed in the 1830s by a "theological revolution," a broad cultural shift away from conservative Calvinism and toward a new faith in free will and human perfectibility. Caught up in a spirit of "romantic perfectionism," this new generation of reformers did not see the poor, the criminal, and the handicapped as symptoms of social decline and disorder but as challenges that had to be met in order to fulfill the promise of millennial progress. "Such a society," Thomas writes, "would tolerate neither poverty nor suffering; it would contain no condemned classes or deprived citizens, no criminals or forgotten men." The result was a "huge rescue operation," and Thomas singles out Howe as an example of this new faith in "Christian individualism."[47]

Thomas offers a convincing portrait of Howe's "conversion" experience, the intellectual and emotional journey that inspired this idealistic young man to dedicate his life to helping the blind. But we can gain a fuller understanding of Howe's motivations by placing this conversion experience into a wider social context. Whatever Howe's personal reasons were for helping the blind—and to a great extent they must remain at least as elusive to us as they were to him—we should remember that he was not alone in his ideals or in his actions. Rather, his work at Perkins was entirely dependent on the financial support and moral approval of his fellow citizens.

What is remarkable about antebellum reform crusades like Howe's, from this perspective, is not the emergence of a small group of individuals willing to devote themselves to a life of good works but the fact that these men and women were admired and richly rewarded by a broad section of the public. When Howe first took up the cause of blind people in the early 1830s, he claimed that he needed only to make New Englanders aware of the plight of the blind in order to win generous public support for the school. "We have never allowed ourselves to suppose, for a moment," he wrote, "that the generous inhabitants of New-England would suffer their blind to remain in intellectual darkness." Just as the European philanthropists were supported by the "munificence of Royalty," Howe told his audience that he was counting on the more democratic "free and hearty support of a New-England community."[48]

However effective as a rhetorical device this appeal to regional pride may have been, it was more than empty flattery. Since the 1790s, New Englanders had created hundreds of voluntary charitable organizations, launching what the historian Conrad E. Wright has called a "transformation" in the way charity was thought about and administered. In the colonial period, Americans generally took care of the needy through informal channels of family, kin, and community. But after the Revolution these personal and often irregular methods of charitable support were replaced by new attempts to rationalize and institutionalize benevolence. Citizens from all social classes joined in the creation of hundreds of voluntary associations, pooling time and money to teach lifesaving techniques and build lifeguard stations, to shelter orphans and support widows, to evangelize Indians, to build a school for the deaf in Hartford, to aid the victims of fires, and to root out vices like drinking and Sabbath-breaking.[49]

These reform movements began as voluntary, grass-roots organizations in the first decades after the Revolution. But by 1830, many of them were headed by a new kind of humanitarian, the professional reformer. These men and women did not create new institutions or launch moral crusades single-handedly. Rather, they assumed a place at the top of a broad social pyramid, a structure of public interest and financial support which grew out of the movement to create voluntary charitable organizations. From this perspective, these new professional reformers might well be understood as performers on the public stage, their professional success and personal rewards intimately linked to their ability to engage the sympathies, and earn the continued support, of their audience.[50]

Howe understood the nature of the professional reformer's relationship with his audience remarkably well. Through his exhibitions and a steady flow of essays and reports, he quickly added the education of the blind to the growing list of New England's publicly supported charities. The press heaped praises on his efforts, devoting lengthy columns to the school's exhibitions and enthusiastically reviewing his annual reports. New England's state legislatures were generous with funds and quick to issue proclamations of support. Women's groups from surrounding towns competed in their efforts to raise an endowment for the school. And within a few years men of influence in Boston pointed to the Perkins Institution with pride, considering it evidence of their city's sophistication and progressive spirit.

At the same time that Americans were building these new benevolent societies and educational institutions, they were also transforming their economic life. In the 1830s, the economy was growing rapidly, fueled by immigration, a loosening of credit, and the beginnings of urbanization and industrialization. Like many Americans, Howe found this economic transformation unsettling; it filled him with anxiety about the centrifugal forces of unfettered greed and ambition. But Howe's own success story reminds us that reform movements provided an alternative career track for ambitious young men, as leaders in their society's parallel pursuit of *moral* progress. No less than the founders of the new wildcat banks and textile mills, Howe was a striving Jacksonian individualist. But he was driven to win a different kind of riches, "the excitement of an active life [and the] hope of rendering myself of use to the country and known to its best and most powerful citizens." Like many middle-class reformers in his day, he was learning that selfless service to humanity coincided beautifully with his private ambition to win middle-class respectability and the psychic rewards of respect and honor afforded to professional philanthropists.[51]

Reminding readers of Howe's earlier claim to the public's esteem, his heroism in Greece, one reviewer for the *Boston Weekly Messenger* suggested that the young man's new cause made him "worthy of renewed admiration." Another saw in the good doctor's countenance an angelic "glow of genuine benevolence." Such public praise aptly reflected the private sentiments of Boston society's leading men and women. For example, Elizabeth Peabody, after visiting the school in 1833, recalled seeing Howe at work, patiently helping his young blind students learn to decipher a raised-letter alphabet he had created by gluing twine on cardboard. "I shall not [for] all time & eternity, forget the impression made on me by seeing the hero of the Greek Revolution . . . wholly absorbed & applying all the energies of his genius to this . . . humble work, and doing it as Christ did, without money and without price."[52]

Howe also enjoyed the respect of other educators of the blind, his peers in this new profession, who often praised him as "the Father in this interesting enterprise." Perhaps the most rewarding expressions of gratitude came from blind people themselves. One blind preacher from Georgia, after receiving from Howe a raised-letter Bible, wrote to say, "I can not, but I hope God will reward you Sir for your labour, & the interest you have taken in it, & if it was not for the greatest reluctance I feel at going to Sea, I would go to Boston & feel with my own hands, & personally present my thanks to those who have manifested so much kindness for the afflicted & unfortunate blind."[53]

Such praises were regularly repeated in the press, their echoes amplified as the news of Howe's work spread. By 1841 his benevolence moved a writer for the prestigious *North American Review* to the point of elaborate inarticulateness: "It is with difficulty that we abstain from the attempt to express,—faintly, after all, it would have to be,—our sense of the worth of his labors; but to those who have the true heart for such, the praise of men is apt to be felt as scarcely better than intrusion and annoyance."[54]

This suggestion that Howe was oblivious to, or even annoyed by, "the praise of men" obscures the complexity of his motivations, setting up an artificial barrier between his love of public praise and his love of humanity. This simplistic view of Howe's motivations also neglects the crucial role that he had to play as a publicist, a shaper of public sympathy. Looking out across the crowd gathered for one of his public exhibitions, Howe thrilled to see men and women moved by their noblest motives. Yet he was pragmatic enough to realize that this "current of popular excitement" could be turned off, directed elsewhere, quite easily. "Men are charitable," as he put it, "by fits and starts only." Perhaps the most important aspect of his job as Perkins' director was not his role as an educator, inventor, or theorist but as a promoter who had to manipulate the emotions of his audience, in person and in print, in order to sustain their interest in his enterprise. The success of his own career, as well as the fate of his blind pupils, depended upon it.[55]

During his first two years as director of the Perkins Institution, Howe rode a wave of public interest in his cause. He settled the school into a permanent home in the Perkins mansion, built a large endowment, experimented with curriculum innovations, and established himself as the nation's leading expert in the field.

Crusading for the oppressed was glamorous, but actually serving them proved slow and tedious work. Howe soon found that most of his tasks as director were quite mundane. His letter-books are filled with the evidence. He bartered with a blind farmer from Deerfield over the price of a year's supply of butter. He consulted with parents over the best way to rid their child of the dangerous habit of masturbation: "My plan is to give him the cold shower bath every time I discover his fault; if this does not cure him, I shall set a person to attend him constantly, and thus shame him before the school." To parents concerned about the rigors of Howe's discipline, he wrote to defend his "cold bath" regimen and 5 A.M. wake-up bell. More than once he had to inform loved ones about the sudden death of their children. He repeatedly wrote to state legislators and town selectmen, soliciting clothing for his pupils: "William has taken a severe cold, and has a cough, which unless carefully treated may prove troublesome. I wish therefore that you would have his flannels got ready immediately." And he was forever soliciting funds, particularly to cover the printing costs of new books and the tuition of new students. All of these tasks Howe handled with firmness of purpose and a vivid prose style, tempered in many cases with remarkable tact and grace.[56]

However, by his own admission, Howe was a better crusader than an administrator and financial manager. His close friend and advisor, Charles Goff of New York, affectionately described him as "a great *hot hearted,* universal, perpetual Philanthropist—and—the *worst—merchant*—in—the—land." Complaining that his field was "too narrow" at Perkins, Howe confided to a friend, "if I am good for anything it is as a pioneer in a rough untrodden path. I want the stimulus of *difficulty.*" Having little patience with the daily details and the endless budgetary concerns of running a public institution, he became restless. His philanthropy was fueled by a strong appetite for heroism and public acclaim, and within a few years of founding the nation's first school for the blind he cast about, looking for a new challenge.[57]

🜚 Visiting the American Asylum for the deaf in Hartford, Connecticut, Samuel Howe had seen Julia Brace, the only widely known case of deaf-blindness in America at the time. Brace had lost her sight and hearing at the age of four, after being stricken by scarlet fever. Over the years she had learned to compensate for this loss through the cultivation of her remaining senses. She learned to thread a needle guided only by the sense of touch, and her sense of smell grew acute enough to guide her to her own clothes when they were mixed in a pile containing those of 140 others.[58] But Hartford's instructors had never succeeded in reaching her intellect and were only able to communicate with her through a primitive set of signs. Her soul, they despaired, remained shrouded in impenetrable darkness. After his visit to Hartford, Howe began to speculate on ways to teach such people to communicate through a manual alphabet, the same one that the deaf students at Hartford were using. "The trial should not be abandoned," he wrote with characteristic optimism, "though it had failed in her case, as well as in all that had been recorded before."[59]

His chance to test his speculations about the deaf and blind came not long after, when he read a newspaper account of Laura Bridgman, a deaf, mute and blind seven-year-old living in her parents' farmhouse in Hanover, New Hampshire. This brief report was written by Dr. Reuben Mussey, a Dartmouth professor of anatomy and surgery. Perhaps fearing that the American Asylum for the Deaf would get her first, Howe "immediately hastened" to Hanover, in the company of such Boston notables as Longfellow, George Hillard, Rufus Choate, and Samuel Eliot. Many years later,

Eliot still recalled Howe's eagerness to bring Laura Bridgman back to Boston, writing that he "drove to the Bridgman house in quest of his prize."[60]

When Howe first encountered Laura Bridgman in the parlor of the Bridgman farmhouse, he found her to be a pretty girl of seven, with long straight brown hair, of average height and with a "well-formed figure." He offered the child a gift, a silver pencil case. Laura was "so much alarmed" by the stranger, she later recalled, that she snatched the present from him and "threw it very impatiently." Drawing on the jargon of phrenology, the new science of the brain of which he was increasingly enamored, Howe noted with approval that she had "a large and beautifully shaped head, and the whole system in healthy action." The only visible flaw in this child was her vacant eyeballs, their contents discharged in the aftermath of her violent bout with scarlet fever.[61]

Howe had arrived at the Bridgman farmhouse at an opportune time. In spite of Tenny's assistance, Harmony was finding it increasingly difficult to keep her daughter occupied. Dreadfully isolated, Laura clung to her mother "wildly and peevishly." Harmony recognized, of course, that her child required special attention but was "so occupied by household cares as to be unable to study her case." Even more troubling, "the child began to have a will of her own." On one occasion, she seized a vial of oil that her mother was using to massage her eyes, and "dashed it to pieces." Another time she tossed the family cat into the kitchen fireplace, an act she later confessed was "extremely indiscreet and ignorant." The cat survived but learned to give the child a wide berth from then on. With only the most rudimentary signs for approval and disapproval, the Bridgmans were finding it harder to control their child, relying increasingly on physical force to check her rebelliousness. That job fell most often to Mr. Bridgman, who signaled his displeasure with Laura by stamping his foot violently on the floor; when that failed to change her behavior, he was forced to resort to physical restraint.

At this point Dr. Howe arrived in Hanover, anxious to win the Bridgmans' approval for his plan to educate their daughter at Perkins. The Bridgmans evidently agreed with Howe's assessment that their present arrangement, with its increasing reliance on physical force to constrain Laura's will, "could not have continued long without deplorable results." "Her parents," Howe later reported, "who were intelligent and most worthy persons, yielded to my earnest solicitations." They agreed to send their child to the Perkins Institution.[62]

Howe "came back to the hotel triumphant," his travelling companion

Samuel Eliot later recalled. "I perfectly recollect his exultation at having se-cured her, and the impression he made on me by his chivalric benevo-lence."[63] But Howe's obvious compassion for the child, and his desire to try his own pedagogical theories, account only in part for this great display of enthusiasm over his new "prize." Howe must have recognized from the start that Laura Bridgman was not just another afflicted child in need but someone he would later call "an object of peculiar interest and lively sym-pathy." Howe, who had become so adept at manipulating public sympathy for the blind, surely understood that this "doubly afflicted" child promised to be a doubly effective means of arousing public support.[64]

Looking beyond the sympathy, curiosity, and tax dollars of the general public to the concerns of the rising class of professional scientists, educa-tors, doctors, and philanthropists, Howe believed that the young girl's ter-rible condition offered a unique chance to shed some empirical light on one of the most vexing problems of epistemology, the role that the senses play in the formation of human knowledge and the shaping of human na-ture. If he should succeed in teaching her to communicate, he surely real-ized, his work would have far-reaching philosophical implications that would capture the attention of intellectuals all over the world.

In short, Howe saw Laura Bridgman as not just another, particularly challenged student in need of his school's services but as an ideal vehicle to continue his quest for righteous adventure, with all the professional pres-tige, public acclamation, and support that a successful experiment would bring. By the time Howe returned to Boston to make arrangements for his new pupil, the young girl's future prospects were intimately entwined with his own.

Chapter 2

Mind over Matter

Laura's parents delivered her to the Perkins Institution on October 12, 1837. Confused and frightened, the young girl burst into "bitterest tears" when they left her. She soon recovered, however, and within a week began to develop strong attachments to the house matron and to Miss Drew, the instructor who had been assigned by Howe to work closely with Perkins' first deaf-blind pupil. She spent her first days engrossed in her knitting and showed obvious signs of pleasure when the women praised her work by giving her a caress on the cheek.[1]

The maternal bond of trust between Laura and her female instructor was balanced by Howe's role as the child's new father figure. During Laura's first weeks at the institution, Howe established his paternal authority by attempting to lead her around the room by the hand. When she resisted, he held her hand firmly, forcing her compliance. She soon submitted, and three weeks after her arrival a visitor to the school noted that she was "very much under the command of the Doctor." If Laura ever felt compelled to submit to Howe's superior strength, those feelings were soon superseded by intense affection toward him, and Howe never had to rely on force again. Once this bond of trust and affection was established and the child grew more comfortable in her new surroundings, he felt ready to begin his experiment to reach her intellect.[2]

Today, growing up as we do hearing the story of the marvelous accomplishments of Helen Keller, we may take for granted the inevitable success of Howe's experiment. It requires an effort of historical imagination to recognize that, as he sat down with the eight-year-old to begin her first lessons, his faith that there was a mind "in there," capable of learning, was an unproven intuition, one running counter to a century of failed efforts to reach other deaf-blind children. Many years later Howe's wife, the writer and suffragist Julia Ward Howe, would capture the excitement of that moment: "The personage within was unknown to him and to all, save in her outer aspect. What were her characteristics? What her tendencies? If he should ever come to speech with her, would she prove fully and normally human? Would her spirit be amenable to the laws which govern our thoughts and conduct for mankind in general?[3]" For searching out the answers to these questions, Howe earned a reputation among his contemporaries as the "Columbus" of the mind.[4]

Unlike Columbus, Howe was not venturing into entirely uncharted waters. Although his educational techniques were untested, his understanding of the human mind was guided along the well-worn tracks of Anglo-American moral philosophy. Like most educated Americans of his day, Howe's notions about human psychology were drawn from the writings of the widely influential thinkers of the Scottish Enlightenment, particularly Thomas Reid and his disciple Dugald Stewart. Howe had encountered these "common sense" philosophers in his undergraduate courses in moral philosophy at the orthodox Brown University, as well as in sermons preached from Unitarian pulpits in Boston.[5]

Following in the philosophical tradition of Descartes, these Scottish philosophers were dualists, insisting that the mind is distinct from, and superior to, the body. Their strong defense of the existence of a nonmaterial human mind is one reason why their writings were so popular with American religious leaders, serving as a cornerstone of American theology and moral philosophy well into the nineteenth century. The historian Daniel Walker Howe has suggested that Boston's Liberal Christians found the mind-body dualism of the Scottish philosophers particularly compatible with their Christian theology. In their view, the philosophers' concept of an immaterial "mind," distinct from the body, was just another way of talking about what Christians had always called the eternal "soul."[6]

Along with dualism, the Scots were strong believers in faculty psychology, the view that the mind is composed of various "faculties." In the common sense tradition, this mind (or soul) was not a passive and ethereal abstraction but an active agent, possessed of certain "powers" of intuition and reason that allow us to clearly and directly perceive the world around us. This idea that the mind is a collection of distinct "faculties," each attuned to a corresponding part of the external world, was first developed by the Greeks and had been commonplace since the Middle Ages. But Scots like Thomas Reid offered a particularly strong defense of the mind's innate "faculties, dispositions, and powers," in response to the epistemological skepticism of David Hume.

As historians of philosophy have often recounted, the terms of this fundamental debate over the reliability of human knowledge were established by John Locke in 1690. In his *Essay Concerning Human Understanding*, Locke argued that we know the external world only through the medium of "ideas," translated by the mind from our sensory experience. Although Reid and his followers greatly admired Locke, they felt that his theory of ideas had proven to be an Achilles' heel, exposing all of human knowledge to doubt. Hume had shown that, if Locke was correct in his claim that the human mind knows the world only through the medium of its own ideas, then the mind can never be certain that these ideas actually correspond to the external world they are supposed to represent. If this is so, Hume maintained, then human knowledge is uncertain and can be accepted only as a matter of faith or convention. All the truths that civilized men and women consider fundamental, from the knowledge of self to the knowledge of God, could never be proven.

Challenged by Hume's skepticism, Thomas Reid and other common sense philosophers came to the defense of human reason by denying Locke's key premise that we know the world only through the intermediary of ideas. Instead, the Scots redefined "ideas," arguing that they were not mental copies of our sense experience, as Locke had maintained, but mental *acts* that directly and clearly grasp the external world, acts performed by the various faculties of the mind.

Howe never appreciated the subtleties of this epistemological wrangling among British philosophers. "The mind is taxed and strained to the utmost," he complained, "to follow the metaphysical authors, and mystical psychologists through their abstruse speculations." In his opinion, the only reward he had gotten for his study of philosophy was "an unsatisfactory headache." Though Howe cared little about the philosophical controversy that had produced the common sense philosophy, he accepted Reid's conclusion that the mind is endowed with a range of distinct faculties.[7]

Pained by philosophical complexities, Howe was particularly attracted to a simple and practical variation of faculty psychology, the "new philosophy" of phrenology. According to phrenologists, the common sense philosophers had correctly identified many of the faculties of the mind but had failed to ground their psychological theory in empirical observation. Phrenologists dismissed the philosophers' concept of "mind" as only an intellectual abstraction, found between the covers of weighty tomes and prone to the abuse of unfounded metaphysical speculation. Fashioning themselves to be scientists and practical reformers rather than philosophers of the mind, the phrenologists argued that a truly scientific and useful psychology had to be grounded in the observable, verifiable material world.

Accordingly, they claimed that the careful examination of hundreds of human skulls and brains had revealed that each of the various faculties of the mind has a *physical* existence, embodied in one of the dozens of separate "organs" of the brain, and usually reflected in the various "bumps" on each individual's skull.[8]

One of the founders of phrenology, Dr. Joseph Spurzheim, arrived in Boston in 1832, the same year that Howe began his career as an educator of the blind. As a young and relatively inexperienced physician cast suddenly in the role as Boston's "expert" on the education of the blind, Howe was no doubt searching earnestly for some firm intellectual foundation. His undergraduate education at Brown had been largely wasted, he later confessed, in the pursuit of youthful pranks. Growing more serious while taking his medical training at Harvard, he found that he had particular talents as a dissector and anatomist. Thus, given his interest in anatomy and his own temperament, long on action and short on systematic reflection, Howe was understandably attracted to this new science, with its self-proclaimed virtues of simplicity and practical utility, all grounded in the science of dissection.[9]

When Spurzheim died in 1832, in the midst of delivering his course of lectures in Boston, Howe was among the prophet's many admirers in that city who viewed him as a martyr who had died in the service of Truth. Howe became a founding member, and recording secretary, of the Boston Phrenological Society, set up to perpetuate both the great man's memory and his science.[10]

Howe maintained his allegiance to phrenology long after most of his peers abandoned the cause, distancing themselves as the science degenerated into carnival sideshow quackery. Yet in the 1830s, his fascination with "craniology" cannot simply be attributed to his peculiar training or his intellectual naiveté. In these years, his interest in the new science put him in the company of some of the most respected medical minds of Boston, including many of his former professors at Harvard's medical school. Howe was not the only one who was attracted to the prospect of replacing the wrangling of the philosophers with an outline of the mind that was "clear, simple [and] natural."[11]

Thus, as Howe contemplated the prospect of educating Laura Bridgman, he consulted the phrenologists' charts of the brain. There his attention was drawn to one particular "organ," the "intellectual faculty" of "Language." This organ, according to Howe's favorite manual on the new science, "gives a facility in acquiring a knowledge of arbitrary signs to express thoughts—a facility in the use of them—and a power of inventing them." In short, Howe's general education in Scottish mental philosophy supported what his more recent explorations in phrenology confirmed with more precision: that Laura Bridgman's brain contained an innate ability to understand and create language. Guided by this premise, Howe reasoned that this power of the mind lay dormant, but unimpaired, inside the child's damaged body.[12]

Of course, Laura had already shown a desire to communicate and had even developed some of her own sign language. In Hanover, Howe had seen her family speak to her through a series of gestures—a pat on the head signaled approval, rubbing her hand meant the opposite, and pushing and pulling were used to tell her which direction to move. Laura had also invented her own signs: fingers held to her face referred to a man with a beard; a hand revolved in the air meant the spinning wheel. Howe recognized that, if left on her own, she would probably continue to develop this nonverbal language, learning to communicate many of her basic needs. But he decided that in the long run this language of gestures would be too limiting, putting blinders on her intellect, shutting her off from the knowledge of more complex, subtle, and sublime human emotions and ideas, locking her in a state of permanent mental and moral childhood.[13]

Howe was determined, instead, to bring Laura into the conversation of human society as an equal, and to prove to the world that, within a damaged body, her mind was intact and fully human. To do that, he felt that he must teach her the use of an arbitrary language, in this case English, founded on an alphabet. She needed, he explained, "a knowledge of letters, by the combination of which she might express her idea of the existence, and the mode and condition of existence, of anything."[14]

The plight of Julia Brace at the Hartford Asylum seemed to prove his point. Her education had failed, Howe believed, because her instructors had allowed her to rely on a "natural language" of simple gestures, rather than the abstract and man-made language of the alphabet. Howe expected that, without his help, Laura would also rely on a primitive language of simple signs, as automatically as water flows downhill by the easiest course. His goal, then, was to guide the stream of Laura's communication into the man-made channel of an arbitrary alphabet.[15]

This distinction between the "natural" language of gesture and the artificial language of the alphabet was not original with Howe but was another theme developed by Scotland's common sense philosophers. In his *Inquiry into the Human Mind*, Thomas Reid devoted considerable attention to the language of pantomime, arguing that this form of communication proved the existence of an innate linguistic faculty in man. Those gestures—the pat on the back for approval, the frown to suggest displeasure, the knitted brow of anger—come instinctively to all human beings, in all cultures. Even the youngest infant, the uncivilized tribesman, and the linguistically isolated deaf person automatically understand the meaning of a smile or a frown or tears. Reid suggested that this natural language of posture and facial expression was the alphabet of humanity's first language, providing the common ground necessary for the subsequent invention of the arbitrary language of words.[16]

Reid believed that this evolution from natural gestures to artificial words came with a price. Our original language of gestures, he argued, was peculiarly well suited to expressing the inner world of emotions. When societies developed artificial languages, their instinctive vocabulary of physical gestures atrophied. By his own time, Reid believed, only orators and stage actors could still speak the true language of the emotions. While such an evolution drew human society further away from the language of its feelings, the transition was a necessary step in the fuller realization of human intellect. "As ideas multiply," Reid's disciple Dugald Stewart explained, "the imperfections of natural language are felt; and men find it necessary to invent artificial signs, of which the meaning is fixed by mutual agreement."[17]

Echoing Reid and Stewart, Howe summarized the distinction between natural and arbitrary language by comparing the former to a "man in his wild state, simple, active, strong, and wielding a club." The spoken language of an arbitrary alphabet, by comparison, was "subtle, flexible, minute, precise [and] is a thousand times more efficient and perfect instrument for thought; it is like civilized man, adroit, accomplished, well-trained, and armed with a rapier."[18]

Howe reasoned that Laura could only develop this facility for language if her one remaining sense of touch could be developed to the point where she could use it to read a manual version of the alphabet. Howe's plan was anticipated by the French philosopher Denis Diderot almost a century earlier. The sense of sight uses a written alphabet, Diderot explained, and hearing relies on symbolic sounds. But he saw no reason why the sense of touch might not develop its own medium of symbolic language. "For lack of this language," he speculated in his Letter on the Blind, "there is no communication between us and those born deaf, blind, and mute. They grow, but they remain in a condition of mental imbecility. Perhaps they would have ideas, if we were to communicate with them in a definite and uniform manner from their infancy; for instance, if we were to trace on their hands the same letters we trace on paper, and associated always the same meaning with them. Is not this language . . . as good as another?"[19]

Diderot's conjecture about the possibility of a manual alphabet was confirmed by a later generation of French educators who worked with the deaf. Until the Abbé de l'Épée began his pioneering work with the deaf in the late eighteenth century, most philosophers who speculated on the subject believed that thought, even the written word, was impossible without sound; signs of intelligence in deaf persons were often greeted as little short of miraculous. But the Abbé's success in teaching a manual alphabet to the deaf proved that the sense of hearing is not an essential component of thought. The manual alphabet cut language loose from its presumed moorings in the voice and the ear.[20]

The Abbé pushed even further. If hearing could be dispensed with, he reasoned, why not sight as well? Anticipating Howe by a half century, he published speculations on a possible method of instruction for the deaf and blind, a problem more hypothetical than real to him since he did not know of any person so afflicted. Sicard, the Abbé's successor at the Parisian school for the deaf, went on to prove that even the blunt sense of touch could become refined enough to serve as the medium of thought. In fact, he had actually used such a language, conversing with one of his students in the pitch darkness of midnight by impressing the signs of the manual alphabet into the outstretched hand of his companion.

Thus, as Howe began his unprecedented experiment with Laura Bridgman, he was guided by the theories of Scottish philosophers and phrenologists, whose map of the brain showed him that the child's mind was endowed with a linguistic "faculty," a capacity to learn and use an arbitrary language. Their theories assured him that, if he could find a way to speak to her through the lone sense of touch, she would eagerly meet him halfway. French educators provided Howe with that language, the manual alphabet of the deaf. Howe's work as a pioneer in the education of the deaf and blind must be understood in the context of these European precedents. Presented with a rare opportunity to help a young deaf-blind student, Howe turned Old World theory into New World practice.

Howe began Laura's education by trying to teach her to associate simple objects with their names, imprinted in raised letters. He attached embossed paper labels on a few simple objects—a knife, a pin, a pen, and others. Laura was first presented with the label itself, detached from its corresponding object. She was then made to feel the object, on which Howe had attached an identical label. To express the idea that the embossed letters "p-i-n" were somehow identical with the pin she held in her hand,

Howe resorted to one of Laura's own signs for likeness—he held his two forefingers together, suggesting identity. According to Miss Drew, Howe's assistant in these lessons, Laura "readily perceived the similarity of the two words." And, rewarded by pats on the head for correct answers, "the natural sign of approbation," the student learned within a few days to match the labels to their appropriate objects. The teachers knew they had succeeded in this first crucial step of Laura's education when they saw that "a light of intelligence lighted her hitherto puzzled countenance." However, Howe recognized that, though his pupil was evidently bright and eager to learn, she had not yet grasped the mysterious power of language. She matched words and objects not in order to communicate but merely as an intellectual exercise of "imitation and memory."[21]

Once she had this first inkling about "words as a whole," Howe then tried to teach her to create words herself. He broke the paper labels up into their component letters. Laura soon learned to arrange these slips of paper in their proper order, recreating the label and matching it to its object. At first she spelled out these words in a "mechanical" fashion. Howe compared her skills at that point to those of "a very knowing dog" who was eager to perform tricks only in order to win approval, the reward of loving pats on the head. Howe searched for a sign that she was beginning to truly appreciate the communicative power of those patterns at her fingertips, and it came at last, after several months of patient, methodical instruction.

> The truth began to flash upon her, her intellect began to work, she perceived that here was a way by which she could herself make up a sign of anything that was in her own mind, and show it to another mind, and at once her countenance lighted up with human expression; it was no longer a dog or parrot,—it was an immortal spirit, eagerly seizing upon a new link of union with other spirits! I could almost fix upon the moment when this truth dawned upon her mind, and spread its light to her countenance. I saw that the great obstacle was overcome.[22]

Howe's 1841 account of Laura Bridgman's linguistic breakthrough—described as a lightning-like burst of spiritual insight—bears remarkable resemblance to the better known story of the great turning point in Helen Keller's education. Howe suggested that, in spite of months of preparation, the obstacle was overcome "at once." The wide threshold, he suggested, between the "knowing dog" and the human spirit was crossed almost instantaneously. Her sudden understanding of the value of language seemed to induce a new birth within her, the creation of an "immortal spirit" right before Howe's eyes.

In her autobiography, Helen Keller described a similar rapid transformation, in the often-told story of her trip to the well. Understanding for the first time that the letters "w-a-t-e-r" spelled into her hand corresponded to the cool water that flowed over her hand, she suddenly realized that all objects have names, and that the manual alphabet was her key to expressing them to others. Keller later described that moment as "in the nature of a revelation."

> There was a strange stir within me,—a misty consciousness, a sense of something remembered. It was as if I had come back to life after being dead . . . I understood it was possible for me to communicate with other people by these signs. Thoughts that ran forward and backward came to me quickly,—thoughts that seemed to start in my brain and spread all over me . . . Delicious sensations rippled through me, and sweet strange things that were locked up in my heart began to sing.

These two accounts of a miraculous and immediate transformation of the soul, of a spiritual birth through language, are remarkably similar. Yet they also share the fact that they were written years *after* the events actually occurred. Setting aside consideration of Helen Keller's experience, it is important to notice that Howe's version of Laura Bridgman's linguistic apotheosis was first published in his annual report of 1841, at least three years after the events he describes. All of his accounts prior to this time failed to mention this singular and powerful moment of intellectual and spiritual birth, and instead described a much more subtle and painstaking process of gradual enlightenment.[23]

Howe's 1841 report of a great spiritual apotheosis exaggerated the contrast between the pre- and postlinguistic child. While Laura's introduction to arbitrary language was undoubtedly of profound importance to her subsequent intellectual development, she arrived at Perkins with an intellectual curiosity that could hardly be described, as Howe had done, as "mechanical" or animal-like. Howe himself noted, in his first report on her in 1838, that she was extremely curious about her surroundings, "constantly active," evidently "intelligent," able to express affection, take part in imaginative play, and mind her manners while at the table.[24]

Howe's later account also ignored his previous testimony about the child's slow and painstaking introduction to language. In his 1838 report, he announced that his pupil had succeeded in learning the nature of words and could use letters to express the names of "substances." In this first published version of the story, Howe found her accomplishment "gratifying," but did not suggest, as he did later, that "the great obstacle was overcome." Rather, he remained cautiously optimistic that her grasp of language could be advanced through the "slow and tedious" process of education.[25]

The only other eyewitness observer of Laura Bridgman's introduction to language was Miss L. H. Drew, her daily instructor during this period. In an account also written much later, Drew made no mention of any single moment of apotheosis, noting only that "whenever she overcame a difficulty, a peculiarly sweet expression lighted up her face, and we perceived that it grew daily more intelligent."[26]

In short, some of the contours of Howe's account of Laura's education seem to have taken shape over the course of his first few years with her. His role as a disinterested observer and reporter of an important psychological experiment may well have been eclipsed by his inclinations as a journalist and a publicist to adorn a tale that might better capture the sympathy and imagination of his growing reading public.

While the story of Laura Bridgman's first breakthrough into the world of language may have developed over the course of her first few years at Perkins, Howe moved much more quickly to assert the important philosophical conclusions to be drawn from his successful experiment. In his first public reports on her progress, he confidently announced that Laura Bridgman was not, as might be supposed, "but a blank." He had broken through her damaged body to discover a soul, "active, and struggling continually not only to put itself in communication with things without, but to manifest what is going on within itself."[27]

In this report, given four months after her arrival at Perkins, Howe believed that he was already beginning to discern the basic outline of that spirit which was "shut up in a dark and silent cell." He marveled at her playfulness and affection for her teachers and classmates, and he took a parent's pride in her physical skills, her ability to sew and knit and dress herself "with quickness and precision"—all skills she had learned prior to coming to Perkins. But most importantly, he rejoiced at what he called her "mental phenomena."

> She has a quick sense of propriety; a sense of property; a love of approbation; a desire to appear neatly and smoothly dressed, and to make others

notice that she is so; a strong tendency to imitation, insomuch that she will sit and hold a book steadily before her face in imitation of persons reading . . . The different states of her mind are clearly marked upon her countenance, which varies with hope and fear, pleasure and pain, self-approbation and regret; and which, when she is trying to study out anything, assumes an expression of intense attention and thought.[28]

At this early stage, Howe felt that he could not say conclusively that his young pupil had a clear sense of right and wrong, apart from the love of approval which she so eagerly sought. But he was convinced that her mind, her conscience, her soul showed all signs of being in healthy working order, unimpaired by her physical infirmity. The mind, Laura's case already seemed to prove, was not only at least partially independent of the body but showed every sign of being able to overcome the most horrendous physical barriers imaginable. "The immortal spirit within her," Howe wrote in the first month of his experiment to a supporter in Maine, "although in darkness & stillness like that of a tomb, is full of life & vigor, is animated by innate power & triumphantly refutes the doctrine that the soul is but a blank sheet upon which education & experience write everything."[29]

By insisting that Laura's mind was not a "blank sheet" but was driven by an "innate power" to communicate, Howe was entering the child as a crucial piece of evidence in one of the most important scientific and theological debates of his time. For more than a century, the role that the senses play in determining human nature and creating human knowledge had been *the* crucial debate in philosophical circles, the sticking point that had divided the various competing branches of Enlightenment thinking about the human mind.

Locke had established the starting point of that debate, with his efforts to place the study of the human mind on the same scientific footing that Newton had placed the study of the heavens. The view held by Descartes and his fellow rationalists that humans are born with certain innate ideas that the Creator plants, fully formed, into the human mind was, for Locke, an unfounded superstition, a remnant of the discredited vagaries of medieval scholasticism and mystical neo-Platonism. Searching instead for the observable mechanisms of mental activity, Locke posited that the mind contains no innate ideas but develops them from the sensory input of the external world and from self-reflection on its own activity. Prior to receiving these sensory impressions, the child is born, in Locke's famous phrase, into a state of *tabula rasa*.

Down to Howe's own time, American intellectuals revered Locke's accomplishment, and college students dutifully worked their way through his *Essay Concerning Human Understanding*. But some also worried that a group of Locke's disciples, particularly among the French, had mistaken him to mean that the "mind is the result of sensation." The mind, these French materialists argued, is born passive and inert and is shaped entirely by its external environment. Today, Locke scholars point out that this has been a common misreading of the philosopher's famous metaphor of *tabula rasa* and show that Locke actually credited the mind with a more active role in converting sensory input into knowledge through certain innate reasoning "faculties." But in Howe's time the materialistic implications of Locke's sensationalist psychology were made dangerously clear by some of the radical thinkers of the French Enlightenment. Condillac, for example, felt that he was only carrying Locke's psychology to its logical conclusion when he tried to prove that the mind contains no innate faculties and that thought is therefore purely the product of physical sensation. Explaining all mental phenomena as byproducts of the senses, the materialists seemed prepared to dismiss the immaterial mind and the immortal soul as unscientific superstitions.[30]

In Howe's time, this philosophical radicalism was not easily dismissed as another Old World madness, safely contained on the far side of the Atlantic. In the 1830s, the fruits of French materialism were ripening in the midst of pious New England. Two years before Howe met Laura Bridgman, he set down his own fears about the rise of an "infidel party" in Massachusetts in a two-part article called "Atheism in New England," published in his own *New England Magazine*. Howe warned his readers that the freethinkers of his day enjoyed growing congregations who gathered each week to hear their "ministers" ridicule Christianity, foment envy and class hatred among the poor, undermine the institution of marriage, and promote "degrading profligacy."[31]

At the bottom of all these threats to "the foundations of the social-fabric" lay the theory of materialism, what Howe called "the doctrines of the French infidels." In an effort to make this perfectly clear, Howe quoted verses from the infidels' "Bible of Reason":

The soul is [only the] principle of sensibility. To think, to suffer, to enjoy—is to feel. When the body, therefore, ceases to live, it cannot exercise sensibility. Where there are no senses, there can be no ideas. The soul only perceives by means of the organs; how then is it possible for it to feel after their dissolution? . . . That the effect, called mind, ceaseth, and is entirely discontinued, is manifest; because, it hath a beginning, and is proved to be nothing without the body: how great a folly it is to imagine what is mortal can be immortal!

In Howe's opinion, New Englanders had "too long been blind, and deaf, and dumb" to this threat of materialism in their midst.[32] He disagreed with those who felt that the best way to contain infidelity was to ignore it, that attacks only stirred up public interest in the freethinkers' ideas. In his opinion, American society was arriving at a crucial juncture, a time when education was "just beginning to be general" and the impressionable, "half-formed minds" of the American people were ripe for influence, either for good or ill. "It is light and purification which the public mind requires," Howe proclaimed.[33]

And so when he succeeded in teaching Laura Bridgman language, Howe seized the chance to instruct his fellow citizens, while dealing a scientific deathblow to the impious doctrines of materialism. If the materialists' ideas about the human mind were correct, Howe reasoned, a person in Laura Bridgman's predicament would be incapable of thinking, since she lacked most of the sensory input essential to the formation of ideas. In a sense, a deaf and blind person would have no mind and no soul; she would be trapped in the vacant state of *tabula rasa* in which Locke had supposedly suggested all babies are born. Howe liked to point out that this bleak view of human nature had even insinuated its way into English common law. Blackstone had classed the blind-deaf as "in the same state as an idiot; he being supposed incapable of any understanding, as wanting all those senses which furnish the human mind with ideas." Now that he had shown that Laura could learn and communicate, Howe believed that no person could take seriously the radicals' claim that "the soul is merely the result of sensation." As Laura reached out to the world around her, Howe thrilled to witness the triumph of mind over matter.[34]

At first, Laura read and spelled out words on a set of raised-letter metal types that Howe had specially made for her. This slow and cumbersome process was soon abandoned in favor of the manual alphabet of the deaf. Laura's instructor, Miss Drew, began each morning's lesson by introducing the child to a new object, spelling out its name in finger letters pressed into Laura's eager palm. "She placed her right hand over mine," Drew recalled, "so she could feel every change of position, and with the greatest anxiety watched for each letter; then she attempted to spell it herself; and as she

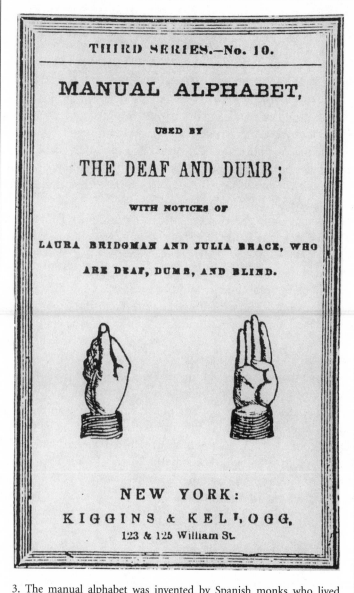

THIRD SERIES.—No. 10.

MANUAL ALPHABET,

USED BY

THE DEAF AND DUMB;

WITH NOTICES OF

LAURA BRIDGMAN AND JULIA BRACE, WHO
ARE DEAF, DUMB, AND BLIND.

NEW YORK:

KIGGINS & KELLOGG,
123 & 125 William St.

3. The manual alphabet was invented by Spanish monks who lived under a vow of silence. It was brought to America by educators of the deaf. Laura sometimes dreamed using the finger alphabet. *(Courtesy of Dartmouth College Library)*

mastered the word, her anxiety changed to delight." Laura made remarkable progress with this finger language, using it "so fast and so deftly, that only those accustomed to this language can follow with the eye, the rapid motions of her fingers." Within a year, Laura was also learning to write, her pencil guided by a grooved pasteboard placed underneath her paper. Before long she was conducting a simple but voluminous correspondence with her family, and recording her daily lessons in a journal.[35]

As Laura's grasp of language continually improved, Howe grew more confident that his protégé had dealt a knockout blow to the doctrine of materialism. He wrote to the English writer Harriet Martineau that "her whole nature seems changed & the now triumphant mind begins to speak out in her countenance with a natural eloquence surprising to those who remember her former situation."[36]

Howe drew his philosophical conclusion emphatically in his 1838 report.[37] In the sentimental prose style that Howe used to appeal to the deepest sympathies of his readers, he painted the scene of a chance meeting in the institution's hallway between Laura and one of her classmates. He described "an intertwining of arms—a grasping of hands—and a swift telegraphing upon the tiny fingers (which communicated) exchanges of joy and sorrow . . . kissings and partings." Moving to the moral, he concluded that such a scene was "a better refutation of the doctrine, that mind is the result of sensation, than folios of learned argument. If those philosophers who consider man as only the most perfect animal, and attribute his superiority to his senses, be correct, then a dog or a monkey should have mental power quadruple that of poor Laura Bridgman."[38]

Howe was fully prepared to give the senses their due. The "French philosophers," he conceded, were correct in asserting that "all ideas of sensible objects are derived immediately or remotely from impressions made upon the senses." In other words, our knowledge of the material world must come from our experience of it, through the senses. Thus, for example, a deaf and blind person could never learn anything about the true nature of color or sound. Where the empiricists had erred, Howe claimed, was in their attempt to overapply this "doctrine of sensation," claiming that *moral* and *spiritual* knowledge were also produced by sensory experience. "All the higher and nobler attributes of the soul, all that part of man which is truly in the likeness of God, is independent of sensation," Howe concluded. "The hope of immortality, the love of goodness, the veneration of justice, the desire of sympathy, the yearning for affection, are all independent of external sensations." Though such claims carried Howe far beyond the evidence provided by his experiment thus far, he was confident that Laura would reveal all of these symptoms of the soul in due course.[39]

æ If popular press accounts of Laura's breakthrough into language may be taken as a measure of general public reaction, Howe's audience was eager to accept his claim that the child's story proved the existence of an immaterial soul. Countless writers echoed Howe's argument that Laura's education was a profound tribute to the human spirit's power to overcome physical barriers. However, very few writers for the popular press took a serious interest in the more intricate philosophical details of Howe's battle against the philosophy of materialism or his hasty attempt to enter Laura's story as evidence in the philosophers' ongoing epistemological debate. Popular Christian belief at the time led most people to accept dualism, a clear distinction between body and soul, as a matter of course, untroubled by the arcane epistemologies of European radicalism. One brief exception suggests the rule. A writer in the *Godey's Lady's Book* recommended, "We hope all who are inclined to the philosophy of materialism will study the facts of this wonderful and well authenticated case." That warning not withstanding, the number of that journal's readers who were drawn to the dangerous French doctrines was no doubt quite small.[40]

But the intellectual community took Dr. Howe's contribution to the mind/body problem quite seriously and praised his vindication of "this imperial mind of ours." Dr. John Kitto, author of a widely read book on the senses, called the moment of Laura Bridgman's linguistic breakthrough proof that "wherever there *is* mind, there is no imprisonment from which it cannot be freed." Kitto praised Howe's work as a "great discovery in the history of man" and urged that the specific moment of the child's linguistic breakthrough should be carefully recorded for posterity. One of Howe's professors at Harvard's medical school, visiting Perkins less than a month after Laura's education began, wrote that the child's "power of ratiocination" was sufficient evidence "to convince the greatest skeptic of the existence of the soul."[41]

The most thoughtful endorsement of Howe's attack on materialism came from the *Christian Examiner,* the leading journal of Boston's Unitarians. Mrs. L. Minot explained to her readers that there were "two grand divisions of metaphysical systems," one which attributed knowledge to the senses and the other which held that the intellect, the human mind, is an essential and active agent in the formation of ideas. Like Howe, Minot freely acknowledged that the input of the senses was necessary to the formation of most human knowledge about the world. But she claimed that the materialists, those prodigal heirs of Locke who had so troubled Howe, were guilty of exaggerating the importance of the senses, downplaying or dismissing altogether the crucial, even "godlike" role that the mind must play. Already anticipating Kant's influence on America's emerging Romantic movement, Minot greeted Howe's experiment as part of a broader intellectual revolution against materialism. "The senses, which in philosophy have long been lord of the ascendant, and claimed to be the source of all the godlike thoughts of the soul, are now hiding their diminished heads. The ideal is regaining its rightful domain, and restricting them more and more to the mere threshold of the soul's temple."[42]

As important as Howe's experiment was for the vindication of the intellect and the ideal, Minot was more impressed by the breakthrough he had made in applying the scientific method to the study of the human mind. Rationalists and empiricists, she explained, had been deadlocked for centuries in an armchair debate over the origin of human ideas in large part because they lacked the techniques for investigating the matter firsthand. Infants, Minot suggested, offer an ideal testing ground for resolving these questions about the workings of the human mind, yet this fertile field of scientific investigation was abandoned to mothers, their own minds hopelessly distracted by the "petty cares and duties" of child-rearing. Facts were needed, data gathered by "the closest attention of a cautious and philosophic observer."[43]

Howe's experiment, Minot suggested, represented an entirely new and scientific approach to ancient moral questions, the chance at last to gather "details such as the philosopher has long sought in vain." Howe had found in Laura Bridgman an ideal specimen to study. Even infants learned at lightning speed, but Laura's mental processes were slowed by her handicaps. "The steps of her progress are laborious," Minot explained, "which enables a careful observer to note them accurately." She added that it was the scientific community's great fortune that fate had entrusted this case to Howe, a philosopher and "a man of candid and accurate habits of mind."[44]

In spite of all the praise heaped upon Howe by his contemporaries for his scientific credentials and careful observation, the flaws in his famous "experiment" on the role the senses play in creating mind seem glaringly obvious to even a casual observer today. To refute the doctrine that "the mind is the result of sensation," Howe would necessarily have had to show that Laura Bridgman's mental life existed independent of *all* sensory input.

After her illness, Laura enjoyed considerably less outside stimulation than the average person, but with her single sense of touch her mind was never devoid of a sensory connection with the world around her.

Perhaps sensitive to this flaw in his experiment, Howe often minimized the importance of the sense of touch, dismissing it as the least articulate and the crudest of senses. He portrayed the girl, prior to her education at Perkins, as little more than a cartesian corpuscle, bouncing in a cold and barren world made up only of space and matter. Even her own younger brothers and sisters, Howe wrote, "were but forms of matter which resisted her touch, but which differed not from the furniture, save in warmth and in the power of locomotion. And not even in these respects from the dog and the cat."[45]

Yet Laura's sense of touch was undeniably an essential stimulus to her mind after her illness; and, judging from the affection she expressed to her family and the number of household duties she performed, the sense of touch conveyed a great deal more to her mind than Howe acknowledged. Without downplaying the severity of the child's plight or the value of Howe's humanitarian act, it seems clear that at no point during her illness and isolation did Laura ever resemble the child which he described as a "soul buried a thousand fathoms deep—so deep that no one could reach it or make a sign to it."[46]

The most important challenge to Howe's claim that his experiment had proven that the mind operates independent of the senses comes from the fact that Laura Bridgman experienced the full range of sense experience for more than two years before her illness, and had even begun to develop her powers of language. Howe repeatedly probed his pupil for evidence that she remembered any of the impressions she received in those years, even resorting to experiments with hypnotism, then known as the new science of "animal magnetism." He concluded that, "to the best of my judgement, she has no recollection." Since she was unable to recall anything of the world of sights and sounds from her first two years of life, Howe concluded that the influence of these sensations had been completely erased from her brain, at least "for all practical purposes."[47]

As years went by, his accounts of the child's earliest years usually omitted mention of her early language skills, or even her experience of sight and sound. She had been deaf and blind, he began to write, "from her tender infancy." When some of his contemporaries expressed skepticism, suggesting that Laura's remarkable progress in learning language was due to "some remembrance of oral language," Howe could only accuse them of being "metaphysical hairsplitter[s]."[48]

Today, with the benefit of a century and a half of empirical research, psychologists tell us that the sensory impressions gathered in the first two years of life are both indelible and enormously important to proper mental development. In fact, subsequent work with the deaf and blind has shown that those *born* into this state face nearly insurmountable barriers to mental development. Howe's breakthrough to Laura was a remarkable achievement of pedagogy, and a great act of human kindness, but in the end it could not resolve the ancient complexities of the role that the senses play in forming human knowledge.[49]

The efforts Howe made to explain away these flaws in his experiment suggest that he was well aware of them. Yet, in all the scientific discussion of Howe's work during his lifetime, there was little explicit criticism of his methodology. Not until the next generation of more empirically sophisticated psychologists arose were the flaws in Howe's experiment made plain. In 1879 G. Stanley Hall, the last scientist to examine Laura Bridgman in person, concluded that she could remember nothing of her first two years. But he added, "Yet, when we reflect on the amazingly rapid self-education of infantile life through the senses and its fundamental nature, it is impossible to believe that its effect can ever be entirely obliterated." Hall conjectured that Bridgman's "insatiable curiosity" about a world she could neither see nor hear was one crucial remnant from her first two years.[50] Perhaps even more important, her relatively rapid understanding of the nature and use of language was no doubt a product of her early linguistic development.

One possible explanation for the widespread uncritical acceptance of Howe's method and conclusions is the fact that they accorded so well with the prevailing wisdom of his time. Laura Bridgman delighted the Anglo-American intellectual community because she seemed to prove what they already believed. Defenders of the Christian faith welcomed what they took to be scientific evidence of an immaterial soul. Others in this era of democratic reform, individualism, and expansion embraced Howe's claim that Laura Bridgman proved that the human spirit, however humble, could conquer the most formidable physical obstacles. Steven Jay Gould, the historian of science, has suggested that scientific attempts to describe and measure the human mind have often been "virtually free from the constraints of fact." One reason, says Gould, is that the study of the mind is typically "invested with very little reliable information. When the ratio of data to social impact is so low, a history of scientific attitudes may be little more than an oblique record of social change."[51]

According to Gould, the likelihood that an observer's bias will corrupt the objectivity of an experiment is increased not only by the social significance of the results but also by the scarcity of reliable scientific evidence. In this regard, the obvious flaws in Howe's experiment reveal the primitive state of experimental psychology in the antebellum period. In the previous century, the thinkers of the Enlightenment had called for a new, scientific study of the human mind. Locke, as a pioneer in psychological speculation, founded his new science of the mind on the method of "introspection," the careful observation of the processes of one's own mind. This approach was vulnerable to the charge that each observer's self-reflections are inevitably subjective, even solipsistic.[52]

Howe, like many in his time, dismissed the introspective approach used by Locke and , later, the common sense philosophers, as hopelessly flawed. "They all hold up consciousness as a mirror before them," he wrote two years before finding Laura Bridgman, "and think they see there an image of man which they attempt to describe; but alas! the mirror is so narrow that it will admit but one image at a time, and that the image of him who holds it up." Echoing the prevailing scientific wisdom of his day, Howe concluded that such an approach "must ever err."[53]

Thus it was left to Howe and other nineteenth-century heirs of the Enlightenment to devise a new model of psychological investigation, based on the systematic observation of the minds of *others*. Howe's work, flawed as it was, must be understood in this context—as an early attempt to find a new method of empirical psychological research. By attempting to study the processes of Laura's mind rather than those of his own, Howe anticipated the course of future experimental psychological research. But clearly his own biases, and those of his society, compromised his observations and his conclusions, making his work no more objective than that of his predecessors.

Because Howe's earliest findings confirmed his society's cherished belief in an immaterial soul, many observers hailed him as a profound philosopher and a pioneering scientist of the human mind. But Howe's work with Laura was just beginning at this point. He vowed to carry on, learning what he could of the operations of the mind as he studied the gradual unfolding of "the moral and intellectual nature of this interesting child." Having proven the existence of the soul, he now proposed to dissect it, to search for clues to its internal nature.

As ever, Howe brought his own biases into this investigation. But at this point his assumptions about what he expected to find veered off from the broad intellectual consensus shared by Anglo-American Christendom. He would find in his exotic pupil a mind and soul that operated according to phrenological laws that mirrored his own liberal faith. While Howe's famous experiment began with universal admiration and acclaim, the doctor would soon find himself mired in controversy.

Chapter 3

In the Public Eye

Six months after Laura's education began, her mother came to Perkins for her first visit. Before being sent to Boston, Laura had been inseparable from her mother, following her around their farmhouse kitchen by day and insisting that only her mother could rock her to sleep each night. When Harmony Bridgman entrusted her daughter to Dr. Howe's care, she feared that his experiment would probably be cut short by her incurable homesickness.[1]

A half-year later Howe wrote to the Bridgmans, assuring them that he did not think that their daughter "repines in the least for home." More tactfully though less truthfully, he hastened to add that this did not mean that the child had forgotten, or even "diminished her affection" for, her parents. Confident that Laura was quite at home at Perkins and that her education would not be disrupted by the distraction, Howe encouraged Harmony to visit.[2]

As he later reported to his readers, Howe watched this family reunion "with intense interest." As the eight-year-old played with her classmates, oblivious to her mother's presence, Harmony Bridgman stood in the doorway, "gazing with overflowing eyes upon her unfortunate child." Laura accidentally bumped into her mother and began feeling the stranger's dress to see if she recognized the person. Concluding she did not, she turned away, "as from a stranger." Howe informed his readers that "the poor woman could not conceal the pang she felt."[3]

Handed a string of beads she had often worn before coming to Perkins, the child recognized them immediately, put them around her neck, and searched for Dr. Howe to tell him that she remembered that the necklace was from Hanover. Still, she rejected her mother's caresses. When another object from home was given to her, she grew more curious about the stranger and then recalled that she too came "from Hanover." But she still did not know her mother and turned away from her indifferently when beckoned by her blind playmates. "The distress of her mother was now painful to behold," Howe wrote, adding that "the painful reality of being treated with cold indifference by a darling child, was too much for a woman's nature to bear."[4]

Before long, however, Howe thought he could see "a vague idea flit across Laura's mind." As she reexamined the stranger more intensely, her face revealed, Howe believed, the contending emotions of hope and doubt. At this point Harmony kissed her child, Laura's uncertainty was dispelled in a "flash" of truth, and "with an expression of exceeding joy she eagerly nestled to the bosom of her parent, and yielded to her fond embraces." Howe hastened to assure his readers that he was not a voyeuristic intruder on this scene but a scientific observer, eager to gather all that could be learned about "the workings of [Laura's] mind." But even the scientist had to acknowledge some sacred ground on which he should not tread. Howe told his readers that, once mother and child were thus united, he "left them to indulge unobserved those delicious feelings, which those who have known a mother's love may conceive, but which cannot be expressed."[5]

This story, woven into his annual report on the Perkins Institution two years after Laura arrived there, was greeted as "a thrilling incident" by the popular press. Several papers and journals excerpted the story from the larger report, promising their readers that Howe's tale "excites the deepest sympathy." Others devoted much more column space, reprinting most or all of his twenty-page report on Laura's progress that year. One reviewer informed her readers that the blind school's report contained "tales of thrilling interest, not surpassed by those of the novelist." Another suggested that the account of the little deaf and blind girl might easily become a favorite of the lending libraries.[6]

As news of Laura Bridgman spread, so did Howe's readers, and by 1841, when Laura was ten, his accounts of her education were regularly reviewed, excerpted, or printed in their entirety in a wide range of newspapers, children's books, "ladies,'" religious, and "family" magazines, as well as more scholarly journals. Within two years of Laura's arrival in the public eye, most editors in the United States and Britain could assume that "our readers are familiar with the history of Laura Bridgman, whose mental development under such apparently insurmountable embarrassments has been watched with much interest."[7]

This wide public fascination with Laura Bridgman was due not just to the remarkable accomplishments of the young student but also to the skillful public relations campaign of her teacher. Inserted into the Perkins Institution's 1838 and '39 annual reports, Howe's first public announcement of his breakthrough presumably reached only a relatively small, specialized audience of doctors, philanthropists, and New England legislators, those interested in the progress of the nation's first school for the blind. But Howe was an astute promoter of his own cause, turning reports which might have been dry and perfunctory reviews of facilities, expenditures, and personnel matters into lively rhetorical articles, full of enough sentiment to move the common reader, as well as the legislator, to take a deep interest in the cause of the blind.

Since 1832 Howe had been presenting the blind to the public in print and in exhibition halls around the country. This experience taught him that the afflicted themselves, their plight as well as their accomplishments, were the most effective means of pricking the public conscience into action. Thus he recognized that his new pupil was an ideal vehicle for arousing public sympathy and enlightening the public mind about the needs and potential of the handicapped. Howe had reduced the process to a simple formula: "Human sympathies are always ready to be poured out in proportion to the amount of human suffering," he reasoned, adding that "when the supposed sufferer is a child—a girl—and of pleasing appearance, the sympathy and interest are naturally increased."[8]

As the fame of Dr. Howe's experiment grew, so did the amount of space he devoted to her story in each of his annual reports. In 1841 he began the practice of attaching a separate appendix to the public document, devoted exclusively to providing an account of the intimate details of Laura's progress for that year. As the reviewer's comparison between Howe's reports and those thrilling "tales of the novelist" suggests, Howe did not simply report the facts of Laura's case in dry administrative prose but wove scientific observation into the conventions of sentimental fiction, ensuring that Laura Bridgman would become "an object of peculiar interest and lively sympathy."

From the outset of his work with Laura, Howe took particular care to send his reports on her case to specialists in Europe, those on the forefront of educational reform and experimental psychology who were likely to recognize the scientific significance of Howe's accomplishment. To a Parisian educator who had already praised Howe's work with the blind in a French journal, Howe sent his latest report on this "most interesting case." "I hope to make some curious and valuable observations," Howe told him, "upon the innateness of ideas, the succession of ideas &c, by means of this most interesting child," adding that "would you desire it, I will communicate further observations upon her case." To the language philosopher Baron

Degerando he suggested, "I think the case of Laura Bridgman will interest you deeply."[9]

In Germany, Howe corresponded with Dr. Julius of Hamburg. Julius had written to Howe to learn more about Julia Brace of Hartford, but Howe assured him that his own deaf-blind pupil was "much more interesting in every point of view" and enclosed his first two reports on her as evidence. Howe recounted Laura's "wonderful and unexampled" accomplishments in her first two years at Perkins. Then, in a rare mood of playfulness, he told the famous doctor that "perhaps I shall send you some further account of this prodigy out of whose case some of your German Psychologists might weave long tissues of beautiful, if not useful moonshine." Julius did, in fact, pass on Howe's reports to his colleagues, and Howe was soon greeted by a request from a professor at Konigsberg for an updated account of Laura's progress, expressing particular interest in Laura's earliest conceptions of death.[10]

Howe evidently communicated with Swiss educators as well. As early as 1838, a Boston lady who was touring the asylum for the blind at Lake Geneva found herself inundated with questions from one of the blind students there about Boston's new celebrity "of whom he had heard so much."[11]

Through the 1840s Howe's annual reports were translated into the major European languages and "read by thousands." One friend, traveling abroad, reported in 1842 that "in Germany, I found frequent passing notices in Books & periodicals of Laura Bridgman's case." While visiting Paris, George Sumner reported back to Howe that his reports were "exciting the admiration of many enlightened Frenchmen" and that papers on her case were being presented and published there.[12]

Howe found that, among Old World intellectuals, the British showed the greatest interest in his new experiment, probably because it promised to accord so well with their own philosophical tradition.[13] A Scottish friend wrote to Howe that "Laura Bridgman is very much admired by the British public, and her case is universally attractive. It is spoken of with deep interest and admiration in every society into which I enter."[14]

By far the most important English tourist to visit the young celebrity was Charles Dickens, who made a visit to the Perkins Institution the very first stop on his American tour of 1842 and recorded the encounter in his *American Notes*. Dickens devoted most of his chapter on Boston to her and reprinted extended sections of Howe's own writings in his book. Dickens's account was the most widely read version of Howe's accomplishment and contributed more than any other work to Laura Bridgman's spreading fame in Europe and America during the 1840s.[15]

In Howe's absence, the novelist and his wife were escorted to the Perkins school by Howe's close friend, Charles Sumner. They found Laura sitting very still in her room. After brief introductions, they followed her to the parlor, where she became quite playful. Laura's teacher, Miss Rogers, recalled in her diary that Dickens "could hardly believe the evidence of his senses, and was much more surprised than people generally are."[16] In fact, he was so moved that he later suggested that, along with Niagara Falls, Laura Bridgman was one of the two highlights of his entire tour of the New World. While still traveling in the Midwest, Dickens wrote to Howe to express his appreciation:

> I never was more truly and deeply affected in my life than on that occasion (except when I read your account of Laura Bridgman a day or two previous). I never more sincerely regretted the not seeing any man than I did the not seeing you. I am one of God's creatures who to the best of his capacity and ability loves the rest;—accept the thanks I offer you, in the name of humanity, for the light you have shed on that dark world by which you are surrounded, and in which you labour, to your everlasting honor.[17]

When the two ardent lovers of humanity actually met in England a few years later, they could muster little love for each other. Dickens found Howe to be "a cold-blooded fellow," while Howe privately complained that fame had inflated Dickens's ego. In spite of these personal differences, the two exerted a strong mutual influence upon each other, one that shaped both of their efforts to explain the "meaning" of Laura Bridgman to the Anglo-American public. In an undated letter to Horace Mann, clearly written well before his unfortunate meeting with Dickens, Howe wrote that he "greatly love(d)" the novelist "for the grace & beauty & tenderness with which he depicts dignity of character in servitude, ideality in rags, & stern morality in squalid wretchedness."[18]

As that comment suggests, Howe appreciated the way Dickens had turned conventional middle-class morality on its head, finding virtue in the poor and sinfulness in those callous rich people who ignored the plight of their less fortunate fellow creatures. This inversion perfectly matched the new spirit of romantic reform that motivated Howe; the blind pupils at an asylum, the students at school, even the prisoners in the new penitentiaries were assumed to be essentially good, always capable of moral and social regeneration if treated with enlightened Christian benevolence.

While a direct link between the writings of the two men on Laura Bridgman is impossible to prove, it seems likely that Howe's previous exposure to Dickens's work led him to see Laura's story the way the novelist might. Howe played up the pathos of a silently suffering child, as well as the redemptive imagery of a child entombed in darkness, miraculously brought into the light. One Dickens scholar has suggested that, when Dickens read Howe's reports, he found echoes of the themes of his own fiction, "isolation and enclosure, personal transformation and spiritual rescue. As cheerful victim and source of spiritual inspiration to others, the Laura Bridgman constructed by Howe resembles Little Nell, and her story, as Howe shaped it, dramatizes Dickensian motifs." Reading Howe's account of Laura Bridgman several days *before* he actually met her, Dickens was no doubt doubly prepared to see her as a moving symbol of his own highest hopes for humanity.[19]

The most compelling proof of this link between Howe's scientific reports and Dickens's fiction is the fact that, in describing his impressions of Laura Bridgman, Dickens borrowed one of Howe's favorite metaphors. Howe had often described her as "shut up in a dark and silent cell." Elaborating on that motif, Dickens told his readers that she was "built up, as it were, in a marble cell, impervious to any ray of light or particle of sound; with her poor white hand peeping through a chink in the wall, beckoning to some good man for help, that an Immortal soul might be awakened."[20]

At the height of the reform impulse in the 1840s, the distinction between the novelist's sentimental tales of spiritual regeneration and the philanthropist's actual practice must have seemed blurred, particularly in America. Many of the same people who anxiously awaited the next installment of Dickens's latest work also flocked to visit the impressive new prisons and asylums that were being constructed in enlightened communities throughout the Northeast. As the historian John Sears argues, American and European tourists thought of asylums and prisons as "sacred places" which offered the possibility of "miraculous transformations." Visitors poured into Perkins, Sears suggests, because they hoped to see "dramatic examples of people passing from darkness and silence into light and joyful sound." And as the writings of both Howe and Dickens had attested, no sight in America offered a better example of this kind of modern miracle than the Perkins Institution's most famous resident.[21]

&) "I would have given a year of my short future life to have witnessed your meeting with Laura," a doctor from South Carolina wrote to Howe. The child, he added, was "a more interesting creation than Petrarch's; endowed by you with fire from Heaven—not stolen." As the story of Laura's breakthrough into full humanity was rapidly passing from fact into romantic allegory, thousands wanted to witness the miracle for themselves. When Howe brought Laura along on his traveling exhibitions, he could be assured of an enormous crowd. A reporter on hand for their visit to the New Hampshire statehouse, for example, wrote that he had "never seen the House and galleries so crowded, except upon the visit of General Lafayette." When Howe brought his most famous pupil to Washington, he secured an audience with President Polk.[22]

The crowds at the school's weekly exhibitions, already large before Laura Bridgman arrived, now swelled to the point that a second show often had to be added. One of Perkins' instructors reported in her journal that the crowd "has become so great . . . and presses so closely about Laura, that we are obliged to surround her desk by settees, thus making a little enclosure to protect her."[23]

"Strange feelings spring up as we gaze upon Laura," one woman in the crowd reported. "Never shall I forget the sentiments which this little being awakened in my mind," another Perkins visitor recalled. A British lady studied Laura's "eloquent face," and wrote, "I might well have been reminded of the illumined alabaster vase to which some one imaginatively compared a celebrated poet's countenance, for really Laura's face appeared almost like a crystal one, and the mighty mystery of mind seemed peering through the transparent casket." Laura's face was perhaps made more mysterious, and more pathetic, by the green velvet band that she always wore over her eyes, shielding those around her from the disturbing sight of her lifeless eyes.[24]

The sight of this child, afflicted yet triumphant, obviously stirred deep emotions in visitors to the Perkins School, emotions that these early Victorians almost invariably attempted to distill into a moral. What answers to "the mighty mystery of the mind," what lessons for life, did Laura's strangely veiled yet animated face offer these touring pilgrims? In many respects, her eyeless face was a mirror, reflecting back to each viewer a symbol of some of the most cherished sentiments of the era.

Many visitors saw in Laura Bridgman proof of the miraculous power of the human spirit, the ability of even the most humble and disadvantaged to rise above adversity. The more optimistic saw her accomplishments as evidence of the "wondrous power and art of mind" shared by all human beings. For others, her achievement was more a chastisement than an inspiration. They left Perkins with the conclusion that the senses of sight and hearing were heavenly gifts that were too often taken for granted, abused through the sin of ingratitude to the Creator. "What a rebuke," a writer for a popular family magazine proclaimed, "to those murmurers who possess all the human senses, and yet complain of their *hard* lot!" Another writer felt Laura's silent rebuke personally. Finding the sight of her "inexpressibly affecting," he confessed that the experience made him "more than ever grateful for my own mercies, and humble at the thought that I had made of them so little and such unprofitable use."[25]

Frequently the moral lessons afforded by this extraordinary child were pointed toward more ordinary ones. A writer for a popular magazine for mothers, finding her "most tender sympathies excited" by a personal pilgrimage to Perkins, thought that she "could not furnish a more interesting story for children." Baptist preacher and children's author W. K. Tweedie depicted Laura as proof of the power of individual effort. He told Victorian girls that she showed that "painstakingness" would be rewarded, that she was "a model of what can be accomplished by pains, and prayer, and well-directed effort." When Laura was ten, a visitor from Nantucket was "amazed" to see her happily learning to write and taking apparent pleasure in the company of others. "Her laugh is quite audible and natural, though she cannot herself hear it," he wrote to his daughter, who was about Laura's age at the time. The father added this admonition: "Think how happy ought those to be who have all their senses, when this poor little girl is so happy with so few."[26]

In this manner, this tragically deformed girl was repeatedly held up to children as a model of Victorian virtue, of happiness in the face of adversity, of gratitude for the blessings of health, of the importance of hard work and individual effort. Young girls poked out their dolls' eyes and named them "Laura," while reluctant pupils grew to resent their elders' constant reminders to compare their own efforts with those of the little deaf and blind girl, who had accomplished so much in the face of such overwhelming obstacles. Writing years later, the journalist Nellie Bly called Laura Bridgman the *"bete noire"* of her childhood. When Bly resisted learning the alphabet, she was often told of Laura Bridgman. "That little girl could not see her letters, could not hear them spoken, could not speak them," Bly was admonished, "But she never said, 'I can't.'"[27]

Dickens was more impressed by Laura's complete sincerity, another favorite in the Victorian pantheon of virtues. "It is strange to watch the faces of the blind," he wrote in *American Notes,* "and see how free they are from all concealment of what is passing in their thoughts; observing which, a man with eyes may blush to contemplate the mask he wears." Another English visitor marveled at "Laura's intelligent and most speaking face." Watching as a letter from a friend was read to her, the woman saw words translated from the printed page into Laura's sign language, while the import of the letter was instantly telegraphed on the child's face. "Wonder, pleasure—sometimes a slight shade of vexation and disappointment—regret, affection, mirth, sympathy, doubt, anxiety, hope, expectation; all seemed to impress themselves by turns on the voiceless and sightless one's features."[28]

Scholars have noted that the early Victorians were extremely interested in the quality of sincerity, sometimes attributing this to the uneasiness that many in the middle class felt about urbanization and the growing rate of social and geographic mobility. At a time when individuals were becoming increasingly anonymous and atomized and yet more economically interdependent, sincerity was a valuable measure of one's trustworthiness. One plausible explanation, therefore, for the era's fascination with children in general, and Laura Bridgman in particular, is the fact that these innocents were so clearly incapable of the kind of dissemblance and guile that seemed to be pervading the rest of society.[29]

Literary historians have sometimes described the era's fascination with sincerity more as an aesthetic quest, a romantic attempt to probe with honesty the inner recesses of the self. Drawing inspiration from the intimate self-revelations of Rousseau's *Confessions,* nineteenth-century romantics were searching for a new language that made the inner workings of the individual heart and soul transparent to public gaze. Many who followed Laura Bridgman's progress, particularly those unable to visit Perkins, relied more on the child's soundless words than on her transparent and eyeless face. As Laura's language skills developed, many of her utterances were carefully recorded by her teachers in a daily journal and then condensed and reported by Howe each year. Judging from the number of times these anecdotes were reprinted in the popular press, Laura's comments evidently delighted many readers. This great public interest in the naive questions and simple statements of a preadolescent girl can, at least in part, be explained by the fact that they epitomized this treasured quality of sincerity. No less than her face, Laura's words were an unusually direct window on the inner workings of her mind, expressed in a language which was distinctly her own. Aware of this appeal, Howe frequently assured his readers that he had not tampered with Laura's language but simply reprinted it verbatim.

Laura learned language with great difficulty. Because the normal process of language acquisition was slowed, Howe was able to make a careful record of the steps she took each year. Unlike other children, she lacked a visible external reference for her words and was cut off from most of the social conversation that provides context and teaches the conventional usage of words and phrases. "Other children learn language by mere imitation and without effort," Howe explained. "She has to ask by a slow method the name of every new thing; other children use words which they do not understand; but she wishes to know the force of every expression."[30]

As a result of this unnatural isolation from human conversation, Laura approached language with an intense literalness. Perhaps even more than most children, she had a tendency to over apply the rules of grammar, expecting consistency where so often it does not exist. Once she had mastered a rule, Howe wrote, she would "admit of no exceptions." When she came down with a case of the mumps, which swelled the glands on just one side of her face, she insisted, "I have mump." She rejected as absurd the notion that "n-a-i-l" could mean both the covering at the tips of her fingers *and* a sharp piece of steel made by the blacksmith; and blacksmiths, she assumed, were "necessarily black men." Learning that when she was by herself she was "alone," she inferred that when she was with another she was "altwo." Laura clung to language with such literalness that for several years she was unable even to fathom the concept of fiction. While this posed pedagogical obstacles, Howe was delighted with what he took to be evidence of the soul's natural truthfulness, its instinctive sincerity.[31]

Laura was not only tripped up by inconsistencies in the language but also by her intense isolation from the world around her.[32] Almost everything that she knew of the world had to come to her through language, and she fed an insatiable curiosity through an endless round of questions which often left her teachers reeling from exhaustion. For example, Dr. Howe reported in 1842 that the child was obsessed by a desire to learn as much as she could about animals and incessantly probed her teachers for more information. Do worms go outside to play? Are they afraid when hens eat them? she wondered. Told that cows have horns to push away "bad cows," she asked if they had two horns in order "to push two cows." After a long string of questions about whales and fish—"Why does not whale live on land like worm?"—her teacher belatedly realized that "she was totally ignorant of the form of a fish," adding, "I could not give her a very perfect idea of it."[33]

One afternoon, at the end of a long train of such questions, Laura asked, "Do horses sit up late?" When told they did not sit up, she laughed and asked, "Do horses stand up late?" When Thomas Carlyle read about the incident in a copy of a report forwarded by Howe and delivered by Dickens, the great English romantic wrote, "That little question of hers stirs us to laughter, to tears,—when one thinks of the good little creature,—and probably to as kind a mood as human speech alone can awaken in a human heart." "Few things I ever read," he told Howe, "have interested me more than this of your dear little Laura Bridgman." Carlyle's heart was melted, clearly, not by the child's profundity but by her simplicity, a naive wonder common to all children but heightened in her case by her sensory isolation. Like others who saw their own favorite values reflected back as they gazed at the stricken child, Carlyle found evidence of the uncorrupted soul's natural curiosity and creativity. Poetic metaphor, she proved to the poet, is the true language of the soul.[34]

Carlyle called Laura "a true angel-soul and breath of Heaven" and heaped praise on Howe for his work with her. But he felt that he must share "one painful apprehension." The angelic qualities that Carlyle admired so much in Laura Bridgman might be ruined, he believed, if she ever learned just how special she was. Her simplicity, her sincerity, her naive wonder at the world might all be stained by "vanities and base confusions" if she should ever come to realize "how wonderful she is." Laura's was not the studied sincerity of the poet, then, but the fragile spontaneity of a child, not yet banished from paradise by eating the "forbidden fruit" of vain self-consciousness. Ironically, Laura's "innocent heart" might be spoiled not by the seduction of a malicious devil but by those well-intentioned spectators who "must gather round her with their wonder and their grimaces." Writing to Howe, Carlyle could hardly contain himself at the thought: "Be far distant; ye unmalevolent blockheads; go; elsewhither, in the name of Heaven!"[35]

Howe shared Carlyle's concern that the public's growing interest in Laura might spoil her purity of spirit, her simplicity and sincerity. In the same year that he received Carlyle's letter, Howe publicly criticized those who unthinkingly lavished attention on the child, serving their own "spontaneous impulse" without regard to the long-term effect on her character. With hundreds passing through Perkins each month, he found it "almost impossible to prevent her receiving such attentions and such caresses as directly address her self-esteem." The result, he fretted, was that this remarkably pure, simple girl might come to think of herself as "a lion, than which hardly a greater misfortune can befall a woman." Howe asked the school's female teachers, Drew and Rogers, to do their best to shield Laura from the corrupting influence of public attention.[36]

While they tried to carry out Howe's orders, Laura's instructors continued to complain about being "interrupted almost every day." On Saturdays, when the school was open to the public, Laura joined the other blind children, demonstrating to enthusiastic crowds her ability to write and to point out locations on an embossed map. The experience often left her "very much excited," a source of concern to her teachers. But they also worried that these events reminded Laura that she was "an object of more interest than any of the other blind girls."[37]

While Laura's guardians felt that exhibitions did the most to inflate her "self-esteem," at any time of the day, any day of the week, the child's routine might be disrupted by those admirers who were influential enough to be permitted a private audience with the famous child. One day in 1841, her teacher recorded this entry in her journal: "While engaged with Laura, not aware there were any visitors in the house, I had not prepared Laura for company, and before I was aware two ladies and gentlemen came in directly to Laura and took her hand, without any ceremony, and wished me to ask Laura if she recollected that they came to see her two years ago. I begged them not to touch her, and to stand without the enclosure, but they only complied with the first request;—merely moved away from her."[38]

Some visitors, like the moral philosopher Dr. Francis Wayland, presented Laura with small gifts, dolls or sometimes dollars. Others hoped to carry away a prized autograph, written in Laura's distinctive blockish handwriting. Laura marveled at the seemingly endless demand for a copy of her name. Other souvenir hunters snatched up the needlework and knitted items that she sold to earn a modest amount of spending money. "A party of foreigners . . . were [sic] here," her teacher wrote, "who took all of Laura's work that I had on hand & wished for more." And a number of Boston ladies, moved by Laura's case, taught themselves sign language in order to befriend her. By the time she was eleven and mastering her own language skills, Laura enjoyed "a pretty wide circle of acquaintances" and a growing number of correspondents that included the state's Governor Briggs. She was spending a few minutes to a few hours of almost every day being introduced to visitors and performing for them.[39]

In the early 1840s Laura was joined by several other deaf-blind students, brought to Perkins in the hope that Howe could repeat his educational miracle. Julia Brace, the woman from the Hartford Asylum who had first inspired Howe's interest in the deaf-blind, was sent to Boston in 1842, at the age of thirty-five. After a year of painfully slow progress, Howe regretfully concluded that Julia was too old to recreate Laura's rapid breakthrough into language. Lucy Reed, a fourteen-year old deaf-blind girl from Vermont, posed a different challenge to the Perkins staff. Difficult to govern and deeply self-conscious about her infirmity, Lucy had worn a kerchief over her face for years and adamantly refused to remove it. At first Howe felt compelled to subdue her with physical restraint. But over the course of months, Lucy gradually became more sociable, removed her veil, and began to learn to communicate with the manual alphabet. Howe rejoiced that "we had broke through the crust, & got at the living spring within." At that point, however, Lucy's mother demanded her return, disappointed that her daughter had not progressed as rapidly as Laura Bridgman. Against Howe's entreaties, she returned to Vermont, to a life of linguistic isolation. Howe had more success with Oliver Caswell, a twelve-year-old boy from Rhode Island who, like Laura, had been blinded and deafened by a bout of scarlet fever at a young age. Oliver followed in Laura's footsteps, learning the manual alphabet, though more slowly than Laura had done.[40]

4. In his 1840 report, Howe included a copy of Laura Bridgman's first letter home to her mother. (*Courtesy of Perkins School for the Blind, Watertown, Massachusetts*)

While Laura shared the attention of her teachers with these other deaf-blind students, she remained the focal point of interest in Howe's reports and in the public exhibitions. Articles about Julia Brace never failed to contrast her primitive use of simple "natural" sign language with Laura's quick and expanding mental life. And public notices about Oliver Caswell and Lucy Reed dwelled most often on the fact that Laura Bridgman had helped them to learn the manual alphabet. A touching portrait of Laura helping Oliver Caswell learn to read was painted by a Howe family friend and widely reprinted by the press.

Although Laura lived in a lively and crowded institution, surrounded by teachers, matrons, and her fellow deaf-blind students, popular press accounts usually stressed Laura's utter social isolation. Howe sometimes played on this theme as well. "Thousands have been watching her with eager eyes," he wrote with characteristic flourish, yet she remained "all unconscious of their gaze." However, her sense of touch was so acute and her curiosity so keen that she often knew a great deal more about her environment than most people could have suspected. She constantly combed the rooms of Perkins with the "feelers" of her hands, examining every object and quickly noticing when something was new or out of place. Howe found that "a person walking across a room while she had hold on his left arm, would find it hard to take a pencil out of his waistcoat pocket with his right hand, without her perceiving it."[41]

Perhaps because language had to bear so much of the load for her understanding of the world around her, she was extremely social, constantly aware of the presence of others. She could identify her friends by the vibrations their voices made in the air, by the tremor of their footsteps on the floor, or by a brief feel of the cut and texture of their clothes. She could recognize past acquaintances from their handshakes, even if she had only met them once, months before. Thus, even though she never saw the parade of curious onlookers, never heard their conversations about her—no doubt held in hushed tones of sympathy and amazement—she was acutely aware that she was, as Howe suggested, "an object of peculiar interest." Through vibrations in the air and floor, she "heard" the thunderous applause which audiences gave the students at exhibitions, the clapping hands and pounding feet. And she soon knew that "such visitors to the school are more interested in her than in her blind companions; and that they remain near her most of the time."[42]

His own claim that she was unconscious of the public gaze notwithstanding, Howe worried that all this attention would ruin his efforts "to preserve her present amiable simplicity of character." He also began to fear that Laura was being exposed to disruptive influences from her encounters with the other blind girls at Perkins. "When I found out that she could talk freely with the other girls, I thought it would be advantageous to her to be separate at times," Howe explained.

But he also recognized a dilemma. Because manual sign language was almost the child's only avenue to the outside world, he could quite easily regulate all access to her mind. He might even develop an alternative sign language alphabet, so that she could not converse with the other blind children and those visitors who had learned the standard manual alphabet. Such an approach would offer some advantages. From the standpoint of the child's moral development, he could then shield her from the corrupting flattery of fawning visitors. Scientifically, the development of her mind would be easier to observe if she was isolated. Laura's character, as well as Howe's experiment, might remain more pure.[43]

But Howe rejected this extreme approach, recognizing that his prize pupil would have to "run the risk of the disadvantages of society, in order to secure its obvious and indispensable advantages." For the child's happiness, as well as the full development of her mind, Howe conceded, she needed the companionship of children, more regular mental stimulation than one or two teachers could provide, and exposure to as much language as possible.

So Howe settled on a compromise, monitoring but not eliminating Laura's exposure to society. He attempted to control her relations with visitors and other blind children at Perkins by allowing her the special privilege of living in his own private apartment at the school. At the age of ten, Laura moved in with Howe and his unmarried sister Jeannette, who was serving as Howe's assistant and housekeeper. Howe, still a bachelor in his late thirties, came to look on the girl not simply as his most important student but also as a kind of adopted daughter. "I am very much attached to Laura," he told one correspondent. "I love her as if she were my own child." The new living arrangement allowed him to closely monitor the child's progress and limit her exposure to what he believed were bad social influences, while providing her with the kind of family atmosphere that he felt was best for any child.[44]

Howe continued to let Laura mingle with other blind and deaf-blind students during parts of the school day, meet some visitors, and correspond with her many admirers around the world. In making the decision not to isolate the child more completely, Howe wrestled with the contradiction between his role as a humanitarian and his role as a scientist. He had an unprecedented opportunity to explore the gradual unfolding of a mind, placing its "operations" under a metaphorical "microscope." Yet he realized that, if he were to preserve the integrity of his experiment by keeping her in more controlled laboratory conditions, he would have to exact a high price from the child, robbing her of some of the very freedom and dignity that he had restored, hurting the one he had helped.

In addition to his evident concern for Laura's well-being, Howe had other strong reasons to place humanitarian concerns before scientific ones. By the end of the 1840s, he noted that "perhaps there are not three living women whose names are more widely known than [Laura Bridgman's]; and there is not one who has excited so much sympathy and interest." As the child's fame spread, so did her teacher's. Praises for Howe accompanied every article on his beloved pupil, a European monarch awarded him a medal for the work, and countless of his contemporaries assured him that, through Laura Bridgman, he had secured a place in the history of mankind that would never be forgotten. As the influential British journalist Mary Howitt put it, Howe was an "excellent man, whose name ought to be reverenced as one of the greatest benefactors of suffering humanity."[45]

Those singing Howe's praises rarely stopped to consider the purity of his data, entranced as they were by the apparent purity of his motives. While a decision to isolate Laura from the public *might* have produced more reliable psychological observations, Howe understood that it also would have diminished her fame, and therefore his own. Even as he fretted over the effect that public adoration was having on Laura, he was encouraging it through his own publicity efforts. Each week the mail, the press, and public exhibitions brought Howe fresh reminders that his own success was intimately tied to the public's fascination with Laura Bridgman.

Since the outset of his work with the blind, Howe had recognized that one of the most important aspects of his job was to ensure that the public remained interested in the work. Glowing press accounts and public exhibitions, jammed with paying customers eager for a glimpse of Laura Bridgman, were not just the publicity stunts of a P. T. Barnum nor petty distractions to a high-minded philanthropist but an essential part of maintaining the financial support which was needed for the ongoing work of teaching New England's blind children. In addition to his efforts to maintain public interest in his own school, Howe spent long weeks each year trying to spread the Perkins gospel, lobbying legislatures around the country to establish similar schools for the blind in each state. Howe's national fame, fed by the enormous outpouring of public interest in his star pupil, was no doubt one of his greatest assets in winning the respect and support of legislatures and public audiences everywhere. Howe's relationship to

Laura Bridgman granted him access to presidents, legislators, philosophers, and a parade of European and American writers and public figures.

In spite of his misgivings, then, about the disruptive effect that visitors were having on the child's character and on his own experiment, Howe continued to feed the public's curiosity and encourage its sympathy. He did this for the sake of her social development, for the sake of his own ambition, and for the sake of blind students in Boston and around the country. But Howe was convinced that the greatest beneficiary was the public itself. "Everything which brings out the hidden but innate virtues of humanity; everything which puts aside for a moment the selfishness and egotism that obscure its native qualities of love and sympathy, and shows the heart of man beating in unison with the joys and woes of his fellows; every such thing I consider a compliment to me as one of the race. The case of Laura Bridgman has done this in a striking manner, and certainly she can say that it has been better for her generation that she lived in it."[46]

Laura Bridgman, Howe had discovered, could be used as a catalyst to activate the "innate virtues" of thousands of men and women around the world. The child's accomplishments showed them what even the most destitute human being was capable of becoming, while the profound sympathy she evoked reminded them of their own best qualities.

But Howe was not satisfied with simply stirring up vague emotions of love and concern and hazy thoughts about the goodness within the human breast. With the confidence of a Yankee schoolmaster, he set out to use Laura Bridgman as a public lesson on the inner workings of the conscience and the soul. As he continued with his experiment, he announced that he would carefully map the gradual unfolding of Laura's physical, intellectual, and spiritual "faculties."

Howe felt sure that the psychological observations he would make as Laura's education progressed would not only affirm the goodness of human nature but prove it scientifically. Through this unique experiment, he would offer the world a blueprint of human development, one which could guide educators, reformers, and parents in the creation of a more enlightened society.

Chapter 4

Body and Mind

In the early 1840s the Perkins Institution was home not only to several dozen blind children and their teachers but also to hundreds of skulls. As the most enthusiastic officer of the Boston Phrenological Society, Howe became the caretaker of the group's extensive collection—a scientific gallery of skulls, busts, and plaster casts of famous heads. He set up many of the specimens in his office. For those visitors who could read the language of the cranium, each one offered a lesson in human nature. Bulges on the bust of Voltaire, for example, showed where the brain housed the organs of "Language, Mirthfulness, and Ideality." A skull of an Indian, shot "while prowling around a house," showed why that race was characterized by "combativeness, destructiveness, and Secretiveness." A protuberance on the skull of a man who "died insane on music" showed where the organ of "Tune" was located, while the head of a famous Irish nomad marked the cerebral home of "Locality."[1]

As this catalog suggests, one of phrenology's great attractions was its ability to explain individual differences, to impose a plausible and predictable order on the apparent chaos of human diversity. No two skulls, and no two people, were quite alike; yet the anatomical studies done by phrenologists seemed to reveal certain underlying laws of human nature, rules which governed the formation of racial and individual character.

One of the most basic of these laws was the idea that human nature is actually composed of three separate, interlocking natures: the physical, the intellectual, and the moral or spiritual. Phrenologists were not the first to suggest this arrangement. For centuries, philosophers and theologians had been proposing variations on the idea that human nature is a compound of body, mind, and soul. Phrenologists insisted that they had also discovered this scheme, not by reading works of philosophy but through scientific observation of the structure and growth of the brain.

Outlining this theory to a Boston audience in 1837, Howe explained that at the base of the brain phrenologists had discovered the organs responsible for the physical, or "animal," dispositions, the instinctive drives for sex and food, for territory and survival. Because these are essential to the preservation of life, God wisely had placed them in the center and back of the skull, making them first in the order of human development. Phrenological studies of "idiots" and primitive savages had revealed that, while the intellectual and moral faculties of such people had remained undeveloped, the "animal region" at the base of their brains was always fully formed. On this foundation of physical drives, God had erected the human character.[2]

The next stage of human growth, Howe explained, was the development of the intellectual faculties. These were the powers of reason and perception, found "where guides should be, in the front of the head." The intellectual faculties provided the individual with powers of rational calculation. Without the guidance of the moral faculties, the intellect offered no insight into the higher truths of life, matters of right and wrong, but simply helped the individual avoid danger and satisfy the needs of the body.[3]

Only after an individual's animal and intellectual nature had matured could one look for the final stage of human development, the emergence of the moral and religious sentiments. These faculties, Howe believed, formed the capstone of human character, and so he was not surprised to find them where they "should naturally be," at the top of the brain. God had placed these nobler sentiments at the crown of the head because He had intended them to rule over the rest of the faculties, infusing the reason with moral purpose and moderating the physical drives.

In short, Howe and his fellow phrenologists believed that the brain was a microcosm of the human character, its hierarchical structure mirroring the proper relationship between body, mind, and soul. The fully developed and civilized human being, by this view, had a strong body and a clear mind, both obedient to the dictates of an enlightened conscience.[4]

Studying brains from around the world, phrenologists concluded that the full range of faculties—the physical, the intellectual, and the moral— were inherent in the human constitution. Yet, as the example of primitive savages made clear, development of the higher faculties was not inevitable. Human nature was raw material, in need of the guiding hand of education. If children were left to their own devices, Howe insisted, they would become like savages. Only their animal faculties would develop, leaving them "little elevated above the brute." The civilizing influence of education was essential, he believed, if children were to be "developed more than the animal."[5]

In his first few months with Laura, Howe felt that he had already demonstrated that, in spite of being cut off from normal human relations, she was clearly more than an animal. Inside her damaged body, he had found a mind that wanted to learn and a soul that yearned for communion with other human beings. But Howe felt that this great discovery would be a hollow accomplishment if he could not succeed in guiding Laura's mind and soul to maturity, educating her to become a conscientious and self-governing adult. This was the next, crucial phase of his experiment, one that would absorb his interest for more than a decade.

As Howe made plans for Laura's education, his phrenological theory of human development provided a road map. His ultimate destination—the highest goal of all education—was the training of her moral and religious faculties. But phrenology told him that these would emerge slowly, only maturing in the later stages of her education. To prepare for this culmination, he would first have to provide the proper training for her physical and intellectual faculties, developing them "in their due proportion, and in their natural order." The first step, then, was to give Laura a sound physical education.[6]

At 5:30 each morning, students at the Perkins Institution were awakened by a bell, clanging through the "large and airy halls" of the school. Laura, of course, could not hear the sound, but she soon learned to rise with the other children, sensing their movements in the vibrations of her floor and door. At times, her teacher was not so disciplined. Her attempts to stay, as Laura put it, "so very comfortably adjusted in bed" were rewarded with a scolding from her pupil, who considered it "a very bad habit to lie in bed till the first meal bell rings for breakfast."[7]

During the morning meal, as at most other times of the day, boys and girls were carefully segregated from one another. Laura sat at one of the girls' tables, usually next to a teacher, conversing with her fingers as she ate the simple fare that Howe insisted should always be served at the school. Justifying this culinary discipline, he wrote that his students "must subsist on plain and wholesome food & banishing all thought of gratifying mere taste, 'eat & drink to live,' never reversing the order even for a holiday." Laura, whose sense of taste was greatly retarded by her near total inability to smell, had little complaint about the blandness of Perkins' fare. She usually ate bread and butter for breakfast and often contented herself with far less food than her teachers felt was healthy.[8]

After breakfast the boys were sent outdoors for exercise, while the girls got theirs by being kept "busy at housework." Laura, like all of the other children, was expected to maintain her own clothes, bed, and room and to do "everything for herself that she could possibly do."[9]

Bathing came next in the morning routine. Convinced of the purifying effects of cold water, Howe insisted that the students should take daily cold water baths or showers, even in winter. Some of the children balked, while their parents feared that the exposure to this element, pure as it might be, would threaten their children's health. Howe, assuming the voice of a firm but benevolent doctor, assured parents that cold water was nothing but "salubrious," and that the children's resistance to the baths nothing but laziness. Laura, always eager to please the doctor, faced her morning shower with what she called "much courage and alacrity." With all the fervor of a new convert, she was soon proselytizing her own family back home in New Hampshire. "A shower bath is very beneficial to the health of the body," she informed them. "Should you not like to attempt it & see if it will do you all much good?"[10]

The bell rang again at nine, signaling the beginning of morning lessons. The boys filed into one classroom, the girls went to another, while Laura usually worked in her own room, instructed by Howe when he had the time or by Miss Drew or Miss Rogers, the two young women who worked as teachers of the female blind students during Laura's first few years at the school. Perhaps remembering the tedium of his own public school education, when children were "kept on school benches six hours, with but one intermission," Howe arranged the Perkins schedule so that his students would never be subjected to academic studies for more than an hour and a half at a time without a break. Lessons on geography, algebra, grammar, and "natural philosophy" were always punctuated by sessions in the music room, which Laura could not participate in, or by half hour breaks for exercise. Howe criticized common school teachers for demanding too much mental activity from their children, while ignoring their need for fresh air, light, and regular exercise. The system he was using at Perkins, he suggested, was a model for others to follow.[11]

While Howe felt that all teachers should pay more attention to their pupils' physical education, he considered this particularly important for teachers of the blind. The first blind students he encountered convinced him that most blind people were physically inferior, characterized by flabby muscles, a stooped gait, and lazy habits. In some cases, he reasoned, blindness was only one symptom of wider health problems; but for most, he insisted, their physical inferiority was simply the result of improper education. Well-intentioned parents, he often argued, made the mistake of coddling their blind children. Sheltered by solicitous adults and unable to keep up with their sighted brothers and sisters, blind children fell into sedentary habits, which in turn caused their incomplete physical development and sometimes even premature death.

Howe was convinced that the health of the blind could be greatly improved through a proper physical regimen. He advised parents of blind children, "Do not too much regard bumps on the forehead, rough scratches, or bloody noses; even these may have their good influences; at the worst they affect only the bark, and do not injure the system like the rust of inaction." At Perkins, he waged a continual war against what he called his pupils' "almost insuperable repugnance to locomotion" and found that he had to be "very rigid in requiring the pupils to go to walk daily; to go through with gymnastic exercises in winter; and to resort freely to sea-bathing in the summer." In order to provide his students with better facilities for physical education—playgrounds, open streets, and a place to swim—Howe relocated his school in 1839, moving out of the Perkins mansion in Boston and taking up residence in the Mount Washington

5. Howe complained that blind children were too often pampered by their parents. Believing that a sound body is the foundation for a healthy mind, he required his students to exercise every day. Laura embraced this strict physical regimen. *(Courtesy of Perkins School for the Blind, Watertown, Massachusetts)*

House, a former luxury hotel located on a hilltop overlooking the bay in South Boston, then considered a rural suburb.[12]

Howe's physical education program was evidently successful. Visitors to the school were sometimes shocked to see the children playing so freely and aggressively, wrestling, running, and even climbing ropes and ladders. The director of Philadelphia's school for the blind, Julius Friedlander, could hardly believe reports that Howe's students could "safely climb up a pole and run out on yard arms, and perform other exhilarating and invigorating evolutions." Howe took great delight in the sight of his pupils joining in the same physical activities that sighted children enjoyed. In the early years of the school, he was even a regular participant in these daily games of "romps."[13]

Laura enjoyed these exercise sessions immensely. In her first few years in Boston, she mingled with the blind girls during recesses and proved to be one of the most physically aggressive children on the playground. As she grew older, she was no longer encouraged to roughhouse with her fellow students. Instead, she began to take her exercise separately, accompanied by a teacher. Often they would take long walks, traveling five or six miles a day along the beach or South Boston's streets, sometimes ranging all the way to Boston itself. Laura embraced the physical challenge wholeheartedly. One exception proved the rule: after a particularly long afternoon walk, her teacher noted with satisfaction, "For once had the pleasure of seeing [Laura] tired, she even confessed as much and said she had 'walked twenty hundred miles.'"[14]

In the long winter months, when walks were less feasible, Laura and her teacher got their exercise through "calisthenics," the new fad then sweeping over middle-class America. At other times she went horseback riding, her mount guided by her teacher. She even tried her hand at bowling in the school's own alley.[15]

The remainder of each afternoon was devoted to work. The boys spent four hours a day in the workshop, where a supervisor taught them to weave manila doormats and baskets and to sew mattresses and pew cushions. The girls, including Laura, did more domestic chores around the school and also worked on knitting and sewing.[16] Howe expected that all of the girls "should be able to wash, iron, set tables, and to keep furniture in order."[17]

Howe saw a twofold value to this manual training. For many, the skills learned at Perkins would someday allow them to earn their own living. For Howe, this was the "object ever kept in view," the prospect of helping the blind win for themselves a "happy independence." But for those who would never need, or be able, to provide for themselves in this way, he still believed that they would benefit from the sense of physical confidence and self-reliance that was developed in the afternoon work sessions. Though Laura could never hope to earn more than pocket money through her needlework or housework, her teachers felt it was an essential part of her education, providing valuable physical training in "habits of application and industry."[18]

After an evening meal also characterized by its wholesome simplicity, the younger children went to bed at seven o'clock, while the older students gathered for a second hour of singing, followed by more relaxed social time, dedicated to "reading, newspapers, and history." After a prayer at nine, all of the Perkins students retired to their bedrooms, warmed in the winter by a furnace that was "scientifically" designed to heat their rooms "without vitiating the air." As the students made their way through the wide and stark marble halls of the school, the very architecture may have reinforced in their minds the school's twin goals of austere living and grand public purpose.[19]

Some considered Howe's tightly scheduled regimen of work, exercise, study, simple food, and cold water to be "severe discipline." More than one mother wrote to him asking that her child be excused from the cold baths or the early morning wakeup call or the daily work schedule. Howe handled these requests with tact but uncompromising conviction. All of his students, he explained, "must conform to all the rules required for the government of children." Howe fully believed, it should be added, that the same rules applied to the self-government of adults, and he struggled to impose a routine of "regular hours, regular habit, pure water & plain beef" on his own busy life.[20]

Through his public accounts of the daily regimen that he had devised at Perkins, Howe turned his school into a showcase of the latest ideas about physical education and health. Although he had received a traditional medical training at Harvard, like many educated Americans in the Jacksonian period he had doubts about some of the practices of orthodox medicine—particularly the use of bloodletting and purges—and was drawn instead to the new and controversial theories of "hygienic" reform emerging at the time.[21] For example, Howe's belief in the value of a simple and bland diet was shared by many health reform advocates, the most notable being Sylvester Graham, a tireless proponent of vegetarianism and the rejuvenating powers of coarse bread made from unrefined flour. While Howe did not carry his dietary restrictions so far, he shared Graham's conviction that improper eating habits were among the great "errors of our social system."

Many illnesses, he believed, could be traced to disruptions of the digestive system caused by an overly stimulating diet. Howe was convinced that much suffering could be avoided if Americans could be taught to stop "eating too much, or too fast, or too hot." These bad eating habits were not only a health concern but also a moral one. Stomach troubles, Howe reasoned, taxed the entire body, drawing vital energy away from a person's intellectual and moral faculties.[22]

As Howe's faith in the medicinal powers of cold water suggests, he was also attracted to the unorthodox theories of hydropathy, often known as the "water cure." Suffering from bouts of exhaustion and fever in the 1840s, probably brought on by the recurrence of malaria that he had contracted while in Greece, Howe sought relief at cold-water spas in New York, western New England, and Europe. In addition to promoting the alleged purifying properties of cold water, hydropathists also encouraged their visitors to adopt other lifestyle changes intended to strengthen the body and prevent disease, including daily exercise and a simple and more wholesome diet. Howe felt so rejuvenated by his own experience at one of these cold-water spas that for a brief time he contemplated starting his own hydropathic resort.[23]

Howe dabbled with another unorthodox medical practice, the use of electricity as a form of physical therapy. Proponents of electrical therapy argued that the body operates on the same principle as a battery, storing and expending an invisible electromagnetic force. This theory received support from the new science of mesmerism, or "animal magnetism," which was introduced to New England audiences in the mid-1830s by the Frenchman Charles Poyen and drew the respectful attention of many leading doctors and intellectuals at the time. Howe put enough stock in this new science to try electrical treatments and mesmerism at Perkins. He exposed Laura to "strong magnets," "magnetic tractors," and "animal magnetism." She sometimes noted in her diary that she had spent an afternoon "taking galvanism." But Howe finally concluded that all of these treatments were "without any apparent result."[24]

Howe may have been introduced to many of these unorthodox therapies through his interest in phrenology. America's leading phrenologists were staunch advocates of health reform. Believing that phrenology provided the first empirical proof that the mind is directly connected to the body, through the organs of the brain, they often claimed that their science demonstrated just how important a healthy body was to the development of a sound mind. As a leading phrenological writer of the time summed up this position, "whatever depraves or vitiates the body, thereby depraves the

NERVOUS system, and through it the BRAIN, and thereby the MIND . . . Mental purity is compatible only with physical health." Finding that the various health reform movements were founded on a similar belief that physical health would yield mental benefits, the editors of phrenological journals gave ample coverage to the latest ideas about dietary reform, hydropathy, exercise, and mesmerism.[25]

Each of these health reform movements attracted only a small group of devoted disciples, but many more Americans were curious about the new practices. Fascinated by what they had heard and often in hope of a cure, thousands attended demonstrations of mesmerism, vacationed at water spas, began a program of calisthenics, or tried to adopt a more natural and "scientific" diet. The broad popular appeal of these new theories about the body may in part be explained by the fact that, for all their apparent novelty, these reforms rested on a firm foundation of traditional wisdom. The idea that the mind is somehow connected to the body, for example, had been commonplace since ancient times. Phrenologists and mesmerists offered new, more mechanical explanations for the links between mind and matter, and intensified interest in the physical component of human nature. But their conclusion, summed up by Howe, that "Man can abuse and destroy the powers of his mind, by neglecting or abusing his corporeal organization" only restated what most Americans would have considered common sense.[26]

Likewise, few middle-class Americans would have disagreed with the code of morality that health reformers derived from their investigations into the natural laws of health. Hygienic reformers invariably claimed that their findings vindicated Christian morality, often adding that this was one proof of the soundness of their science. Thus Howe and other advocates of physical education praised temperance, moderation, and self-improvement while condemning sexual excess, drunkenness, gluttony, laziness, the hectic pursuit of wealth and fame, and the vanities of fashion. While they were more likely to describe these vices as "unhealthy acts" rather than as sins, most reformers placed themselves in the service of conventional Christian morality.[27]

If many of the moral lessons derived from the new sciences were commonplace, their methods of investigation were more radical, signaling important changes in thinking about the meaning of health and illness and the emerging importance of science as a source of moral authority. Since ancient times, medical scientists and doctors had treated the body as an object of nature, subject to certain regular laws. But most of these laws had remained a mystery until the late eighteenth century. Then, as part of the research program of the Enlightenment, the new science of physiology developed remarkable insights into the structure and function of the brain, the nervous and respiratory systems, and the activities of the various tissues and organs. Increasingly, the body was seen less as a metaphoric vessel, an earthen container for the soul, and more as an intricate mechanism guided by predictable laws of nature.[28]

Howe, like most of his contemporaries, drew religious conclusions from these scientific findings. The complex mechanisms of the human body, he felt, offered powerful evidence that the world was designed by a benevolent Creator. And he, like others, assumed that this "natural revelation" of God's will provided by physiology was generally consistent with the supernatural revelation provided in the Scriptures. But Howe added to this the more radical claim that, whenever the scientific laws of health seemed to contradict religious teachings drawn from the Bible, science should be taken as the final authority. Christianity, he felt, had been "corrupted" by centuries of human error, while the natural laws discovered by physiologists offered a plain, reasonable, and unchanging record of God's will. Speaking as a "true phrenologist," Howe announced that whenever religious doctrines or practices contradicted the findings of physiology, he would choose to see religion yield, casting off "all forms of . . . observance which are injurious to the physical health, or which tend to undue excitement of the cerebral functions." Many health reformers shared Howe's conviction that the body, not the Bible, was the best guide on matters related to human health and morality.[29]

And, in Howe's opinion, the new physiological sciences contradicted some of the most important orthodox Christian ideas about the human body. According to the Calvinist view which had prevailed in New England for two centuries, the body was stamped not only with proof of the Creator's wise design but also with the evidence of humanity's subsequent corruption. Orthodox Christians believed that all humans, as the inheritors of original sin, suffered from disordered constitutions, an affliction which could only be set right through the healing power of God's grace. The weakness of the will, the fallibility of the reason, and the strong pangs of passion and appetite were all proof that human nature had been corrupted by sin. The physical decay and ultimate death of the body offered further evidence of Man's fallen state. Orthodox theologians often explained the harsh realities of early death, disease, and pain as punishments from God, the just fruits of Man's sinfulness.[30]

In most cases, physiologists thought quite differently about the human body. Viewing the body as a biological mechanism rather than as a repository for the soul, they saw it not as corrupt and fallen but as marvelously intricate, beautifully adapted to perform its appointed functions. The lesson which phrenologists and other health reformers drew from these investigations was that the human faculties and dispositions were not inherently sinful but good, all intended by a kind God to help His creatures attain happiness.[31]

These reformers, most of whom shared Howe's liberal theological views, did not deny the orthodox Calvinists' observation that evil and misery existed in the world. But they insisted that these were not inherent in the human constitution and therefore were not inevitable. Evil and illness existed, Howe and his colleagues believed, only because the human constitution had been improperly developed. Some faculties were being overly stimulated, others left to atrophy. These were not flaws in the body's design but distortions introduced by human error. A poor social environment, along with improper training and education, had caused humans to leave the path of health and well-being, straying into habits which caused disease and early death.

And in Howe's opinion, the problem was getting worse every day. The year he began his work with Laura, he warned a Boston audience that the nation was suffering from a disastrous neglect of the laws of hygiene, and a subsequent decline in physical beauty, that was masked by the frills of fashion. One needed only to compare the Pilgrim Fathers, "a band of erect, full-chested, robust, and ruddy youth," to the "round shouldered, lank-sided, weak, pale, and puny abortions" who were seen on the city streets in the 1830s. The hectic pursuit of wealth, the vanity of ambition, and the over-stimulation of urban living were all taking their toll on the physique of American men. Women were suffering a similar degradation, Howe scolded. Proof of their "defective physical organization" was seen everywhere in the "narrow chests, projecting collar bones, pallid faces, and decaying teeth," as well as in the proliferation of dentists, milliners, and hairdressers, all feeding like fungus on the decaying body politic.[32]

Howe, who was considered by his peers to be remarkably handsome, felt that his neighbors' physical ugliness was not only a matter of medical concern but also one of profound moral importance. Their unhealthiness was just one symptom of American society's general ignorance and neglect of the "organic laws." At a personal level, disregard for these divine rules of right living was being punished by disease, ugliness, and early death. At the level of "social relations," the cumulative effect of these individual acts of disobedience was moral and social chaos, and ultimately the physical decay of the race.[33]

Like so many other antebellum reformers, Howe mingled deep pessimism about the state of his society with an even greater measure of optimism. Now that the laws of human health were being uncovered by physiologists and applied and disseminated to the public by health reformers, phrenologists, and educators like himself, he expected that the decline of the American race could be reversed. The human body, he speculated, could be not only greatly improved but even perfected. Once the laws of health were universally understood and obeyed, he prophesied, disease and physical afflictions would be eliminated; all could look forward to robust health, enjoyed throughout a long life.[34]

And Howe held up Laura Bridgman, who took to his regimen with almost alarming intensity, as evidence that obedience to the laws of hygiene was rewarded with health and beauty. After she had spent two years under his care, he noted that "she has improved very much in personal appearance." In subsequent reports he made repeated references to the excellence of her health, the grace of her movements, and the ever-increasing beauty of her "countenance."

> When her features are all exposed, your attention is so painfully drawn to the hollow sockets in which are seen the shrivelled remnants of what were her eyeballs that nothing agreeable can be seen. But she is never thus seen except by friends, for it has become as much a habit for her to put a clean green ribbon over her eyes when she dresses herself, as it is to put on her gown. When thus dressed and her eyes shaded, her features are comely and pleasing; and the regular oval of her face, surmounted by her broad, lofty brow, and set off by her fine, glossy hair, makes her quite handsome.[35]

With Laura's lifeless eyes hidden behind a green ribbon, Howe presented her to the public as a model of physical health. As the nation's leading advocate of physical education for the handicapped, he felt that her vitality and attractiveness proved his point that all children could benefit from such training. Even among those who suffered severe liabilities, he had demonstrated, proper care of the body could do much to restore health and happiness.

Howe may have had another, unspoken reason for shielding Laura's vacant eyes from public view. A central premise of his theory of education was the claim that the body, mind, and soul were interconnected, that the proper development of each was dependent on the health of the others. "The non-development of any organ," he once explained, "the non-performance of any function, deranges and injures the whole system." While Laura's health was excellent, her eyes were a reminder that she had organs that would not function, a body that would never be whole. If Howe had remained true to the logic of his theory about the relationship between the mind and the body, Laura's physical imperfections, her deafness and blindness, should have imposed sharp limits on his expectations for her mental and moral growth. Even the single handicap of blindness suffered by his other students, by this view, should have been seen as a serious obstacle to full human development.

Howe was not unaware of this implication but, in the early years of his work with the blind, he chose to ignore the contradiction. "We have too great confidence in the faculties of the human mind," he announced in 1839, "to admit that the deprivation of one bodily organ can destroy or repress them. Hence we have claimed for the blind an equal participation in the blessings of education with seeing children." Trusting that his program of physical education had done much to compensate Laura for her physical liabilities, and hopeful about her mind's power to overcome the serious obstacles that lay before her, he began her intellectual education with great optimism.[36]

In her first three years at the Perkins Institution, Laura spent most of her classroom time on the slow and arduous task of expanding her vocabulary. When she was nine, completing her second year of schooling, Howe estimated that her language skills were no better than those of a normal three-year-old. A year later she had mastered most common nouns but still struggled with the more abstract elements of language. By way of example, Howe wrote, "Some idea of the difficulty of teaching her common expressions, or the meaning of them, may be found from the fact that a lesson of two hours upon the words *right* and *left* was deemed very profitable, if she in that time really mastered the idea."[37]

While Laura labored to master English words, she also invented her own unique language, a series of high-pitched vocal sounds she used to "name" many of her family and friends. Howe noted that when Laura entered a room full of blind girls at Perkins she embraced each of them, "uttering rapidly and in a high key the peculiar sound which designates each one." Howe believed that Laura's vocalizing was further evidence of the mind's innate linguistic faculty, but he considered these "natural" signs to be an intellectual dead-end and did nothing to encourage her use of this "rude and imperfect language." Because her sounds were usually loud and shrill, he more often tried to stifle Laura's voice, hoping to guide her expression into the more socially acceptable medium of the finger alphabet.[38]

By the time Laura was eleven, Howe was pleased to note that her language skills had improved greatly. Perhaps because she was not distracted by the often misleading sound of words, she spelled with remarkable accuracy, pressing letters from the deaf alphabet into the hands of her teachers. One of her greatest delights became catching others in errors of grammar or spelling. On one occasion, Howe informed Laura, "Doctor will teach Laura." The child laughed and chided him, informing him that he should have said, "*I* will teach *you.*" At this point, Howe evidently felt that her language skills had progressed to the point where she could begin working with a more conventional common school curriculum.[39]

Laura spent the morning classes learning the same subjects that the other blind children did, beginning with a session on mathematics, first adding and subtracting and then multiplication. She disliked math, often complaining after a lesson that "my think is tired." Her teachers' daily journals are full of entries which suggest that the child often did all in her power to avoid her math lessons. "Allowed her to converse instead of the arithmetic lesson, which always pleases her." "Laura asked to talk about animals, so excused her from the much less interesting lesson in arithmetic." Asked to compute the price of a quarter barrel of cider, given the price of a full barrel, she evaded the question by asking one of her own: "How did the man who wrote the [math] book know I was here?" to which she added, "I can not give much for cider because it is very *sour.*" On another morning, the child pleaded, "I do not want to study to cipher, I want to talk about things."[40]

Laura's formal education in the nature of "things" began with introductions to objects around the Perkins Institution. As a proponent of the latest pedagogical innovations, Howe used his reports on Laura Bridgman to criticize the traditional classroom techniques of rote learning and recitation. This approach, he charged, only gave children a knowledge of "mere words," and made the lessons drilled in at school far less interesting than the knowledge they gained gladly and effortlessly through their interactions with the wide world beyond the schoolhouse.

Attempting to recreate this natural learning process, Howe was determined that all of his students would learn as much as possible from direct interaction with objects, rather than words. He filled many cabinets with wooden models and specimens of flora and fauna, feeding his students' tactile understanding of the natural world. Likewise, he devised and printed raised maps, mathematical diagrams and musical scores, and even had a large metal globe specially forged in Germany and set up in the central hall of the school. Howe felt that this direct, tactile approach to education was particularly important for blind children. But he also believed that, at Perkins, he was showcasing a new and enlightened pedagogy that would improve the learning environment in any classroom.[41]

As Laura grew older, her lessons in the nature of "things" also came from interactions on the streets of Boston, a world almost as distant and mysterious to her as if it were on the other side of the globe. During her long daily walks with her teacher, she often played a game, stopping in the middle of the walk and insisting that her companion describe to her in full detail everything she could see and hear from that spot. "She will not be content," one teacher noted, "if she thinks I have not told her objects enough to make up the scene."[42]

On these excursions, Laura learned about the various trades practiced in the Boston area and, most interesting of all to her, about local animals. She asked endlessly about flies, cats, birds, horses, and people. "Can birds study?" "Why do not flies and horses go to bed?" "Are horses *cross* all day?" "What did man make red for?" Suffering from the "hiccoughs," she wanted to know "if they were black & where they went when they went away?"[43]

This tumult of questions was so great that Howe decided at first that it was useless to pursue a "definite course of instruction." Instead, her teachers usually let the child's intense curiosity direct the subject of each day's lessons. Recording these sessions in their journals, Laura's teachers evidently enjoyed the naive poetry of the child's eager questions, but they also took them as sobering reminders of the deep gulf which separated their student from the world around her.[44]

Many of these conversations occurred in the early afternoon, after lunch and recess, when Laura usually practiced language skills with her teacher. The time was spent reviewing the morning's lessons, learning new words, and satisfying the child's insatiable desire to get some clear understanding of every new word she encountered. "I want you to tell me many new words," she pleaded at the start of one afternoon class. "What does language, syllable, divided, evil, mean?" In a lesson about the senses, her teacher informed her that most people had five, while she only had three. Laura was "much displeased" to learn this, but returned to her lessons the following day and proudly announced that she actually had *four*. In addition to touch, and a partial sense of taste and smell, she also had the sense of "think."[45]

Laura's comment is revealing, because the medium of language had become her single most important source of knowledge about the world around her, carrying a full burden which for most people is shared by their senses of sight and sound. She clung to words intensely because they were her only clues to the mysterious world beyond her limited horizons. When alone, she conducted finger-language soliloquies and even "imaginary dialogues." In his second report on her education, Howe observed: "In this lonely self-communion she reasons, reflects, and argues; if she spells a word wrong with the fingers of her right hand, she instantly strikes it with her left, as her teacher does, in sign of disapprobation; if right, then she pats herself upon the head and looks pleased. She sometimes purposely spells a word wrong with the left hand, looks roguish for a moment and laughs, and then with the right hand strikes the left, as if to correct it."[46]

By the time Laura was eleven, these inner musings were conducted so swiftly that even a trained eye was unable to read the flashing of ideas across her fingers. But she always longed, above all, for the mental stimulation she could attain only by conversing with others. "If she becomes sensible of the presence of any one near her," Howe wrote, "she is restless until she can sit close beside them, hold their hand, and converse with them by signs." Encountering the other blind students passing her in the hallway, she often held them against their will, insisting that they talk with her. Thus the afternoon hours devoted to conversation passed quickly for Laura, and she looked forward to these sessions enthusiastically.[47]

One of her teachers observed that this complete dependence on language gave Laura one advantage over children who have all their senses. "If interested in anything especially," the teacher noted in her journal, "she does not forget it, but while dressing, or working, or however occupied, her mind is upon it, while other children go from their lessons into a world which presents so much to take their attention that the lesson is hardly thought of before another school-day comes."

While this intense concentration made educating the child much easier, it could also leave her teachers reeling. In their daily journals, they frequently complained of mental exhaustion and headaches, evidently a product of the stress caused by trying to satisfy the girl's endless questions, her constant efforts to use her teachers' words almost as a "fourth" sense, as a way to compensate for her extremely limited direct experience of the world.[48]

When Laura reached the age of thirteen, her understanding of the immediate objects around her became more settled and she progressed to more advanced common school subjects, beginning with geography and composition and soon adding astronomy and history. History proved a challenge for her teachers, who wanted to shield the child's unsuspecting nature from the disturbing examples of human cruelty that seemed to lurk on every "dark page." "I find it difficult to tell her a connected story without alluding to wars," one teacher confessed to her journal when Laura was fourteen, adding that "this would be so terrible to her that I cannot think of beginning it yet."[49]

Geography was safer, and Laura quickly learned to identify such things as the river systems of Georgia and Ohio, the port cities of the world, and the states of New England on raised relief maps that Howe had designed himself. Her teachers' journals frequently report that she was "much excited" to be learning such things. "It seems to me," one wrote, "that few children make a geography lesson so completely their own as she does."[50]

While her ability to point out exotic locations on the globe always impressed the crowds who came to see her at exhibitions, such worldly knowledge actually masked the child's seemingly insurmountable naiveté about the world beyond the reach of her fingertips. After a geography lesson on Niagara Falls, for example, her teacher was pleased to report, "I explained to her about the water falling & I think she understands it." Yet Laura's "understanding" was clearly of a curiously limited quality, as her teacher added, "Told her about the noise that it made. She said, 'can you hear it?' NO—'try very hard & see'—she held my hands very still for me to listen." In an astronomy lesson, Laura might be able to recall the number of miles that separate the Earth from the Sun, yet still wonder why humans could not sail there "in boats." Though she could promptly identify the cities of New England on a raised map, while walking through the streets of Boston she once asked her teacher if she could see the windows of her parents' house in New Hampshire.[51]

In short, Laura's understanding of the external world was, in spite of many long hours of instruction, strangely uneven. While Howe tried all in his power to prevent Laura's education from becoming a training in "mere words," her knowledge of symbols, her ability to use words, far surpassed her ability to comprehend some of the most fundamental aspects of the physical world all around her. She could learn, with "great interest," about the economic products of the Barbary States, while the sights and sounds of South Boston remained shrouded in mystery.

This abstract and partial quality of the child's growing knowledge of the world was well noted by one of her teachers. After giving the child a lesson on the Erie Canal and Niagara Falls, received by Laura with her usual enthusiasm, Mary Swift wrote, "It might be supposed that [these subjects] would be mere commonplace topics to her, and that the most vivid description could not convey to one, who had never even seen water, the faintest idea of their beauty and grandeur. Just what ideas she did receive, it is impossible for us to know, and also the cause of the excitement she manifested when told about them."[52]

Given the fact that so many of the subjects in the common school curriculum could only provide Laura with the most tenuous, abstract kind of understanding about the world, Howe's decision to instruct her in these fields calls for some explanation. On what grounds did he justify training Laura to identify river systems in distant states and to name the fruits and vegetables shipped out of exotic ports? Why teach her history when most human activities and motivations would always remain far beyond the scope of her understanding and possible experience? Why train her to conduct mathematical calculations which she would evidently never need to apply in real life, destined as she was to remain sheltered in the care of the institution or her family for the rest of her life?

Howe often reported the extreme difficulty which he and his teachers were encountering as they tried to convey this information to Laura, but he apparently never felt compelled to justify his choice of curriculum. Given Howe's wider assumptions about the education of the blind and about the best way to educate all children, the decision to teach Laura the full complement of common school courses must have seemed to him self-evident, the natural outcome of his democratic ideals and his theory of human development.

From the start, Howe worked tirelessly to convince the public of its moral obligation to provide an equal education to all, *adapted* to each individual's particular needs, regardless of the cost. And he urged his students to live up to this opportunity for a common school education, to seize their birthright as citizens of an increasingly enlightened democracy. "You must not think because you are blind," he advised them, "that you cannot learn as much as other children." Armed with an equal education, he told them, they were no longer doomed to becoming "mere objects of pity" but could look forward to full membership in the "body social and political."[53]

Thus, when the students at Perkins performed well in advanced common school subjects, he offered this to the public as the ultimate vindication of his claim that the handicapped were capable of receiving, and entitled to, an equal education and the chance to earn a respectable station in life upon their graduation. When Laura Bridgman, the most famous of the school's pupils, amazed Boston audiences by promptly pointing out river systems on a raised map or by writing a composition or completing mathematical problems, Howe believed that this child, doubly deprived, offered twice the proof that all of the nation's children can, and should, be given the opportunity to learn.

Howe's understanding of human development also led him to believe that no field of the common school curriculum could be sacrificed without injuring the full mental and moral development of the individual. While Laura would never make practical application of much of the information she learned, each different branch of the curriculum was particularly adapted to develop a distinctive mental faculty. In phrenological terms, each academic subject provided the ideal stimulation to a corresponding "organ" in the child's brain. Just as Howe believed that a full program of calisthenics was needed to bring each muscle into use, he also felt that Laura's academic routine should give exercise to each part of the brain. The study of arithmetic, for example, called into action the intellectual faculties of "Order," "Number," and "Size." Geography was particularly suited to exercise the child's organ of "Locality." The scientific study of Nature brought the organs of "Individuality" and "Eventuality" into healthful action.[54]

Thus Howe believed that, even though Laura might never make practical use of much of the information she learned, exposure to the full range of common school subjects was important to her health. In mental training as in physical exercise, the educator's ultimate goal was the balanced development of all the child's faculties, the cultivation of a "well organized" mind, seated within a strong and healthy body.[55]

Toward that end, Howe parceled out the hours of the school day with great care: "In general terms, the pupils devote four hours daily to intellectual labor; four hours to vocal and instrumental music; four to recreation and eating; four to manual labor, and eight to sleep. Or if we consider music as intellectual labor, and work as physical labor, then they devote eight hours daily to intellectual education, eight to physical education, and eight to sleep." Howe partitioned the day into equal parts because he believed that this would ensure that the "different faculties of the mind are called into operation in succession" throughout the day, with none being neglected.[56]

Another tenet of the phrenological gospel which Howe followed faithfully was the idea that a teacher should never have to force a child, against its will, to exercise its mental faculties. The Creator who had designed the various organs of the brain had also wisely decreed, through a law of Nature, that each one would derive pleasure from its own exercise and naturally seek out experiences that would provide this stimulation. "With regard to intellectual education," Howe wrote the year after Laura entered Perkins, "our principle has been, that the mind has an appetite for knowledge, as the body for food; and that the exercise of any of the mental faculties in the acquisition of knowledge, is accompanied and rewarded by vivid pleasure."[57]

Howe could not have asked for better proof of this phrenological theory than Laura Bridgman. From the start he noted "the eager delight with which [Laura] lends all her attention, and the strong effort she evidently makes to gain new ideas." Visitors to the school were sometimes even alarmed by the "great excitement" that the child could display when learning a new lesson. When the meaning of a new word suddenly dawned upon her, Laura would often break into loud laughter and hug and kiss her teacher, leaving her audience to wonder aloud, "What is it pleases her so much?"[58]

Howe had a phrenological answer to that question. The child was simply feeling the natural, spontaneous pleasure which arises from the healthful exercise of her mental faculties. "The innate desire for knowledge, and the instinctive efforts which the human faculties make to exercise their functions is shown most remarkably in Laura," Howe wrote. Resorting to the semibiblical prose style that he always used to remind his readers that they were treading on the sacred ground of natural theology, Howe informed them, "so doth the soul thirst for knowledge, that it will attain it even when half its avenues are blocked up."[59]

Howe claimed that Laura's "insatiable curiosity" demonstrated the wisdom of the Creator's design, showing the perfect compatibility between the faculties of the brain and the "external world." But he also argued that her craving for knowledge proved that society had bungled the job of educating most of its youth. While God equipped each child with a natural love of learning, ignorant teachers had too often squandered the Creator's blessing by stifling this curiosity. Occasionally Howe joined the chorus of popular moralists who laid the blame on the students themselves, charging them with sloth and ingratitude for their natural advantages. "By the cheerful toil and patient labor with which she gleans her scanty harvest of knowledge, she reproves those who, having eyes see not, and having ears hear not." But much more often, Howe presented Laura's case as an indictment of the educational practices of the state's common schools.[60]

According to Howe, most common school masters never allowed children to satisfy the prompting of their natural curiosity but instead tried to turn students into "passive recipients" of knowledge, drilled in by rote. Because schoolmasters had failed to take advantage of each child's internal love of learning, they were often forced to resort to the basest of motivations, the carrot of flattery and external rewards and the stick of corporal punishment. "Truth and knowledge," Howe proclaimed, "when presented in the proper form, are so attractive to [the students at Perkins], that it has not to be whipped in, nor coaxed or bribed in."[61]

Howe described Laura's startling thirst for new information not as a distinctive trait of her own character nor as the product of her unique isolation from the world. Rather, he presented her to the public as the standard by which all other students—and their teachers—should be judged. She was nothing less than scientific proof of the innate potential for education enjoyed by *all* children, a gift from God squandered each day by teachers bereft of a true understanding of human nature and its potential.

Howe's close friend Horace Mann perfectly understood the wider symbolic value of Laura Bridgman to the cause of educational reform. "The history of Laura," he announced, "is more important than that of a rabble of common kings."[62] Mann had been involved with the Perkins Institution from the start, serving as its attorney and a founding member of the school's board of directors. Through the middle years of the 1830s, his post as the speaker of the state Senate made him a valuable ally of the Perkins School, able to use his political connections to insure that Howe's reports, as well as tickets to school exhibitions, made their way into the hands of influential legislators.[63]

In 1837, the same year Laura entered Perkins, Mann stepped down from the Senate, abandoning his immediate political ambitions in order to accept the job of secretary of the new State Board of Education. Because most Massachusetts communities valued their traditional right of local control over their children's schooling, the state granted Mann's new board little direct power to change common school practices. His assignment was simply to gather information about the state of public schooling in Massachusetts and to advise the legislature about possible reforms. If he were to have any influence at all, Mann knew, it would lie in his powers of persuasion, his ability to transform his post into a pulpit for educational revival. Toward that end, he founded the *Common School Journal* the following year. Although this journal was a privately funded enterprise, Mann presented it to the public as the voice of the State Board of Education, a vehicle for debating and promoting the latest innovations in all aspects of schooling.[64]

The *Common School Journal*'s debut coincided with Howe's earliest public report on Laura Bridgman. Mann printed Howe's remarks in their entirety, and over the next decade he devoted a considerable number of pages to reprinting a full transcript of Howe's annual reports on "this wonderful child." Mann eagerly seconded Howe's suggestion that Laura's story contained important lessons that should be applied to the education of all children. "The mental phenomena manifested by Laura," he announced, "commend her case, in an especial manner, to the study of the educationist."[65]

Praising Howe as a "profound and philosophic observer," Mann repeated his claim that Laura's handicaps provided science with a unique chance to observe the very essence of human nature. He explained to his readers that philosophers had been embroiled for centuries in a debate over the relative importance of "the force of nature, and the force of education." Embracing the crucial but dubious premise of Howe's experiment, Mann described Laura as "a case of mental isolation,—a development and growth, equally unaided by external cultivation and untrammeled by coercion, and hence borrowing little or nothing from a foreign source." Thus, the child offered the first empirical look at the "original tendencies" that all children are born with, prior to being educated, for better or worse, by their environment.[66]

Mann found Laura's insatiable curiosity particularly useful for his own purposes. In his inaugural address as the leader of the state's educational reform movement, he declared that there was "one rule, which, in all places, and in all forms of education, should be held as primary, paramount, and, as far as possible, exclusive." This pillar of Mann's pedagogical theories was the maxim that "Acquirement and pleasure should go hand in hand." In other words, students should be motivated to learn by the natural, God-given pleasure of learning itself, not by the external inducements of rewards or punishments.[67]

Mann could cite no better evidence for this pedagogical principle than the example being set in Boston by "the blind, and the deaf and dumb." The blind students at Perkins, whose eyes were "curtained," eagerly sought knowledge through their ears. And, as Laura Bridgman had shown the world, when both eyes and ears were blocked, a child would even use "the nerves of touch" in her eagerness to carry ideas, those "offerings of delight," upward to the "sovereign mind." Howe's experiment with Laura seemed to prove that a child's love of learning was not the creation of outside forces of punishment and reward but was an internal urge so strong that, with the enlightened help of a wise educator, it could overcome the most unfavorable of external circumstances.[68]

Though Laura's case evidently proved that human nature is a positive, creative force, Mann never dwelled on this conclusion for long without attempting to draw sharp comparisons between her character and that of other children. "Why is it," he asked his readers to contemplate, "that she loves to learn, and regards her instructors as her dearest friends, while so many others hate books and teachers?" And he wanted to know, "Why should so many other children be morose, petulant, ill-tempered, quarrelsome, while this lovely being is tender, charitable, and overflowing with affection towards all around her?" Mann's answer to those questions was that all children would be as eager to learn, as happy and kind as Laura Bridgman, if they had more enlightened teachers. "She has such a love of knowledge, that the most trivial acquisition is a luxury, which love, indeed, all children would have were it not destroyed by mismanagement."[69]

In their effort to transform this singular child into a symbol of pure and natural human nature, Howe and Mann's attention to the actual details of her case clearly suffered. Her character and her educational experience were much more complex and multidimensional than Howe ever admitted, and as a result his public reports on Laura offered only half-truths. He mentioned her victories but almost never her setbacks. He praised her pure character and love of learning and ignored instances of perversity, apathy, and deceit. Publicly, he described the child's education as "a kind of triumphal march"; privately, her teachers recorded a much more difficult journey. "I find Laura very averse to close application," one teacher noted when she was twelve. "She very well likes to have a question put on the board and perform it mechanically, but as soon as I give her a question that requires a little more reflection, she grows nervous and irritable."[70] Laura's dislike of mathematics has already been noted. While she usually resisted in a good-natured fashion, by simply trying to change the subject, at times she resorted to more extreme measures. When Laura was thirteen, her teacher made this entry in her journal: "[Laura] tried unsuccessfully to tell me how much a quarter of eight was, and said, 'I do not know.' I replied, as I always do when she does not take time, 'If you think, you can tell me.' Instead of receiving it as usual, she caught my hand and twisted it very hard. At first I thought it was play and was surprised to see her face scarlet, and that she was in a passion."[71] The next day, Laura apologized for trying to break her teacher's arm.

While such acts of violence were rare, her lessons were often delayed or disrupted by the child's alternating bouts of apathy and nervous excitement. One morning class was consumed in discussion of why Laura was "so unwilling to write, and . . . so fitful."[72] Another time a whole month of study was lost, as she was too "nervous" to concentrate. "I almost *dread* to teach her," one teacher confided after a particularly frustrating math lesson, "she gets so nervous and impatient." To her teachers' embarrassment, Laura's streak of perversity sometimes flared up when she was on the public stage. More than once, she spent her first class on Monday morning discussing why she had been unwilling to write her name or answer geography questions for the "ladies and gentlemen" who came to see her on exhibition day.[73]

Howe also provided a selective portrait of the child's motivation to learn. According to his theory, the only proper reward for learning came from within, when the child enjoyed the pleasurable sensations caused when a mental faculty was exercised. Any external motivation to learn was, he often said, an undignified appeal to the child's less worthy emotions, his or her fear of pain or love of flattery. Howe correctly reported that Laura took remarkable pleasure in learning new things, but he neglected to mention that one of the child's greatest desires was always to win the approval of "Doctor." While Laura never had to fear the schoolmaster's rod, she could be stricken by the possibility of falling out of Howe's favor. Her teachers regularly appealed to this motivation to get the child to do her lessons. For example, when she was eleven, a teacher made the following entry in her journal: "Oct 6 1841—She grew impatient and said, half in jest, 'I cannot learn . . . because I am very dull.' I said then I will tell Doctor you can not learn and write about it in my journal . . . Thinking I was in earnest, she said, 'I think I will *try*.'" As this passage suggests, Laura was ever aware that, even when the doctor was not in the room, he was always watching her progress via the daily journal. Whenever she did something that she thought the doctor might not approve of, she would beseech her teachers not to note it in the journal, so "Doctor" would not hear about it.[74]

From today's perspective, Laura's transgressions seem almost trivial. Most observers might consider her outbursts of anger and impatience quite "normal" behavior, particularly for a child who was daily facing such frustrating barriers to communication. And her desire to please her great mentor, the man who brought her into the world of language and who became a second father to her, hardly seems to suggest that Laura's motivations for learning were external and therefore not sincere. Yet Laura's teachers were deeply troubled by these small incidents, and Howe, while claiming to make a careful and scientific record of the facts of her case, presented the public with a selective version of Laura's classroom experiences, swept clean of all troubling ambiguities. His professed commitment to Baconian science, the careful and unbiased gathering of the "facts" of his experiment, was eclipsed by his desire to turn Laura into a symbol, a rhetorical tool placed in the service of educational reform.

In the first few years of their work together, Howe had good reason to be pleased with Laura's rapidly developing language skills. But Howe viewed this aspect of her education as only a preliminary step. He looked forward to the next, more important stage in the gradual unfolding of her faculties, the development of Laura's *conscience*. In his 1840 report, he speculated, "If the same success shall attend the cultivation of her Moral nature, as has followed that of her Intellect and her Perceptive Faculties, great will be the reward to her, and most interesting will be the result to others." "The intellectual progress of this child is most gratifying to me," Howe wrote to a German psychologist when Laura was ten, "but I watch with much more interest for the development of her moral sentiments; and hope thereby to resolve many doubts which have arisen in my own mind of the correctness of our commonly received notions of psychological phenomena."[75]

While Howe often suggested that he was interested in these questions simply from a scientific and philosophical point of view, he privately conceded that he was most anxious to use his experiment to promote practical reforms. Howe believed that, if Laura could help him prove that children were not only innately curious but also innately *moral*, his work with her might serve as a blueprint for sweeping changes in the way Americans thought about, and taught, their children. But first he would have to show that the child not only had a natural eagerness to learn but also an instinctive impulse to be good.

Chapter 5

The Instinct to Be Good

In the autumn of 1838 the Scotsman George Combe embarked on a tour of the United States to promote the new science of phrenology. After the untimely death of Dr. Spurzheim in 1832, Combe had assumed the mantle of leadership in the phrenological movement. Arriving in Boston to give a series of lectures, he found two admirers waiting to meet him, Horace Mann and Samuel Gridley Howe. Combe was delighted to hear that the two New England philanthropists were already laboring to put his ideas about human nature and educational reform into practice. By the end of his sojourn in America, Combe informed Howe, "You and Horace Mann are parts of my entire future existence."[1]

For their part, the two Americans found Combe to be everything they could hope for in a prophet. "It was like the voice of God," Mann wrote after hearing Combe lecture, "revealing eternal truths to men, to make them wise, not merely to their own salvation, but to the salvation of others." Like most phrenologists, Combe not only expounded his ideas in public lectures but demonstrated them by reading skulls and predicting the character of their owners. During one of these exhibitions in Boston, Combe was shown the skull of an Italian immigrant who, unbeknownst to him, had "killed himself for love." Mann was delighted to watch his phrenological mentor identify the man's tragic character flaw "as tho' it had been printed in Roman character." "He will cypher up a man," the educator marveled, "and give you the answer fearfully quick."[2]

During the course of a three-year stay in America, Combe visited the Perkins Institution numerous times and, with Howe's endorsement, presented it to his own readers as a successful experiment in the practical application of phrenology. Combe found Laura to be "the most attractive of all the pupils" there. Probing her skull with his calipers, he reported that her head was "of full size and well formed." The child's tidiness was explained by her large organ of "Order," and Combe was pleased to note that the other "organs of domestic affections"—self-esteem, love of approbation, cautiousness, and conscientiousness—were all "in the best feminine proportions."[3]

Over the course of several visits, as the child's education progressed, Combe noted "a distinct increase" in her brain size. Howe enthusiastically agreed and only regretted that the initial measurements of her head taken when she first arrived at Perkins had been misplaced. Most importantly, Combe noted that this growth was in the "coronal" region, the throne of the brain where the moral sentiments would ideally come to reign over the entire body and soul. In short, Combe found the child to be the perfect raw material for an experiment in moral education, and by the time she was ten he felt that her moral nature was already beginning to develop.[4]

Combe also placed his calipers upon Howe's skull. "It is not difficult to analyze your mental constitution," he told his new American friend in 1840. The phrenologist saw the undeniable marks of "genius" on the cranium of the man who had found his own ideas so compelling. In the con-

6. Laura Bridgman's story helped turn the Perkins Institution into a popular tourist attraction. But Howe hoped that his investigation into her moral nature would also attract the attention of scientists and philosophers around the world. *(Courtesy of Perkins School for the Blind, Watertown, Massachusetts)*

tours of Howe's head, Combe also saw a physical explanation for his driving ambition, his keen desire to win a "brighter destiny" for himself. Howe had a bulging "Love of Approbation," as well as "Large Combativeness," the very qualities, Combe suggested, which had already led him to fly impetuously to the aid of the Greek revolutionaries. Fortunately for the underdogs of this world, Howe's desire for fame and his love of combat were counterbalanced by an equally large organ of "Benevolence," which explained why he had since applied his love of glory and combat to the humble work of educating the blind. Combe assured him that, after all these accomplishments, he still had enormous untapped capacity for "moral enterprize." As illustrious as his work at Perkins was, he could look forward to even more "honourable fame" if he could find "the right place . . . to set [his] faculties to work."[5]

Clearly, Combe's insights into Howe's character could have been divined more easily from the young reformer's recent history than from his cranial bumps. Yet, although his science was delusionary, Combe did provide a remarkably accurate forecast of Howe's future. For the rest of his life, Howe suffered from acute bouts of restlessness, always searching for what Combe called "a still wider sphere of action." Even in 1840, as he was winning international fame for his experiment with Laura, he thought of abandoning his work with the blind in order to seek a diplomatic post in Spain. Mann, who looked to Howe as a personal advisor and partner in educational reform, dissuaded him.[6]

Howe remained the director of Perkins for the rest of his life, but his subsequent career was marked by bold, combative, and sometimes reckless forays into other arenas of reform. In the three decades following Combe's prediction, he founded the first school for the mentally handicapped in the nation, served as one of Dorothea Dix's staunch allies in her work for the insane, championed common school and prison reforms, and took a leadership role in a number of abolitionist organizations. And, as Combe had suggested, he always conducted these campaigns with a volatile mixture of sincere compassion and social conscience, personal vanity, and outright love of confrontation. Howe's biographer Harold Schwartz described his approach to moral combat as "patronizing when agreed with, but wild with rage, contemptuous, and vituperative when opposed." No incident in Howe's reform career better typifies this constant struggle between his organ of "Benevolence" and his organ of "Combativeness" than his clandestine support of John Brown's raid on Harper's Ferry. As a member of the "Secret Six" who funded Brown's failed attempt to incite a bloody slave rebellion, Howe had to temporarily flee to Canada in 1859 to avoid extradition to Virginia. He was truly a field commander in what Emerson called that era's "soldiery of dissent."[7]

Howe aimed his phrenological organ of "Destructiveness" at numerous villains in his long career as a reformer, from the "barbarous" Sultan of Turkey to the "slavocracy" of the South. But he always found his greatest foe much closer to home. Calvinism, he believed, was "the greatest obstacle to all kinds of human progress." Howe was particularly opposed to the Calvinist doctrine of original sin. "I cannot believe in the total depravity of man," he told a gathering of phrenologists. "And if there is any one thing which is certain to excite my disgust, it is the spirit of those who in one breath exalt, praise, and adore God, and in the next, insult Him by vilifying and degrading man, made in His own image." To his friend Horace Mann he wrote, "I can't keep my hand off John Calvin. And if I could, I would not. Why should I: is not my mission belligerent: did not God intend my destructiveness for something; & though my gun be but a pop, shall I not pop with all my might?"[8]

The Calvinist doctrine of original sin, these two partners in reform believed, not only slandered God and humanity but also had devastating social consequences. The science of phrenology confirmed for them that a benevolent God had designed human nature as a complex organization of physical, mental, and spiritual "faculties." In their proper place, even the lowest physical drives were inherently good, only causing evil when abused or improperly educated. Phrenologists believed that they could use their new scientific insights into the nature of the various "organs" of the brain to improve the human condition and advance human happiness. By following the guidelines that God had so clearly imprinted on the human cranium, they planned to reform institutions to conform to the phrenological laws of human development. Once schools, churches, families, and prisons were reorganized along phrenological lines, they felt, all individuals would be able to develop their natures to the fullest. The potential goodness in human nature would be fully realized, just as God had always intended. Howe was convinced that, on the day when that happened, all "rivalry, war and crime" would be eliminated.[9]

Howe and Mann believed that instead of following this divine blueprint for human progress, Calvinism was thwarting God's plan by teaching that human nature is profoundly flawed, that the moral law within is a message hopelessly scrambled by sin. Making matters worse, the orthodox were among the most vocal critics of phrenology. By thus shutting out the light of new science and clinging to their pessimistic view of human nature, Calvinists were fatalistically resigning themselves to Mankind's sufferings and moral failures. Under the sway of their gloomy theology, Mann believed, Boston society had created schools, prisons, and churches that not only expected but actually promoted the worst in human conduct.[10]

Calvinism, Howe once told Mann, was "the greatest enemy of God, the libeler of his noblest son, our great older brother [Adam]." And Laura Bridgman provided him with the ideal opportunity to restore Adam's and Eve's reputations by refuting the doctrine of original sin. If Howe could show that this child had a pure moral nature, this would prove that human sinfulness was not innate, inherited from Adam, but was produced by the corrupting influences of a bad environment. Through his experiment with Laura Bridgman, he planned to convince the world in general, and Boston's Calvinists in particular, that it was social institutions, and not human souls, that were in desperate need of renovation.[11]

When Howe began his work with Laura Bridgman, his faith that she could be taught and his subsequent conclusions about the relationship between her mind and her body were drawn, as we have seen, from the philosophical tradition of the Scottish Enlightenment, which reached Howe largely through his interest in Unitarianism and phrenology. As he moved to the next phase of his experiment, hoping to prove that her mind was endowed with a pure and reliable conscience, Howe returned to the same sources for guidance. The Scottish common sense philosophy, particularly its moral sense tradition, was ideally suited to his purposes. The Scottish philosophers had developed a theory of human nature in response to the ideas of a more secular philosophical gadfly, the English philosopher Thomas Hobbes. In his *Leviathan* (1651) Hobbes had described human beings as creatures driven to seek power and glory, their selfish deeds restrained only by a fear of death at the hands of competitors and by the threat of eternal punishment waiting for sinners in the afterlife. While Hobbes and Calvin shared little else in common, both felt that humans were motivated primarily by self-interest, and both offered a similar intellectual challenge to those who placed more faith in human nature.[12]

Locke offered an alternative explanation for human morality, but even many of Locke's admirers felt that he had done little to improve the reputation of human nature. While Locke denied Hobbes's claim that humans are innately selfish, he held that children are born neither good nor bad, capable of reason but morally neutral. Through careful reflection on the information provided to our senses, Locke felt, the human mind can discover the rational moral order that God has imposed on our world. But he conceded that the majority of men were incapable of this kind of so-phisticated moral reasoning. Most, he felt, could be motivated to behave themselves only by a more primitive appeal to their most basic interests, the desire for pleasure and the fear of pain. Thus, human laws might be reasonable, and God's commandments certainly were, but to influence human behavior both had to be reinforced by the threat of punishment and the promise of God's reward in heaven for those who avoided sin.[13]

Many English moralists in the eighteenth century were disturbed by Hobbes's bleak view of human nature and deeply dissatisfied with Locke's rejoinder. At a time when enlightened Europeans on the continent were praising the power of human reason, England's foremost philosopher, Locke, seemed to suggest that people are ultimately motivated by a rational but rather narrow calculation of self-interest and that God rules his creation through commandments and threats rather than through reason and love. One of the most successful attempts to provide a more dignified explanation of human motivation came from Locke's best-known student, the Earl of Shaftesbury (1671–1713), a founder of what came to be known as the moral sense or sentimentalist tradition of moral philosophy. Shaftesbury charged that Hobbes's catalog of human motivations was incomplete, that he had "forgotten to mention Kindness, Friendship, Sociableness, Love of Company . . . or anything of this kind." Challenging Locke's assertion that we are born morally neutral, Shaftesbury claimed that these impulses were expressions of an instinctual human love of goodness and social harmony. We have an innate and emotional attraction to the good, he argued, that is similar to our spontaneous appreciation of beautiful objects. While some might refine and develop their conscience more fully than others, Shaftesbury and his fellow moral sense philosophers held that we all are born with an impulse to recognize and approve of human goodness.[14]

This moral sense theory entered the Scottish philosophical tradition with Frances Hutcheson, a thinker who one historian has called "the most influential and respected moral philosopher in eighteenth century America." Hutcheson described human knowledge of right and wrong as the product of an "inner sense," attuned to know the moral world as naturally and reliably as our five physical senses know the physical world. Locke had claimed that human minds may come to know moral truths through a gradual reasoning process, building up evidence from the analysis of sensory data. Hutcheson argued instead that the moral sense acts spontaneously, stirred by the heart rather than convinced by the mind. Hutcheson also took issue with Locke's claim that good behavior flows from self-interest, a hedonistic calculation of potential punishments and rewards. We instinctively feel compassion for the afflicted, Hutcheson countered, even when their misfortunes have no possible impact on our own lives. And we despise the wicked, even if their misdeeds advance our own welfare.[15]

Moral sense philosophers did not deny that virtue has its rewards. Hutcheson observed that when individuals perform good deeds they often experience an immediate sense of pleasure. This, he suggested, was part of the Creator's wise design. God did not resort to the enticement of heavenly rewards, or the threat of hell, to bribe human beings to be good. Instead, He had wisely constituted human beings so that they would feel an immediate gratification when they did the right thing. Thus, according to Hutcheson, the moral sense informs humans of right and wrong, inspires them with an instinctive urge to be kind, and rewards them with pleasurable feelings for satisfying this moral impulse. In short, through God's wisdom, the line between self-interest and benevolence was erased.[16]

While this moral sense tradition developed in England and Scotland as a response to Hobbes and Locke, Boston's Unitarians imported these ideas about the conscience to use in their battle against the Calvinist doctrine of innate depravity. Contrary to New England orthodoxy, human beings were not born with sinful and rebellious natures, according to the Unitarians, but were endowed by their Creator with a deep instinct for selfless benevolence. William Ellery Channing, one of Howe's most important mentors in Unitarianism, was profoundly influenced by the moral sense tradition's more hopeful view of human nature. After reading Hutcheson's moral philosophy as a young man, Channing declared, "I do and I must reverence human nature. Neither the sneers of worldly skepticism nor the groans of gloomy theology disturb my faith in its godlike powers and tendencies."[17]

The Unitarians' faith in the fundamental goodness of human beings seemed to receive scientific confirmation in the researches of the phrenologists, who had also embraced the moral sense tradition, recasting it onto their own peculiar map of the mind. According to George Combe, for example, the organs of benevolence, hope, conscientiousness, and ideality could all be found in the privileged position at the top of the cranium. These "moral sentiments," Combe explained, generate the virtuous impulses that come naturally into play whenever the mind is presented with the appropriate "external objects." Just as the ear automatically responds to sounds, the organ of conscientiousness is a "higher instinct," triggered spontaneously whenever a person encounters what Combe called "moral relations." Phrenologists believed that one of the most sublime proofs of "the divine administration of the world" was the fact that God had created human beings so that the exercise of these moral faculties provided the purest and most long-lasting experiences of pleasure available to human-kind. God, in His wisdom, had made it *feel* good to *be* good.

 Guided by phrenology, Howe expected that Laura Bridgman's mind was endowed with this inner moral sense. Certain of what he was looking for, he found evidence almost from the start. After Laura had been at Perkins only four months, while she was still struggling to understand the simplest nouns, Howe discerned rudimentary moral impulses in the child's behavior. In his first public account of her, he was pleased to report Laura's "quick sense of propriety." She had good table manners and showed a strong desire to "appear neatly and smoothly dressed." Because Laura was so hopelessly cut off from the world of external appearances, Howe concluded that these behaviors could not have been learned; rather, they were "mental phenomena," the spontaneous actions of the child's innate moral intuition.[18]

When Harmony Bridgman read in Howe's reports his enthusiastic speculations about the child's "natural" good manners, she was incensed. Why should the doctor be so surprised to find that their child had table manners? Did he think her parents had taught her nothing in the first seven years of her life? Mrs. Bridgman might well have made the same objection to Howe's surprise at finding that her daughter had a "sense of property." "She will retain nothing belonging to another," Howe reported to the world. "She will not eat an apple or piece of cake which she may find, unless signs are made that she may do so." Ignoring the probability that these behaviors were learned at home before she came to Perkins, Howe intimated that he was witnessing the spontaneous, natural impulses of the child's moral faculties.[19]

In his next annual public report on her case, Howe was pleased to announce further evidence that the child was being directed by these internal moral sentiments. After fourteen months of education, her intellectual achievements lagged far behind those of other children her age. But he was pleased to report that "her moral nature—her sentiments and affections, her sense of propriety, of right, of property, &c, is equally well developed as those of other children."[20] Taking aim at Locke's theory that good actions are performed as a result of calculating self-interest, Howe suggested that the child's moral behavior was instinctive, expressing itself independent of her powers of reason. Several years later, he made this point more explicitly. Addressing himself to those of his readers who were not already "conversant with metaphysics," he explained:

According to Locke's theory, the moral qualities and faculties of this child should be limited in proportion to the limitation of her senses; for he derives moral principles from intellectual dispositions, which alone he considers to be innate . . . Now the sensations of Laura are very limited; acute as is her touch, and constant as is her exercise of it, how vastly does she fall behind others of her age in the amount of sensations which she experiences; how limited is the range of her thought—how infantile is she in the exercise of her intellect! But her moral qualities—her moral sense—are remarkably acute.[21]

Laura was "scrupulously conscientious," he insisted, not because of any lessons she had received. Her extremely simple vocabulary and the enormous barrier to her mind would have prevented her from learning abstract moral rules even if he had tried to teach them to her. She did not, then, understand the concepts of right and wrong intellectually but "*felt*" them through the actions of an innate "moral disposition."[22]

Shaftesbury had described the inner moral sense as a single powerful emotion, rooted in the aesthetic appreciation for harmony and the public good. As the sentimentalist tradition evolved over a century and a half down to Howe's time, proponents had dissected the moral sense into an increasing number of distinct and more specialized moral sentiments. Throwing philosophical economy to the winds, the phrenologists had been particularly willing to add new moral "faculties," "sentiments," and "dispositions" to their scheme of the mind. Each Victorian virtue found a home in its own separate lobe of the brain. As Howe's experiment progressed in the early 1840s, he devoted the bulk of his annual reports to a detailed analysis of Laura's moral nature. Without precise definitions or systematic order, he found in her character a large and shifting number of these innate moral sentiments.

As the very name "common sense" implies, the philosophers of the Scottish Enlightenment believed that morality was founded on humans' natural love of society. God had wisely constituted human nature with a craving for companionship, a desire which forged the bonds of mutual concern and affection that held together families, communities, and nations. Echoing this common sense tradition, Howe instructed his readers that "the social state is not elected by men, but . . . they are impelled to it by the irresistible cravings of their nature." The "natural tendency to social union" was the very foundation of morality. Accordingly, Howe found the first and most basic expression of Laura's moral sense in her remarkable "sociability." From her earliest days at Perkins, the child had shown an intense desire to communicate and exchange affection with those around her.

In fact, Howe's faith that she could learn language was based on this evidence that, in spite of her extreme isolation, she had an innate craving for communion with others. The urgings of this "social organ," Howe deduced, would drive her forward in the search for some way to express her thoughts and feelings.[23]

One clear example of this social faculty at work, Howe believed, was her remarkable desire to imitate others. In her first months at Perkins, she would sometimes hold a book in front of her face for long periods of time, mimicking the process of reading aloud which she had felt others doing. Such actions, Howe wrote, "must be entirely incomprehensible to her, [and] can have no other pleasure than the gratification of an internal faculty." According to phrenology, this faculty of imitation was God's way of urging human beings to copy the good moral example of their peers.[24]

The most important expression of the social organ was affection, and Laura displayed this in abundance. Howe noted that "when she is sitting at work, or at her studies, by the side of one of her little friends, she will break off from her task every few moments, to hug and kiss them with an earnestness and warmth, that is touching to behold." As Laura grew older, she learned to be quite happy by herself, but whenever she knew that another was in the room, she became "restless" to sit close by them, and to converse in the manual alphabet.[25]

According to Scottish thought, this craving for companionship was not just another emotional need but the very foundation of human morality. Because we feel this natural affection for our fellow human beings, we learn to sympathize with them, we are motivated to help them, and we come to seek our own well-being in the common good. Laura Bridgman had amply proven the power of this natural sympathetic impulse, not by her own behavior but by the interest and concern that she had elicited in so many others. Howe's entire philanthropic enterprise rested on the reliable human law that the sight of another's afflictions "calls at once for our sympathy with the sufferer," and he often pointed out that Laura Bridgman, above all other children at Perkins, was particularly able to "excite the tender compassion of all who feel."[26]

While Howe was gratified by this show of public sympathy, in his battle to restore the reputation of human nature he was anxious to prove that the child was just as capable of expressing compassion as she was of evoking it. At times he fretted that Laura's physical limitations would prevent her from developing her sense of concern and compassion. "All exercise kindly offices to her, and are themselves made better by the practice of the kindly feelings," but Howe noted that there was little Laura could do to reciprocate. He feared that, without exercise for her feelings of sympathy, she might come to expect the public's kindness as a unilateral "right," thus breaking the circle of mutual sympathy and support which was the foundation of all social relations.[27] But Howe was pleased to find that, in spite of the stark limitations imposed by her own handicaps, she still felt a keen sense of sympathy for the afflicted. "She loves to be employed in attending the sick," he was proud to report, "and is most assiduous in her simple attentions, and tender and endearing in her demeanor." He added that she even showed such compassion for the sufferings of those children whom she normally disliked, further evidence that the child was motivated not by the rational calculations of self-interest but by an instinctive sympathetic response to all human suffering.[28]

Howe noted only one obvious exception to Laura's altruistic instinct. The single "unamiable part of her character" was her "contempt" for the children at the institution whom she judged to be mentally inferior. She took advantage of those unfortunates, making them "wait on her." Howe did not seem too troubled by this flaw, however, and explained it simply as an irrepressible manifestation of her "Saxon blood."[29]

Howe also found evidence of what he believed to be Laura's innate honesty. While it posed pedagogical obstacles at times, he was delighted to find that for the first few years she could not even fathom the idea of fiction. He claimed in his reports that he could only "recollect" one or two occasions when the child had attempted "deliberate deception," and then "only under strong temptation." The conclusion Howe reached was that Laura had proven that "truth is plainer and more agreeable to children than falsehood." Unless disturbed by some bad influence, he claimed, children will spontaneously follow their "natural tendency to tell the truth."[30]

Howe also found her sense of propriety remarkably pronounced, especially for such a young child. "With no need of instruction," she ate and drank moderately and paid scrupulous attention to her cleanliness and appearance. "Never, by any possibility," Howe reported, "is she seen out of her room with her dress disordered; and if by chance any spot of dirt is pointed out to her on her person, or any little rent in her dress, she discovers a sense of shame, and hastens to remove it." Howe carried this argument further, suggesting that Laura's moral faculties were more attuned to "natural" morals, even minor ones, than to those based on "mere, arbitrary social conventionalism." For example, she only had to be told once that blowing her nose at the dinner table was disagreeable, a practice that Howe believed violated "natural" decency. But she had to be repeatedly reminded about the proper use of a fork and knife. Howe found this fact "remarkable and most gratifying," further proof that Laura's moral education was not being imposed on her from without by social pressure to conform to arbitrary standards but was guided by the natural, spontaneous stirrings of her own soul. No less than a Transcendental ascetic, the child seemed to be stripping away layers of arbitrary convention, the accumulated burden of the past, and pointing the way toward a new morality rooted only in the natural and spontaneous intuitions of the soul.[31]

One of Laura's most mysterious and controversial manifestations of the moral sense was what Howe called her "natural feeling of delicacy," her innate instinct for modesty and sexual purity. Even at the age of eight, she rejected "every approach to familiarity" from most men, though she showed no such uneasiness with women. Visitors to Perkins often commented on what George Combe described as the child's "sensitive delicacy in regard to sex." She would welcome and return the hugs and caresses of women. When introduced to other females, she would scan her fingers over them, exploring the details of their garments and the contours of their faces. But with male visitors she avoided, even repelled, all physical contact. Dickens encountered this during his visit. "My hand she rejected at once," he reported in *American Notes*. "But she retained my wife's with evident pleasure, kissed her, and examined her dress with a girl's curiosity and interest."[32]

Some quite plausibly suggested that the child's reaction to men was not a natural moral reflex but was caused by her relationship with her father. In Howe's early reports on her case, they reminded him, he had noted that Daniel Bridgman had sometimes resorted to threats of physical force to make his child obey. While Howe never discussed the fact publicly, the child did seem to generalize her feelings about her father, telling her teachers that she feared him "because he is a man." While there is no evidence that Daniel Bridgman was abusive toward his daughter, or uninterested in her welfare, he was evidently a distant and unaffectionate father, perhaps not unlike many hard-working Yankee farmers of the day. Laura's anxiety about her relationship with her father may well have influenced her feelings about other men.[33]

Howe countered this argument by pointing out that Laura felt no such fears with Tenny, the eccentric bachelor who had been so kind to the child in the first years after her illness. And she was quite comfortable around Howe himself, according to his reports; the two had enjoyed daily games of "romps" together throughout her childhood. Furthermore, though she avoided physical contact with most men, she enjoyed their company and befriended many. (The only regular male visitor to Perkins whom she clearly disliked was Charles Sumner. With her typically shrewd insight into human character, she found him to be aloof and "not gentle," a view shared by many of the haughty senator's friends and foes.)[34]

Thus Howe insisted that Laura's unusual reaction to men could not be explained as a quirk of her personal history but as the spontaneous expression of her "innate tendency to purity." In his eagerness to draw universal moral lessons from her case, he transformed the child's distinctive personality traits into a law of human nature. "I think it forms an important and beautiful element of humanity," Howe proclaimed, "the natural course of which is towards that state of refinement, in which, while the animal appetites shall work out their own ends, they shall all of them be stripped of their grossness, and, clad in garments of purity, contribute to the perfection of a race made in God's own image."[35]

Some criticized Howe's claim that Laura Bridgman proved the existence of such an innate faculty of purity by pointing to "the want of delicacy in savages." But Howe argued that Laura Bridgman was more uncorrupted than any noble savage, whose habits were debased by inherited social customs. Isolated as she was from the world around her, Laura Bridgman afforded the chance, for the first time, to study a completely "unsophisticated child of nature." Curiously, the calamity which so clearly distinguished her from her fellow human beings made her seem truly natural, unbiased by environmental influence.[36]

As Howe's comments suggest, one of the influences from which he felt Laura had been liberated was the past, the weight of inherited tradition and superstition. While he was speaking in this instance about the customs of "savages," his comments are suggestive of his feelings about New England's Calvinist past as well, a legacy as riddled with bigotry and backwardness as any exotic customs of the Hottentots or the Hindus, in Howe's view. Literary historians have suggested that many Jacksonian writers shared Howe's fascination with the possibility of making a complete break from the inherited mistakes of the past. Many felt that the New World offered a fresh start, a symbolic return to Eden. The virgin soil of a new continent and the nation's unique experiment with democracy might combine to produce "a radically new personality," one "emancipated from history, happily bereft of ancestry, untouched and undefiled by the usual inheritances of family and race," an individual whose only obedience was to the natural moral law within.[37]

In his eagerness to tear down the past, to level Calvinism in preparation for a new, enlightened, and purified Christian republic, Howe transformed Laura Bridgman into a mythical symbol of Edenic innocence and purity.

She was the perfect reminder that the human character was not permanently and irremediably disfigured by sin, that the human race once was, and could again become truly made in God's image. In his mind, this child had restored the reputations of Adam and Eve, those archetypes of human nature who had been so libeled by the Calvinist doctrine of the Fall. And if there was no reason to doubt that those ancient ancestors were inherently sinful, Howe reasoned, then there was no good reason to think the same of the children of Jacksonian Boston.

Horace Mann shared Howe's conclusion that Laura Bridgman's "original tendencies" had proven to be remarkably pure. Following his friend into this more controversial theological territory, Mann used his *Common School Journal* as a platform from which to promote Howe's findings to reform-minded educators in his state and beyond. Mann announced that Laura "exhibits sentiments of conscientiousness, of the love of truth, of gratitude, of affection, which education never gave to her. She bestows upon mankind, evidences of purity, and love, and faith, which she never received from them. It is not repayment, for they were not borrowed. They were not copied from the creature, but given by the Creator."[38]

Mann told his readers that Laura's natural innocence demonstrated how important environmental influences are in human development. "Were other children shrouded from the knowledge and example of artifice, of prevarication, of subterfuge, of dissimulation, of hypocrisy, of fraud, in all its thousand forms, as she has been, what reason have we to suppose that, as a general rule, they would not be as just, ingenuous, and truthful as she is? What a lesson to parents and educators!"[39]

Lacking hearing, Mann explained, the child had not learned about all the deceits of "social intercourse." Without a strong sense of taste, she could not be bribed to good behavior by misguided appeals to her appetite. Ignoring much evidence to the contrary, Mann also concluded that since Laura lacked sight she was immune to fashion; "a copious fountain of envy, rivalry, pride was at once dried up," destroyed along with her eyes. Deprived of most social intercourse, her natural instinct for justice had been undisturbed by society's "changeful absurdities of conventionalism," its tendency to "place the applause of others above the approbation of conscience, and of the sacred, inborn, God-implanted sense of duty." In this manner, Mann turned every one of Laura's virtues into a condemnation of Jacksonian America's vices.[40]

Though Howe and Mann were optimistic about the powers of human nature, they were not blind to human frailties and faults. Few people were perfect, they conceded; all made mistakes, just as Adam and Eve had. But if humans were sometimes led astray from their natural moral impulses, these reformers placed the blame not on human nature but on the "tempting apples" of a bad social environment. The way back to Eden, then, lay in the elimination of those tempting apples through the reform of society's institutions—its schools, prisons, families, and churches.

With unconscious irony, Howe reached back to a favorite metaphor from Boston's Puritan past to describe the significance of his experiment to disprove orthodox Calvinism. Laura, he declared, was "as a lamp set upon a hill, whose light cannot be hid," a beacon radiating from Boston, giving guidance and hope to the friends of reform and the foes of orthodoxy everywhere.[41]

Laura was between ten and fourteen years old when Howe made most of his public observations about her moral sense. Then and ever after, she was unaware of these pronouncements about her own self. She understood that her daily lessons and some of her comments were recorded in her teachers' journals, and she knew that many adults wanted to meet her and watch her demonstrate her penmanship and knowledge of geography. But she had no idea how closely she was being watched, how public her most intimate thoughts had become. "Could Laura be suddenly restored to her senses," Howe wrote, "and clothed with our faculties and intellect, which so far transcend hers, she would stand amazed to find herself the center of so much observation."[42] Laura sat silently in the midst of a whirlwind of words, never participating directly in this exhaustive search for the meaning of her own life story.

Yet Laura, too, was struggling to understand human nature and human motivation through an examination of the only evidence she had close to hand, her own moral, and immoral, impulses. On this subject, she was never as eloquent as Dr. Howe. Nor was she as optimistic about her own goodness, and the goodness of others. When she was thirteen, her teacher made this entry in her journal: "I read to her a letter from a friend who was teaching school—She spoke of her scholars as very pleasant & kind. Laura said 'Are all scholars kind?' I answered 'I think so,' supposing she meant to ask if all *her* scholars were kind. She repeated the word '*all?*' with emphasis."[43]

As Laura's own doubts suggest, the mythical Laura Bridgman that Howe presented to the antebellum public, the perpetually happy child with a natural instinct for truthfulness, kindness, and modesty, was an alluring vision but only a half truth. Just as, in his effort to present her as naturally curious, he had ignored glaring trouble spots in the child's educational progress, he now glossed over many inconsistencies in her moral development in his eagerness to prove that she was endowed with pure and strong moral intuitions. While Howe presented the child to the public as almost unerringly honest, privately her teachers fretted over Laura's frequent attempts at deception, her "many little lies." For example, one teacher caught Laura trying to deny that she had broken a water glass; the child once told another she had completed some knitting when she had not; she was caught slipping into a blind girlfriend's room for a visit without permission, and so on. When she was fourteen, Laura asked her teacher, "Are you tired of teaching me not to tell a lie?" The teacher saw no need to record her answer.[44]

As proof that the child's steady progress along the broad path of virtue and education was rewarded with happiness, Howe often reported that Laura was constantly joyous. "Her whole life is like a hymn of gratitude and thanksgiving," he rhapsodized. While Laura was a remarkably happy and good-natured child, her teachers also knew a darker side to her personality. Their journal entries take notice, time and again, of the child's bouts of irritability, nervousness, and even rage. Once when Laura was twelve she was overcome with "anger and resentment" when corrected in a math problem, and in defiance she extinguished her teacher's oil lamp, temporarily plunging her teacher into the same darkness with which she struggled every moment of her life. The symbolism of the act was lost on her teacher, who only mourned that the child was "decidedly wrong in her conduct." Other times, Laura struck her teacher or tried to bite her.[45]

The other children at Perkins were also a focus of Laura's wrath. For a time she was in the habit of shoving children she met in the hallway, and her fellow students endured occasional bites and other "very rough" and "rude" behavior. No one better understood the gap between the real Laura Bridgman and Howe's interpretation of her than the other blind children at Perkins. Troubled over Laura's habit of shoving her classmates when she met them in the hall, one teacher confided that "the opinion among the scholars now is, that Laura is the *opposite* of amiable—& the assertion that she is so causes many *sneers*."[46]

Even in her more calm and reflective moments, Laura's moral intuitions sometimes seemed to lead her off the path of virtue. After one of her teachers gave Laura a long lecture on the evils of being "selfish," she was dismayed to find that the child still insisted that she would "like to be a *little* selfish." Exasperated, her teacher noted, "I did not succeed in getting that idea out of her mind." In this case, Laura got little credit for the competing virtue of honesty.[47]

None of these incidents would seem particularly serious to most parents or educators today. Small lies, outbursts of passion, a little selfishness are generally accepted as a "natural" part of growing up, and indeed of being human. Given the incredible burdens Laura struggled under, her transgressions are particularly understandable, and her good spirits and generous nature do seem, as Howe often claimed, quite remarkable. Some of her bad behavior might even be understood as an effort to clarify the true meaning of the moral rules that her teachers were trying to instill in her. After taking a key and hiding it, locking Howe's sister in another room, she told her teacher, "I know it was wrong—was it 'deceive'?"[48]

But the moral regimen that Howe developed for Laura suggests that he was deeply concerned about his student's white lies, her mood swings, and acts of defiance. Harmless as most of these incidents were, he treated each one as though it might be the first step toward moral ruin. Observing most of every waking hour of the child's day, Howe and his female assistants never failed to note the smallest wrongdoing, always brought it to the child's attention, and attempted to root out any bad actions before they might become habitual.

In his public statements, Howe often appeared more tolerant of the child's lapses. On those few occasions when he acknowledged one of her acts of disobedience, he was quick to point out extenuating circumstances. "Two or three instances are recorded in her teacher's journal," he wrote when Laura was twelve, "of apparent unkindness on Laura's part to other children, and one instance of some ill temper to a grown person; but so contradictory are they to the whole tenor of her character and conduct, that I must infer either a misunderstanding of her motives by others, or illjudged conduct on their part." Privately, Howe was concerned about the child's moral setbacks, but publicly he presented them not as a natural part of the child's moral development but as the product of others' thoughtlessness.[49]

As the discrepancies between his public statements and the teachers' private accounts suggest, Howe did not present his readers with a balanced, objective account of all of the "facts" of Laura's moral development. Influenced by his growing affection for the child as well as his eagerness to disprove Calvinism's doctrine of innate depravity, he excused or ignored aspects of her behavior that contradicted his claim that she was governed only by pure and reliable moral intuitions. With the help of his writings, he hoped that the public would agree that there was "no depravity in her nature."[50]

"Laura outruns my hopes," Howe reported to a German philanthropist in 1841. This was the high-water mark of his optimism, and he enthusiastically combed the book of nature for metaphors that might capture the meaning of Laura Bridgman. "She is to other children," he announced, "what the simple wildflower is to the pampered product of our gardens." "The different traits of her character," he wrote on another occasion, "have unfolded themselves successively, as pure and spotless as the petals of a rose; and in every action unbiased by extraneous influence, she 'gravitates toward the right' as naturally as a stone falls to the ground." Howe's extravagant organic metaphors betray the influence of romanticism on his thought. In these exciting early years of his experiment he could sound like a disciple of Rousseau, one who trusted in the goodness of untutored instinct and longed to return human nature to its natural state.[51]

But Howe's organic metaphors are better understood as polemical jabs against Calvinism, rather than as complete expositions of his theory of human nature or his educational practice. Though influenced by the romantic images and ideals that were imported into New England at this time by the Transcendentalists, he always remained a practical Baconian, an heir of the Enlightenment who was more interested in scientific progress than in a return to nature. Thus, while Howe sometimes portrayed Laura as a wildflower, putting forth beautiful blossoms entirely on her own, he more often used a quite different metaphor: he referred to himself as a gardener, cultivating the tender seed of Laura's emerging conscience and carefully pruning away her bad moral impulses. Howe assumed that Laura's moral faculties, no less than her body and mind, would need his careful guidance in order to develop fully.

Chapter 6

Punishing Thoughts

By proving that Laura was endowed with a natural moral sense, Howe felt that he had discredited one of the most important tenets of Calvinist theology, the belief in original sin. But he was anxious to expand the scope of his experiment, taking on orthodox *practice* as well as theory. According to the Calvinist doctrines which had guided New England's social institutions for two centuries, children were born with natures disordered by inherited sin. In the words of the great Puritan theologian Jonathan Edwards, they were "by nature the children of wrath and the heirs of hell." Because the young were incapable of reason, their elders believed that they were particularly liable to be ruled by sinful appetites and passions. Consequently, parents and educators were advised to thwart these inclinations "without compromise." "Children should be regularly checked, and subdued, in every ebullition of passion; particularly of pride and anger," suggested Timothy Dwight, a respected Calvinist authority on education in the early nineteenth century.[1]

The most common way to do that was with a quick and consistent application of "the rod" for every transgression. This reliance on the use of "fear," Howe believed, not only failed to curb a child's bad behavior but actually created it, planting the seeds of "hypocrisy and distrust" in the souls of innocent children and leading them to dread and resent "the iron face of authority." Because they doubted the purity of their children's motivations, he argued, Calvinists were fulfilling their own expectations by "degrading" the characters of the young, appealing only to their "lowest motives."[2]

Howe's parents, who were not Calvinists but Unitarians, evidently used the rod very sparingly and provided him with a great deal of love and affection. But as a student in Boston's schools, he had experienced Calvinist discipline first hand. A high-spirited child with a passion for practical jokes, he often felt the sting of a Boston schoolmaster's rod across his knuckles. If Howe's teachers aimed to break his will, they must have been disappointed with the results, but the memories of his school days left him with a smoldering resentment against traditional forms of discipline, practices which he associated with orthodox religion.[3]

Horace Mann shared Howe's view on corporal punishment and made this philosophy a cornerstone of his educational reform program. Both conceded that corporal discipline was sometimes needed as a last resort, but they joined forces to promote what Mann called the "anti-flagellation system," urging teachers to use "moral suasion" rather than physical force.[4]

Howe and Mann believed that the practice of using physical threats to maintain order in the schoolroom was not only ineffective but dangerously at odds with the ideals and practical needs of a democratic republic. Both men considered themselves patriots, proud defenders of their nation's democratic heritage. Howe, who had even taken an active part in supporting democratic revolutions in Europe, paid the United States his highest compliment by proclaiming that its political system was "in accordance with the principles of phrenology" because it stimulated each citizen's natural faculties of self-government.[5]

Though Howe and Mann agreed that America's institutions were "the best in the world," they—like many in their social class during the Jacksonian period—were uneasy about how the ideals of the American Revolution were being translated into practice. The fate of America's fifty-year-old experiment in individual freedom still seemed precarious, its success far from assured. More than any other people in the world, Americans enjoyed their liberty, but Howe warned that this was a mixed blessing; they were "free for good or for evil." All too often, he thought, his fellow citizens only squandered this freedom in the hectic pursuit of wealth and fame. Though he felt that democracy was the fairest system of government on earth, Howe feared the mass hysteria of democratic party politics. And while he considered himself a champion of religious freedom and tolerance, he hated the spiritual frenzy unleashed by the evangelical revivals of the Second Great Awakening. All around him, individual liberty seemed to be releasing centrifugal forces of selfishness and irrationality which threatened to tear society into fragments.[6]

Howe, Mann, and their allies in reform believed that the best way to solve the problems brought on by democracy's excesses was to improve the moral education of the young. Democracy had liberated Americans from the authority of a state church and government; but the blessing of liberty would become a curse if citizens did not learn how to replace these external constraints with self-control. They no longer had to bow before the will of a priest or a king, but they had to learn to hear and obey their own consciences. The success of the nation's democratic experiment depended on the ability of each citizen to develop these internal powers of self-discipline.[7]

Educational reformers in Howe's day concluded that the crucial time to learn this self-control was during childhood, when the will was still malleable and the moral sense had not yet been corrupted. This moral training, they believed, was the most important part of a child's education. But in common school classrooms, the "intellectual nature alone is cultivated; knowledge, practical and useful, is imparted, but the moral nature is neglected." Howe feared that not only were children not learning to obey their own consciences, but they were also being forced to submit to the tyrannical authority of an orthodox schoolmaster who ruled over them with the constant threat of punishment. As a result, students grew to resent all authority and left school without having learned a measure of self-control, so important to the health of a democracy. "When the boy escapes from school," Howe explained, "he never hears the word "Master" again . . . Unless he sinks down to absolute crime, he scarcely comes into contact with penal law, or knows what legal authority means. Nine tenths of the lives of nine tenths of our citizens are passed with no sense whatever of coercion or compulsion, beyond that which may come from social usages, or their own sense of interest or right; and what must be the condition of him who comes into such a life as this, with no habit and no idea of self-government, beyond that which he could derive from corporal punishment?"[8]

Howe applied the rod at Perkins in some rare cases, with particularly recalcitrant male students. But he believed that a democratic educator should always strive to replace corporal discipline with "moral discipline." Rather than trying to break a child's supposedly perverse will, the teacher ought to "cultivate the good that is in him" by creating an atmosphere of "kindness, firmness, and consistency." In this reformed school environment, students would learn to obey voluntarily, not because they feared punishment but because their natural love of learning and admiration of the teacher's moral example had been stimulated. In such a classroom, and in such a household, "the habits of order, of intelligent self-government, of obedience in freedom," would be painlessly developed within children, preparing them to enjoy, but not abuse, the promise of American liberty.[9]

There was nothing particularly original about Howe's political and social ideals or his theory of child discipline. In his call for a society of self-governing individuals, whose freedom was tempered by a conscientious concern for the common good, he invoked the legacy of the moderate Enlightenment, of the American Revolution's republican ideology, and of the reform wing of his own Whig party. Howe was also not unique in believing that the best way to achieve that goal was through education. His trust in the innate goodness of children and his call for education based on nurture and positive influence were common concerns of most educational reformers by the 1830s.[10]

What distinguished Howe from other reformers was not his political ideals or his theory of child nurture but his novel means of advancing his cause, through a public and "scientific" experiment with Laura Bridgman. Howe felt that his work with Laura afforded an unprecedented opportunity to observe the growth and development of the conscience in its pure form. Through her moral training, he believed that he could prove those ideas about human nature which served as the foundation of republican political and social theories. Specifically, he would show that, when the degrading practice of corporal punishment was replaced by enlightened "moral discipline," children would learn to become self-governing, needing only the clear voice of conscience to keep them on the proper path.

From the outset, Howe had used Perkins as a showcase for his ideas about discipline. Setting the rod aside, he tried instead to appeal to the higher moral sentiments which he believed were present, however feebly, within each wayward child's soul. His reports rarely failed to make pointed comparisons between this approach and that practiced by most of the state's common school masters. Because he always presented knowledge "in the proper form," he explained, his children's natural appetite for learning was excited. As a result, he argued, new ideas never had to be "whipped in, nor coaxed or bribed in." Howe felt that the success that he was enjoying at Perkins using moral discipline was a chastisement to "the mistaken career" of all those teachers who had "spoiled so much good birch, blistered so many soft hands and hardened so many tender hearts."[11]

The Christian Examiner, Boston's leading Unitarian journal, endorsed Howe's effort to model a new approach to school discipline. Reviewing the remarkable progress that his students were making at Perkins, Mrs. L. Minot suggested that those teachers who were "disposed to complain of the dullness and frowardness of their pupils" would benefit from a visit to one of the institution's regular exhibitions. There they would find that, "so far from there being a necessity of severity to induce the young to learn, it will here be found that kindness and encouragement are the atmosphere in which the faculties most readily expand." The "old answer" to student apathy, "the fear of punishment," had proven insufficient; "though it may bring immediate relief, like a drastic medicine, it leaves the patient more subject to the disease than ever." Howe had shown that near miraculous results could be achieved by appealing instead to each child's natural feelings of "curiosity, sympathy, and emulation."[12]

Howe considered Laura to be the perfect example of the existence of these innate faculties, and in his reports he sometimes used her case to critique the practice of corporal punishment, lending support to Horace Mann's wider campaign to change disciplinary practices in the state's common schools. After describing Laura's enthusiastic approach to her grammar lessons, he wrote, "The eagerness with which she followed up these exercises was very delightful, and the pupil teasing the teacher for more words, is in pleasing contrast with the old method, where all the work was on one side, and where the coaxing, and scolding, and birchen appliances to boot, often failed to force an idea into the mind in the proper shape. But Laura is always ready for a lesson."[13]

However, because the physical punishment of girls was frowned upon even by most orthodox defenders of the rod, Laura's case was not a particularly useful vehicle for assaulting the practice of corporal punishment. Even the sternest Calvinist schoolmaster would not have defended the need to strike such a helpless young female. Howe made more effective use of Laura's case to criticize a quite different approach to classroom discipline, the use of positive incentives such as treats and prizes. The leading proponents of this idea were not orthodox conservatives but the followers of the early nineteenth-century English reformer Joseph Lancaster. Struggling with large class sizes, Lancaster had arranged his students hierarchically. The best scholars monitored the progress of their peers, rewarding their accomplishments as they competed to win recognition and move ahead in the carefully regimented system. Students were motivated to learn not by fear but by what Lancaster called the more positive impulse of "emulation."[14]

Some reform-minded American educators embraced Lancaster's "monitorial" system, preferring the symbolic carrot of classroom honors to the literal stick of corporal punishment. But Howe was convinced that this appeal to a child's love of praise was as misguided as the threat of physical pain. Prizes, he argued, encouraged students to perform well only for the external reward of being admired and indulged rather than for the internal experience of learning itself. Howe felt that these motivational devices might inspire children to great mental accomplishments but also stirred up their dark feelings of pride, selfishness, and envy. Under such an approach, the natural pleasure of learning was displaced by pangs of "lassitude and dissatisfaction."[15]

In Howe's estimation, Laura proved that such motivational techniques were entirely unnecessary. Her education was inspired only by her natural curiosity, yet she never grew tired of learning new things. The more Laura studied, the more she was enveloped in "joy, that oxygen of the moral atmosphere." In his opinion, this proved that all children arrive at school as fountains of enthusiasm and remain so, as long as the deep well of their souls is not poisoned by misguided discipline.[16]

In the first five years of Laura's education Howe rarely reported those times when she "swerve[d] for a moment from the right," because, like a compass in a storm, her moral sense always returned her "unerring to the Pole."[17] But as Laura entered adolescence, Howe began a more open, though still guarded, public discussion of the setbacks in her moral education, those brief but troubling incidents with which her teachers had been privately struggling for several years. Howe's account of these incidents was still quite selective; he never acknowledged the full extent of Laura's bouts of bad humor, deceit, and selfishness, perhaps because he was concerned that any mention of the child's small acts of rebellion could be used by the Calvinists to claim that the child was not as pure as he had claimed. But a few carefully selected examples served Howe's purpose; they expanded the moral import of his experiment by allowing him to use Laura's story as a showcase of enlightened discipline.

Howe began this new direction by confessing in his 1843 report that, during the previous year, he had encountered one small lapse in the child's marvelous instinct for honesty. As Laura was preparing for a walk one day, he had teased her about some gloves she was wearing, which gave her hands "a clumsy appearance." While Laura usually entered into such games with delight, in this case Howe had unknowingly wounded her "personal vanity." Returning from the walk, she hid the gloves and allowed her teachers to suppose they had been lost. But, Howe reported, Laura was "uneasy under the new garb of deceit" and soon betrayed herself by asking repeated questions about the whereabouts of her gloves. When he realized that the child was lying about the gloves, he was "exceedingly pained."[18]

An orthodox parent or teacher might have interpreted Laura's lie as a dangerous act of insubordination, a willful sin that should be countered with firm, though not necessarily physical, punishment. Howe believed that such an approach would not teach the child to obey her natural instinct for truthfulness but would only encourage her to tell the truth to evade future punishment. He insisted that, this small lie notwithstanding, truthfulness came more naturally than deceit to Laura, and to all children. The enlightened educator, he argued, should use an incident such as this one as a chance to exercise the child's inner moral sense, letting her own conscience provide the corrective. Taking Laura up "in the most affectionate way," he told her a story about an imaginary family which had always treated its child with great love and truthfulness. Yet the child had chosen to deceive them, an act which caused the family "great pain."[19]

In Laura's moral education, Howe frequently employed this kind of thinly veiled parable, hoping that she would enter into the story, drawing connections between her own behavior and that of the stick figures in his little wooden morality tales. He believed that children first experience morality as an instinctive feeling, an impulse, rather than as the rational assent to abstract rules of conduct. With young Laura, whose grasp of language was still so limited, the prospect of giving her some clear understanding of "moral rules and precepts" seemed virtually impossible. He had to rely instead on "examples in conduct which she shall imitate," calling into play her instinctive feelings of admiration for the goodness of her teachers. And he also hoped to exercise her moral impulses through stories, "relations of actions which shall call into play her sense of right and wrong." As she grew older, she would one day move beyond this immediate intuitive response, as she learned to generalize these sympathetic emotions into abstract moral rules. But the foundation first had to be laid by cultivating her moral *feelings*, and he felt that stories with clear moral lessons best served that purpose.[20]

At times, Laura found Howe's parables more oppressive than enlightening. "Dr. read me a story," she told her teacher one afternoon. "I do not like many stories, they make me sad." But in the version of the lying incident that Howe related to his readers, his story-telling technique had worked perfectly. Laura took the moral hook hidden within the story's bait and soon began to grow pale, "evidently touched." The child asked how the fictional parents responded when they learned that their beloved child had betrayed their trust. Howe told her that "her parents were grieved, and cried," a twist in the plot which brought Laura to the verge of tears herself. Suffering what Howe believed were the self-inflicted pangs of her own conscience, Laura then confessed that she had hidden the gloves.[21]

Mirroring the parents in his parable, Howe responded to the child's confession with a show of grief and instructed the other teachers in the room "to manifest no other feeling than that of sorrow on her account." Believing the social affections to be the cornerstone of morality, Howe wanted the child to feel that she had sundered the bonds of mutual trust, thus casting herself off from the human community. Laura clung to Howe, "as if in terror of being alone," but he broke away from her. She then went to the others, seeking comfort, but found "only sadness" and soon became agonized with grief. Howe informed his readers that this was difficult to watch but that he was "forced . . . to inflict the pain upon her."[22]

Howe did not let her suffer long, fearing that if her punishment became too harsh, his efforts might backfire, leaving her with such a dread of future punishments that she might try to hide one lie with another, falling "insensibly . . . into the habit of falsehood." Howe went to the child and assured her of "the continued affection of her friends." He reinforced the moral of the incident by explaining to her that the painful feelings she had just suffered were "the simple and necessary consequences" of her lie: "[I] made her reflect upon the nature of the emotion she experienced after having uttered the untruth; how unpleasant it was, how it made her feel afraid, and how widely different it was from the fearless and placid emotion which followed the truth."[23]

In short, Howe wanted her to see that it felt bad to be bad. Her feelings of discomfort, he believed, came not from his emotional coercion but from self-induced distress caused by the natural actions of the moral sentiments which God had implanted in her soul. His decision to withdraw all affection from her, to isolate her, was simply a matter of showing her the "natural" consequences of antisocial behavior. As long as Laura followed her innate inclination to tell the truth, her moral sentiments were rewarded with a pleasurable "placid emotion" and she enjoyed affectionate relationships with those around her. When she went astray, the social bonds dissolved, and those same sentiments instantly sounded an alarm of unpleasurable feeling, warning her that she had strayed off of the path of good conduct.

Howe offered this incident to his readers not simply as a curious anecdote in Laura's peculiar biography, and certainly not as an admission that the child was not as pure as he had initially claimed. Rather, he felt that he was providing the public with a model for the proper moral discipline of all children, as well as for wayward adults. Having proven to his own satisfaction that Laura Bridgman's moral impulses were pure and natural, he was now trying to demonstrate how an enlightened educator should work with this raw material, nurturing the moral sense so that it became a strong internal authority, capable of helping the child turn good inclinations into right actions. By teaching the child to hear and submit to her conscience, Howe suggested, he was preparing her to become a self-governing adult.

Readers of Howe's public reports were led to believe that the story of Laura's lie about her gloves was a rare misstep in the otherwise "triumphant march" of her moral development. But the private journals kept by her teachers show that Laura afforded them many more opportunities to experiment with Howe's theory of punishment. Watching over her almost every waking hour of the day, these women felt it their duty, as one put it, to "almost incessantly advise, check, or point out little faults to be corrected." When these infractions were more serious, they responded not by threatening physical punishment or promising heavenly rewards but by holding out the dreadful prospect of social isolation. On the morning that Laura announced that she would like to be "a *little* selfish," for example, her teacher recorded that she had tried to root out this perversity by "all the usual means, such as that ladies did not love selfish girls & she would not be loved when very old." Caught in "another instance of deception," her teacher told Laura that, if she lied again, "I could not love her and I should feel very sad & she would be very unhappy." When reprimanded for pushing the other children at Perkins, she was warned that "the girls would not love her" anymore, a possibility that brought her to tears.[24]

When these verbal threats of social isolation failed to move the child, her teachers reinforced the message by resorting to physical isolation. They battled Laura's regular bouts of anger or impatience by withdrawing their attention and affection, canceling her lessons for the day and leaving her alone with her conscience. For example, when a teacher found that Laura had lied about the amount of knitting she had accomplished one day, she isolated the child, advising her to "think much about deceiving." Laura, who could be formidably stubborn, would sometimes resist this emotional coercion for a time. On this particular occasion, her teacher fretted that Laura "did not seem to be moved at all" by her banishment. But inevitably the following day the child would repent, confessing her fault and seeking readmittance into the circle of social affection. Bursting into tears, she pleaded with her teacher, "I want you to love me many times much." Summing up Howe's own theory of the moral sentiments with admirable brevity, she added that her punishment had taught her that "bad is sad."[25]

Perhaps more than most children, Laura was acutely vulnerable to this punishment of social isolation. All children are dependent on their parents, teachers, and guardians for support and threatened by the prospect of losing their protection and affection. But Laura's unique condition made her particularly reliant on others. While her sense of touch was acute, the knowledge it conveyed was too oblique to ever fully compensate for the solitude of her double affliction. Only language reconnected her with others and gave her information about the world around her. Conversation was, in this regard, her most important "sense."

Because of this linguistic dependence, Laura clung to her teachers. Anxious to preserve the crucial link they provided to the outside world, she poured an enormous—indeed exhausting—amount of affection on her female guardians. For good reason, she called them her "constant companions." Thus, whenever they punished her by breaking off conversation and withdrawing, they were not just depriving her of their company but severing her very being from the world around her. Laura was quite understandably terrified by the threat of being plunged back into sensory and social darkness.

Perhaps because of her unique vulnerability to this form of punishment, Laura threw herself into her moral training with even greater intensity than she brought to her physical and intellectual education. While she did not understand that Howe had turned her moral development into a celebrated public experiment, she knew almost from the start that the details of her daily activities, her comments and her actions, were recorded in a book and judged by Dr. Howe and her teachers. As her education progressed, she began to internalize this process of moral scrutiny, conducting her own inquisitions into her daily conduct. When she was thirteen, one teacher noted in her journal: "After breakfast [Laura] was very much interested in discussing her conduct during the past week, & in comparing it with the previous weeks. She came to the decision that she had only done one or two things wrong this week." Laura's teachers were surprised to find her turning again and again to moral questions. "Children usually prefer to skip the moral of a story," one marveled, "but Laura always wishes to discuss it; she never seems quite satisfied with the results of her own reasoning, or with my verdicts on such questions."[26]

This voluntary self-examination soon became as routine in Laura's life as calisthenics, cold baths, and math exercises. For example, at the breakfast table one morning she announced, "I hope I shall not be cross or make any noises or fret or deceive or tell any wrong stories this week." Her teacher used that opportunity to teach the word "resolutions," a concept Laura understood "very quickly." Another time, Laura asked, "Was I good all day yesterday?" When told that she had been "rude two or three times," she replied, "It makes me sad in eyes & something troubles me when I am not good—does your think trouble you when you are not good?" Those troubling emotions, Laura was told, were caused by her conscience. Like the word "resolution," conscience was a concept that she quickly grasped. Summing up this new feeling of moral duty which was growing within her, she announced, "My thoughts tell me when I am good & when I am

7. Laura and her "constant companion," Mary Swift, conversing with the manual alphabet. *(Courtesy of Perkins School for the Blind, Watertown, Massachusetts)*

wrong." Just as Howe had hoped, Laura was developing a keen conscience. Along with her teachers, she closely monitored her daily behavior, probing her own motivations and judging her actions with puritanical devotion. By the time she was thirteen, she found that after any misdeed she was soon racked by pangs of guilt. Howe had instilled in Laura a hatred of sin and a powerful desire for moral perfection.[27]

Yet, as Laura struggled for self-mastery, she found that her "wrong feelings" of impatience and anger and selfishness would not submit. She was now governed, as she put it, by "two thoughts," a new voice of conscience competing with an equally powerful voice of temptation. In spite of her deep and growing interest in discussing matters of right and wrong, she continued to defy and deceive her teachers, to slap and shove them and her fellow students, to refuse to do some of her lessons. After each of these infractions, she was overcome with guilt and anxiety and repented in tears. But soon she would succumb again to the voice of "temptation." As Mary Swift described it, her student was in the midst of a great moral "crisis": "She was to conquer herself, or ever after to be subject to her passions."[28]

Working closely with Laura each day, her female companions often bore the brunt of the child's struggle to constrain her "passions." Though they were Laura's primary source of companionship and paternal care, as well as her crucial link to the outside world, at times she clearly resented this dependence on her guardians. By the time she was twelve, Laura tried to establish some small measure of autonomy, sometimes countering her teachers' emotional coercion by offering some of her own. In 1842 Miss Rogers was troubled to find that her student had "within the last month withdrawn from me as much as possible—and today has said that she did 'not love me & was not friend of mine'—talked about it to her but can not find any reason for the change." While Laura's moods of defiance passed quickly, they suggest that, now on the verge of adolescence, she was becoming more assertive, trying to carve out some measure of independence in her relationship with her teachers.[29]

When the threat of social isolation and their own disapproval failed to move Laura, her female teachers usually fell back on the last, most effective appeal, the final judgment of "Doctor." Although she repeatedly tested the bounds of her female teachers' affections and authority, Laura dreaded the possibility that any of her misdeeds would be recorded in "the book" which she knew Dr. Howe would read. During one confrontation, for example, when Laura remained unrepentant, Mary Swift reminded her that "Dr. would be very sad when he read in my journal about it." At this stage in Laura's education, Howe was an increasingly distant presence in her life. Relinquishing most of the daily responsibilities of educating her to her female tutors, he was absorbed in other reform projects, and was often away from the Institution for weeks at a time. Perhaps because of this distance, rather than in spite of it, he continued to hold remarkable power over Laura; his authority was not diluted by too much familiarity, and his attention and affection were less frequent and thus more valuable emotional commodities.[30]

In Laura's mind, Howe's special authority was also related to his gender. After a lecture on the virtue of patience, she told Howe's sister, "I am impatient with you & with my teacher but I am never impatient with Dr." When asked why that was so, she replied, "because I never like to let men see me *impatient*."[31]

Thus Howe, as a distant and male authority figure, was able to exert an influence over Laura's behavior that her female teachers, interacting with her on a daily basis, could rarely hope to achieve. Howe was blind to this difference and unwilling to concede that Laura's moral lapses might be caused by either flaws in her character or flaws in his theory of moral discipline. If her female companions still struggled with the child's acts of disobedience and anger, he could only attribute this to a lack of moral magnetism on their part. "There are persons who have had much influence over her education," he wrote after one of Laura's violent outbursts, "who have labored most diligently, and displayed great tact and ingenuity in developing her intellect, but who have never succeeded in inspiring that perfect love which casteth out fear."[32]

Thus, as Laura entered adolescence, there were several storm clouds on the horizon of Howe's famous experiment. Laura's ongoing power struggle with her female teachers intensified; she continued her adoration of Howe just as he was becoming increasingly absorbed with other concerns and distant from her daily life; and she continued to suffer fits of violent anger and frustration, followed by strong feelings of guilt and despair. These were the ingredients for an impending emotional crisis, one which would erupt the following year.

But for the time being Howe ignored these ominous developments, convinced that his plan for Laura's moral education was progressing remarkably well. He was concerned about the child's small acts of misbehavior but was pleased to see that her moral intuitions were developing into a strong internal voice of conscience. While he believed that Laura's moral education was still a work in progress, Howe felt sure that she was well on her way to becoming a conscientious, self-governing adult. He could ask for no better testimony to the success of his experiment in moral discipline than two questions Laura asked one day. "Why do you not punish me any more?" she wondered. And "Why do my thoughts punish me?"[33]

Chapter 7

Sensing God

Laura Bridgman had one of the most scrutinized souls in a city famous for its spiritual introspection. From the moment she entered the Perkins Institution at age seven until Howe's last report on her when she was twenty one, hundreds of Bostonians took an interest in the details of her religious life. Howe often remarked that he received more inquiries about her faith than any other aspect of her education. Almost as soon as Laura emerged out of social and linguistic isolation, some of her admirers looked forward to the day when she might be delivered from spiritual darkness as well.

For those of the orthodox faith, that meant instructing the child in the tenets of the gospel, the sooner the better. They were eager to tell her that she was born guilty of sin and deserving of death but that, by accepting Christ's atoning sacrifice, she could enjoy God's forgiveness and win the salvation of her soul. One visitor summed up the feeling shared by many when he wrote that he could not leave Perkins without "dropping a word on the high privilege and honour which might be in store for [Laura's teacher], of communicating to one, apparently so far beyond the reach of all knowledge, the truths and hopes of the gospel."[1]

But Howe had very different hopes for Laura's religious education. As a liberal Christian, he rejected the notion that Laura, or any other child, was born guilty of inherited sin. Believing her not to be sick, he had no use for the orthodox cure. The doctrine of Christ's sacrificial atonement, he felt, was entirely unreasonable and therefore false. True knowledge of God, he believed, came not from the supernatural revelation passed down in an ancient Hebrew text but from the rational study of the Creator's natural laws, urged on by religious feelings implanted within human nature itself. As Laura's education progressed, Howe devised a plan for her religious training based on these principles, a practical application of the teachings of his mentors in the Unitarian church and the science of phrenology.

As with all of the prior phases of Laura's education, Howe began Laura's

religious training expecting not only to instruct the child but also to en-
lighten the many who were looking on. He believed that, by exhibiting a
pure character and an intuitive moral sense, Laura had already disproven
the doctrine of original sin. Carrying the experiment deeper into controversial theological territory, he next hoped to prove that the child's mind
was also endowed with innate religious sentiments, intuitions that could
lead her beyond a knowledge of right and wrong, all the way to God.

✿ As a young man growing up in the first two decades of the nineteenth
century, Howe's ideas about religion were influenced by the theological
struggle that was then being waged between New England's liberal and orthodox Christians. Howe was eighteen, a junior at Brown College, when
William Ellery Channing delivered his famous ordination sermon, "Unitarian Christianity," a manifesto for liberal Christians that accelerated the
division of New England Congregationalism into two opposing camps.[2]

In this widely circulated and debated address, Channing outlined a
number of points of disagreement between New England's liberals and
their orthodox brethren. At the heart of all these differences lay a dis-
pute over the ultimate source of spiritual authority. While agreeing with
the orthodox that the Bible was an essential, supernatural revelation of
God's will—particularly the "most perfect revelation of his will by Jesus
Christ"—Channing and his fellow liberals declared that they could no
longer accept the traditional view that the Bible was clear and infallible, its
meaning self-evident, and its commands deserving of unqualified obedience. Influenced by advances in textual analysis—the Higher Criticism
then being developed in Germany—Channing and other American liberals argued that the Scriptures were, like any other human record, laced
with the concerns and prejudices of the men who wrote them. The only
way to distinguish human bias from God's truth was to cross-examine
scriptural revelation before the "bar of reason." Channing believed that
God had implanted rational power into the human mind for this very purpose, expecting the true spirit of His nature and commandments to be
clarified by the light of human reason.[3]

Channing pointed to several places where Boston's liberals believed that
the orthodox had mistaken God's true meaning. As the name "Unitarian"
suggests, he found no justification, in the Bible or in human reason, for
the doctrine of the Trinity, the idea of a single God with three natures, in
the form of the Father, the Son (Jesus), and the Holy Spirit. Likewise,
Channing saw no scriptural or rational sanction for the doctrine that Jesus

had a dual nature—both God and man at the same time. This idea, he scolded, placed "an enormous tax on human credulity."[4]

Most importantly, liberal Christians rejected the Calvinist theory of human nature, specifically the doctrines that all humans were condemned by Adam and Eve's original sin, that God had predestined who would be saved and who would be damned, and that Christ died as an atoning sacrifice for human sin. Liberals felt that these principles of orthodox theology turned God into an angry, capricious, and even immoral tyrant, punishing human beings for sins they were helpless to prevent, since their wills were rebellious from birth, their reason was clouded by sin, and their spiritual freedom was negated by predestination. Channing rejected these doctrines inherited from the founding fathers of New England Puritanism as abhorrent to reason, a defamation of God's character, and a slander on human nature.

Reading the Scriptures through the filter of their own standards of reasonable and just behavior, liberals found a quite different God to worship. Theirs was a God who inspired respect rather than fear, One who encouraged rather than bewildered human reason, One whose actions and laws never affronted the conscience, but proved Him to be the perfect model of moral behavior.[5]

Channing's published address added fuel to a controversy already more than a decade old, one which soon culminated in the disintegration of New England's Congregational order. While his sermon included a plea for religious tolerance and Christian brotherhood, both sides retreated into the citadels of their own seminaries. The liberals maintained their grasp on Harvard, while the orthodox, setting aside their own doctrinal differences, formed a united front at their recently founded Andover seminary. The two factions then engaged in a bitter struggle, carried on in both courts and congregations, over the ownership of church property. Liberal and orthodox theologians fanned the flames of controversy by publishing dozens of pamphlets on their controverted points of doctrine.[6]

Howe, raised in a liberal church, naturally sided with Channing. Although there is no evidence that he read Channing's sermon while a student at Brown, he later spoke of the Unitarian leader as an important mentor, praising him as a "democratic Moses" who bravely smote the "rock of truth," releasing its "everlasting waters." As early as his college years, he shared the minister's view that the truths of religion should be determined by the free exercise of human reason. A year after Channing's controversial address, Howe wrote to a school friend that "there are certain principles of truth, implanted in the mind of man, to which he gives implicit belief, and by mingling Errors, with these truths, they become, as it were, interwoven with his very nature, so that it is next to impossible to eradicate them. Upon these, and some other principles, have been reared those structures of religion, which have stood the test of ages." For too long, Howe claimed, orthodox Christians had worshipped the false idol of tradition, mixing their faith with the superstitions of the past. The only solution, he wrote more than a decade before becoming a professional educator, was education. "Knowledge, alone, can free men from error."[7]

Coming of age during the most turbulent years of this "Unitarian controversy," Howe's approach to religion was forever after stamped with the partisan spirit of those times. As the scornful tone of his early letter suggests the young man not only shared Channing's theological views, but also the minister's willingness to confront his Calvinist brethren. Howe declared that New England's orthodox believers would never yield their mental chains without a struggle, and even then he seemed to be preparing to give it to them.

While Howe considered himself, from this early age, a determined foe of orthodoxy, he took little interest in the theological gist of the Unitarian controversy. Though he professed a liberal faith in reason, he saw no need to expend that reason haggling over doctrinal debates. Unlike Channing and Harvard's liberal theologians, he never attempted to explain the true configuration of the Godhead, never tried to define the nature of Jesus's divinity, and never discussed the plausibility of the various Biblical miracles, all central concerns to the first generation of Unitarian theologians.

Howe paid as little attention to the theological complexities of orthodoxy. By the 1820s, as he was entering adulthood, orthodox Christianity was undergoing a profound change in New England, as strict Calvinist doctrines were undermined by the more optimistic evangelical spirit of the Second Great Awakening. Under the influence of the Awakening's revivals, many orthodox Christians came to reject, or at least qualify, the Calvinist doctrine of predestination. While orthodox ministers and theologians still held that all humans are born sinful, some added the radical innovation that sinners still enjoyed enough free will to deliver themselves from this bondage. Through an act of the will, these revivalists suggested, each soul could accept God's grace and win salvation. While this transition away from the traditional Calvinist doctrine of predestination represented an important victory for the proponents of liberal Christianity, Howe either did not notice the change or found it of no consequence. For the rest of his life, he continued to use the terms "orthodox" and "Calvinist" interchangeably, with no regard for the admittedly subtle theological distinctions that preoccupied his adversaries.

As Howe's lack of interest in theology suggests, he was drawn to Unitarianism more by its spirit than its doctrine. He admired the liberals because he felt they had cast off the manacles of clerical authority—a blind obedience to Scripture and a conformity to creeds. While Harvard's professors continued to train Unitarian ministers in Biblical exegesis, girding them for doctrinal warfare with the orthodox, Howe was one of the many "lay-Unitarians" who became liberal Christians not because of the closely reasoned scriptural proofs of Unitarian theologians but because the church served as a broad umbrella, tolerant of diversity, promoting a comfortable and reasonable piety without demanding assent to a rigid catechism. What Howe found compelling about Channing's declaration of faith, then, was not so much his theology as his willingness to defy traditional authority and to claim for each individual the right to choose his or her own spiritual path. In Howe's view, this point of disagreement between the liberals and the orthodox had profound social consequences. In his mind, the orthodox represented the forces of superstition and conservatism, while liberals seemed to be the guardians of intellectual freedom and enlightened reform.[8]

As he began his own career as a reformer, Howe felt that this view was confirmed by experience. Boston's liberal Christians, through their journals and financial contributions, proved a supportive audience for his work with the blind. Likewise, he found the liberals to be the strongest supporters of school and prison reform—a natural outcome, he concluded, of their generous faith in human nature, their eagerness to emulate God's benevolence, and their willingness to question inherited wisdom. In addition, Unitarian society, priding itself on its respect for rational inquiry in religious matters, provided him with a relatively safe community within which to pursue the latest currents of scientific thought. Among the rational liberals of Boston, he could delve freely into the speculations of phrenology without fear of being branded a heretic. Some Unitarian leaders were uncomfortable with the materialistic implications of the new science, but Channing himself befriended George Combe and, though never a convert, was willing to consider phrenology's claims.

Ignoring the enthusiastic interest which the orthodox evangelical press and public had taken in his work at Perkins, Howe considered these Calvinists to be "the greatest obstacle to all kinds of human progress." He characterized them as unwilling to question the authority of the past and as suspicious of all change. They refused to let go of old myths about man's sin and God's anger. Their journals ridiculed phrenology and branded it atheism. They clung to outmoded and unworthy views of punishment and were hostile to reform of the state's common schools and prisons. In

Howe's opinion, the orthodox were victims of the twisted logic of their dreary faith; their demeaning views of human nature had become self-ful-filling prophecies, making them superstitious, stubborn, and ungenerous.[9]

In short, as Howe entered into the Unitarian controversy, he understood the conflict more in cultural than in theological terms. The battle, he felt, was not simply over the proper reading of Scripture or the control of church property. Rather, it was a conflict between darkness and light, big-otry and enlightenment, fear and hope. When he dedicated his life to the service of others and the steady improvement of the human condition, Howe believed that he was also committing himself to a lifelong battle against the orthodox.

⟡ By the time Howe had begun his work with Laura Bridgman in the late 1830s, the focus of the conflict between liberal and orthodox Christians in Boston had moved from the pulpit to the schoolhouse. There Horace Mann was waging his own very public battle against Calvinism. As secre-tary to the state's new Board of Education, Mann considered it his sacred duty to drive the Calvinist dogma out of the state's common school curric-ulum, protecting the rising generation from what he called the "terrors" of orthodox theology.

But Mann was a savvy enough politician to recognize that he could not afford to wage a direct assault on orthodoxy. In 1841 he confided to his journal, "People will bear truth expressed in one way, which they will cru-cify one for expressing in another; & I have to select the way, if possible, that does not lead to crucifixion."[10] Mann knew that liberal Christians were a minority in the state, making up only a quarter of the population. As sec-retary of education, he had to depend on the good will of an eight-mem-ber state Board of Education that included a few prominent orthodox men. Mann's position was political, and he had to maintain a fragile legis-lative consensus.[11]

From the outset, Mann had found this a difficult thing to do. Most citi-zens shared his view that public schools were an essential pillar of a demo-cratic society, but there was much less agreement about the form those schools should take. In Massachusetts and elsewhere, these disagreements often concerned matters of school structure, funding, and political author-ity. Mann, along with reformers in other northeastern states, called for greater centralization of schools and better teacher training, while their opponents resented the state's encroachment on local control and teacher autonomy.[12]

But the religious content of the curriculum was the greatest source of controversy. Like many other common school reformers, Mann championed a "non-sectarian," pan-Protestant curriculum. Catholics and some orthodox Protestants resisted this innovation, claiming that the slate of "universal" religious truths which reformers advocated for America's classrooms looked suspiciously like the tenets of the liberals' own faith. From the outset of his work as secretary, Mann had suffered public attacks from some orthodox Calvinists who saw his effort to eliminate "sectarian" books and teaching from the common schools as a blatant attempt to drive the fundamental doctrines of orthodox Christianity out of the curriculum, replacing them with his own "sectarian" views. In the early 1840s, at the height of Howe's work with Laura Bridgman, these dissenters joined with the proponents of local control to mount several unsuccessful campaigns to abolish the Board of Education, and with it Mann's job.[13]

In the midst of the theological struggles of the Unitarian controversy and Mann's political battles with the orthodox over common school reform, the religious education of the blind children at Perkins was a delicate matter. Privately, Howe had nothing but scorn for the orthodox but, as the leader of a quasi-public institution dependent on the good will of state legislators, he had to proceed cautiously, maintaining a policy of religious impartiality. Mann's example made it clear to Howe that open confrontation might place his entire reform enterprise at risk. Thus Howe took care to ensure that no critic could charge him with running a *Unitarian* school for the blind, using tax dollars and donations collected from a citizenry that was still predominantly orthodox in faith.

In his annual reports, Howe repeatedly assured his readers that the pupils entrusted to his care were receiving a nonsectarian religious education, one which inculcated a broad, ecumenical Christianity without ever trespassing on his students' spiritual freedom. To accomplish this delicate feat, Howe required his pupils to attend a service in the school chapel every morning at 6 A.M. and another each evening. There Howe read a passage from Scripture "without any comment." "We have no comment upon God's word as set down in Scripture," Howe told one concerned inquirer. "But by frequent reading and putting the Testament into each pupil's hand, we leave them to form their own opinion." After the Bible reading, the brief service concluded with a recitation of the Lord's Prayer and the singing of a hymn.[14]

A visitor to the school, though initially skeptical about Howe's religious views, returned from Perkins impressed by the "tones of deep reverence" which he heard the director use while reading from the Bible during the morning service. Howe's respect for the Bible was quite sincere. The New Testament was the first raised-letter book he produced on the institution's printing press, followed soon after by a collection of the Psalms. By 1843 he proudly announced publication of a complete, eight-volume, raised-letter Bible, the first in the world.[15]

But like most liberals, Howe's admiration for the Scriptures was tempered by a rational skepticism. While he may have adopted a reverent "tone" when reading from the Bible in the Perkins chapel, he was doubtless quite selective when choosing the passages to read each morning. Although he felt that the Bible contained sublime truths, he was equally convinced that these truths were mingled with human errors. The Old Testament made him particularly uneasy. Exposing his students to the angry and vengeful God of the ancient Hebrews, he thought, "might do more harm than good."[16]

While Howe could shield his charges from the harmful parts of the Bible during the week, the school's policy of religious neutrality compelled him to yield control of them on the sabbath. Each Sunday, students were expected to attend morning and evening services outside of the institution, at the church of their choice. The younger ones went to hear ministers approved in advance by their parents, while the older students were free to worship where they chose. Howe assured the public that the school never interfered with the religious preferences of its students.[17]

Yet despite this effort to maintain the appearance of neutrality, there were times when Howe could not resist the temptation to warn his students from walking down paths that he believed would lead them to mental and spiritual disaster. In 1841, for example, he barred a fourteen-year-old student from being "baptized by immersion in the sea" and joining a local Baptist church. Howe wrote to the child's parents, explaining that their daughter was, in his opinion, too immature to make a responsible decision about her faith. "She can but very imperfectly give any reasons for her belief in commonly received truths; much less can she assign any satisfactory reason for choosing one form of faith rather than another." Believing in a reasonable religion himself, Howe argued that the child should delay making any decision about her faith until her intellect was more fully developed. But he concluded this letter to her parents with the assurance that he had no sectarian motivations for his concerns and would yield to their wishes if they did not share his objections.[18]

On another occasion, Howe wrote to the parents of a boy named William, warning them that their child had fallen into what revivalist preachers were calling "the anxious state." This condition, Howe explained, was "induced by gloomy and fearful representations of human depravity, divine wrath, and torments of a material hell, with all the appendages of gnashing teeth and undying worms." In Howe's opinion, the child was consumed by orthodox superstitions, "degrading views of the human soul and of the Divine Nature," which he felt were "at utter variance with true religion." He warned William's parents that, if their boy could not be rescued from these morbid anxieties about the fate of his soul, he might suffer physical harm and possibly even end up in "the mad house." In this extreme case, Howe made no offer to defer to the parents' wishes. Throwing his usual veil of impartiality aside out of concern for William's welfare, he declared that, as long as the boy was under his care, he would do everything in his power to "counteract" the harmful effects of orthodox evangelicalism. "I shall teach him to love all his brethren of mankind; to fulfill all his human duties faithfully; to improve all his time, and all his talents; to enjoy gratefully and cheerfully every bounty which his Creator vouchsafes to him without repining for those he has withheld; and to trust himself fearlessly to his tender mercy."[19]

While Howe would reject the notion that he ever adhered to anything like a "creed," this passionate outburst of Unitarian verities serves well as a statement of his faith. Personal virtue, attention to duty, benevolence toward others, and gratitude for one's blessings were all that a reasonable Creator expected from His creatures, and any human who faithfully fulfilled those earthly obligations could look forward to the afterlife without fear. To Howe, this summarized the essence of "true religion," a view of the relationship between God and man that was capable of inspiring believers to think for themselves, improve themselves, and act with Christian charity toward others.

As far as Howe was concerned, William's morbid anxieties were just one example of a religious mania that was sweeping the country, robbing many Americans of their dignity, self-control, and sense of social responsibility. As he began his work at Perkins, the revivals of the Second Great Awakening had swept thousands of converts into mainstream Protestant churches since the turn of the century, "convincing" men and women through emotional appeals rather than carefully reasoned theological arguments. Even Boston's rationalistic Unitarians were influenced by this new spirit of romanticism, leading them to take an increasing interest in religious "feeling" and "sentiment" and to launch their own relatively unsuccessful efforts to win new converts. Though the liberals played a part in this Awakening, they were repulsed by what they considered to be the emotional excesses of the revivals. Evangelical converts had yielded their self-control, losing their ability to temper religious feeling with rational judgment. As Channing put it, revivalism "subverts deliberation . . . The individual is lost in the mass, and borne away as in a whirlwind."[20]

Howe added a medical objection, warning that the religious ecstasies induced by revivals were nothing less than a threat to the health of the brain. "Religious excitement," he warned an audience of Boston phrenologists, "in the extent to which it is often carried out in this country, violates the laws of nature, by causing excessive cerebral action. This is unhealthy, and whatever is unhealthy cannot really be from God."[21]

Howe felt that revivals were only one example of the way orthodox religion robbed people of their ability to make reasonable decisions about their own faith. While he denounced revivals, he was even more concerned about the orthodox practice of providing children with early religious education. Howe believed that, through the use of catechisms, primers, and other forms of Sunday School instruction, orthodox Christians were indoctrinating their children, practicing a quiet but insidious form of religious coercion. He saw no other way to explain the fact that so many adults in his society still believed that God was jealous, angry, and vengeful, that He held humans responsible for the sins of Adam and Eve, and that "another person, suffering for us by proxy, could make us merit more than we otherwise should." Grown men and women clung obstinately to these "absurd doctrines" only because they had been "trained in infancy" to believe them. Once their elders had fastened these "shackles of superstition" on their impressionable young minds, few were ever strong enough to break them. Howe explained, "So, in morals, those two magic lines of the primer,—'In Adam's fall / We sinned all,'—will weigh more with many people, than most logical and philosophical arguments that can be brought forth; for, not all the shrewdness of Locke—not all the force of Bacon, can equal the sway exercised over their minds, by that self-sufficient sage, the nursery maid."[22]

Boston's orthodox leaders were, as Howe suggested, strong proponents of early religious instruction. Almost every issue of their newspapers included articles urging parents and teachers to pay careful attention to the spiritual training of their children. Editors joyfully reported stories of precocious toddlers who could recite long passages of Scripture or who had shown a keen commonsense understanding of one of "God's decrees." Reviewers urged parents to take advantage of the new evangelical children's books and tracts that were being produced for the first time at affordable prices, thanks to the invention of the steam-powered press. Orthodox writers warned parents never to assume that their children were too young to learn about the gospel or to experience an evangelical conversion. Even children under the age of four, one suggested, had been known to experience "deep convictions of sin against God," guilty feelings that had finally been relieved by conversion. Another orthodox editor urged parents to make their children memorize "the great doctrines of Revelation . . . as soon as [they] are capable of understanding the use of language." He anticipated that some might object that this early training would "bias the mind on a subject in which it should act freely," but he countered by asking, "Is it [not] impossible, in the very nature of things, that the mind should be biased for or against religion—then why not for it?"[23]

Howe had a ready rejoinder to that question, based on the teachings of phrenology. According to the phrenological map of the mind, the religious sentiments developed last in the human brain. As the loftiest and most godlike faculties, they enjoyed a privileged spot at the top of the cranium, resting on the foundation of the previously developed physical, intellectual, and moral faculties. Religious belief and feelings were, as Howe put it, "the last and noblest fruits of the growing mind." Early religious instruction, then, violated the laws of human nature, forcing a premature growth of religious feeling and a hardening of religious ideas that disrupted the orderly development of human personality.[24]

᪒ Just as his phrenological manuals had led him to expect, Howe found no evidence of an active religious sentiment in Laura during her first few years at Perkins. As she entered her fourth year of education, a growing number of onlookers wanted to know, "Can she be taught the existence of God, her dependence upon, and her obligations to Him?" Howe assured them that she probably could, in due time, but he hastened to add that "no religious feeling, properly so called, has developed itself yet; nor is it yet time, perhaps, to look for it." Howe admitted that Laura knew the word "God" and sometimes asked questions about Him. But he insisted that her interest was only superficial, an accident caused by chance encounters with books and with other students. He assured his readers that she "has formed no definite idea on the subject."[25]

To ensure that Laura's curiosity about God would not be further encouraged by these chance encounters, Howe instructed her teachers not to answer any of the child's questions that might be considered theological in nature but promptly to change the subject. If Laura persisted, Howe instructed them to tell her that she was not yet old enough to understand such matters and that the doctor would explain it all when she grew older.

He also asked them to use "great caution" in protecting the child from further exposure to religious ideas from her classmates and visitors. Her teachers dutifully attempted to carry out these orders. Whenever they reported in their journals that Laura had asked a question which might be construed as religious, they were sure to add a disclaimer: "As to conversing with her about God," one assured her employer, "I have always avoided the subject."[26]

Since he had isolated Laura, however imperfectly, from the religious ideas of her society, Howe believed that any spiritual feelings or ideas which she subsequently developed would prove that she was guided by innate religious intuitions. If Laura showed an instinctive curiosity about her Creator, Howe believed, this would prove that the human soul was not deeply alienated from God, as the orthodox maintained, but was drawn to Him instinctively. Explaining this theory to another philanthropist, Howe wrote, "I see in every human being a feeling, a sentiment, a part of his nature, which inclines him to worship—to be religious." At other times, Howe described this religious dimension of human nature as "an innate disposition, or adaptation" that caused human beings to naturally recognize and adore their Creator. "When the idea of God is presented," he explained, "we embrace it."[27]

Howe's claim that the human soul is drawn toward God by the urgings of an innate "sentiment" was not original with him but an echo of the writing of both his Unitarian mentors and his favorite phrenologists. These guides told him that all human beings are endowed by their Creator with a spontaneous desire to "adore and worship a superior being." By describing this innate religious component of the mind as a "sentiment" rather than as an intellectual faculty, they suggested that man's desire to know God preceded rational reflection. Humans were first drawn to worship God by their feelings, and only subsequently used their reasoning powers to better *know* Him.[28]

Unitarian divines could be vague about the details of these spiritual sentiments. Some described them as the sum of all human parts, a yearning for holiness that emerged in the human heart once an individual attained the harmonious perfection of the various moral and intellectual faculties. Others identified specific faculties of the mind which were responsible for the religious life. Phrenologists, priding themselves on their ability to transfer vague philosophical notions about faculties into specific neurological "organs," identified three key lobes of the brain responsible for giving mankind its "tendency to religion." These were the moral sentiments of wonder (the instinctive admiration for "the grand and extraordinary"), hope (a confidence in the future which "cherishes faith"), and, most importantly, veneration (an innate human urge to "worship, adore, venerate, or respect whatever is great and good").[29]

True to this religious anthropology, Howe discovered the first stirrings of Laura's spiritual faculties when she was twelve, after her intellectual and moral training were well underway. He reported that Laura had shown a "disposition to respect those who have power and knowledge, and to love those who have goodness." Following the map of the mind laid out by phrenology, Howe attributed this impulse to the child's faculty of veneration, the same sentiment which inspires humans in every time and place to intuit and worship a higher power.[30]

Howe had previously observed similar expressions of the religious impulse of veneration, "the first yearning of the soul for something to adore," in his other blind students at Perkins. These "early aspirations of the spirit," he claimed, refuted the longstanding libel against blind people that they had "a tendency to Atheism." This popular superstition went back at least as far as the Enlightenment, when Saunderson, the great blind mathematician from Cambridge, made some "ingenious objections" to religion while on his deathbed. Diderot, another "ingenious" infidel, publicized these remarks in his *Letter on the Blind,* apparently staining all blind people with the "reproach" of atheism. Howe, after carefully observing "a great number of cases," pronounced that the blind were not less religious but were in fact *more* "susceptible of religious impressions, and have a more devotional spirit, than seeing persons." The blind in general, and Laura in particular, proved that a yearning for God came early and naturally, as much a part of the healthy "growing mind, as any other of its attributes." Following the secret promptings of human nature, children naturally sought to adore a Higher Power, long before they were intellectually capable of thinking about such lofty matters.[31]

Howe was delighted to discover that Laura had thus far confirmed his theory. Just as he had predicted, though she was shielded from the religious language of her society, her religious feeling of veneration seemed to emerge spontaneously, at the divinely appointed stage in her soul's development. But, as these first traces of religious sentiment appeared, Howe did not intend simply to let nature take its course. Rather, he felt it was his duty to help the child trace the sacred clues provided by her own heart and mind, following them all the way to her Creator. The key, he believed, was to strengthen Laura's inchoate spiritual intuitions by giving her lessons in natural theology, teaching her to use her reason to discern God's presence and His will in the natural world. "When her perceptive faculties shall have taken cognizance of the operations of nature," he predicted the year he announced her first religious feelings, "and she shall become accustomed to trace effects to their causes, then may her veneration be turned to Him who is almighty, her respect to Him who is omniscient, and her love to Him who is all goodness and love!"[32]

The idea that God could be known through the study of His creation was not new in the nineteenth century, nor was it the exclusive domain of liberal Christians. For centuries, Christians had been searching nature for proof of God's existence and as a way to confirm and clarify biblical revelation. This respect for the study of nature, as a complement to the study of the Scriptures, was brought to New England by the first generation of Puritans.

Interest in the rational revelations of "natural theology" intensified in the aftermath of the Enlightenment, and by Howe's time the intellectual leaders of all major Protestant denominations considered the scientific study of the Creator's handiwork to be an important branch of religious knowledge. This was the golden age of Protestant science, a time when the Baconian method of induction promised to turn Christianity from a faith into a fact, silencing skeptics and atheists once and for all. Boston's Unitarians were particularly fond of the divine evidence afforded by natural theology, and eagerly searched the "book of nature" for evidence of "God's attributes," religious truths derived from reason and observation rather than scriptural revelation.[33]

As an heir of this tradition, Howe believed that the best religious training he could offer Laura was to teach the child to "trace effects to their causes." Beneath the vast diversity of facts and phenomena in creation, God had decreed wise natural laws, sacred edicts which humans could discover through their powers of scientific observation and analysis. Howe called these laws "angelic messengers," guiding the human mind "upward to the Creator." By training Laura to see and conform to these laws, Howe believed that he would help her channel her feelings of veneration into a worthy conception of God, without the help of the Scriptures or religious indoctrination.[34]

The year after he announced that Laura's sentiment of veneration was stirring, Howe was delighted to report that the child was showing "very great inquisitiveness in relation to the origin of things." As part of Laura's daily lessons about the world around her, she learned that bakers made bread, that carpenters built houses, and so on. Laura soon wanted to know who made wheat, who made wood? Furthermore, she wondered who made bakers and carpenters, who made all people? Her mind, as Howe put it, tended "naturally toward the causes of things." In this way Laura, guided only by her own "natural" curiosity, had stumbled upon one of the Unitarians' favorite proofs for the existence of God, the teleological argument that the design of Creation proves the existence of a Creator. According to this argument, if an object as complex as a tree or a baker exists, then it follows logically that there must also exist a being who designed and created those things. While moral philosophers and Unitarian theologians wrote countless tomes elaborating on this argument from design, Howe felt that Laura sensed this truth intuitively. "She perceived the necessity of superhuman power," he later recalled, "for the explanation of a thousand daily recurring phenomena."[35]

This, Howe believed, was the natural road to religion, and he hastened to leave provocative clues in her path. "I am now occupied," he reported when she was twelve, "in devising various ways of giving her an idea of immaterial power by means of the attraction of magnets, the pushing of vegetation, etc., and intend attempting to convey to her some adequate idea of the great Creator and Ruler of all things." As Laura continued to study nature, Howe felt, she would learn that God exists, that He is loving and benevolent, that He arranged the universe to provide for every human need, and that obedience to His laws of health and morality would ensure her earthly and eternal happiness.[36]

꒰꒱ Howe's attempt to guide Laura's religious intuitions by giving her lessons in botany and physics illustrates the desire felt by New England's liberal Christians to balance the impulses of the heart with the calm rationality of the head. Howe claimed that religious belief "should rather be an affair of the heart than of the head; of the feelings, than of the intellect." But, as Laura's lessons in natural theology suggest, his respect for religious feelings never led him to conclude that religion was a purely subjective, emotional experience, ungrounded in demonstrable truths. Even less did he sanction all expressions of spiritual emotion, as his contempt for evangelical revivalism makes clear. The yearnings of the pious heart, he believed, should never be allowed to cloud or contradict the more dispassionate conclusions reached by the head.[37]

To illustrate the point, Howe cited evidence from the fledgling field of anthropology. As Western explorers and missionaries spread out across the globe in the early nineteenth century, they returned with evidence that a belief in some form of deity was a nearly universal phenomenon. But, as the bizarre and debased gods of the heathens suggested to these enlightened Protestants, man's religious instinct was not sufficiently precise to lead to a proper understanding of the one true God. Howe believed that the great jumble of notions about God held by various cultures around the world proved that humans have no innate idea of God; if they did, they would all agree on His "attributes." However, the universal belief in some sort of deity did seem to prove his claim that all humans have "an innate disposition, or adaptation, not only to recognize, but to adore [God]." The feelings generated by this religious sentiment had to be guided by enlightened reason; the primal urge to adore God had to be tempered, for example, by the ability to trace effects to their causes. To illustrate his point, Howe suggested that a bolt of lightning might well inspire strong feelings of veneration in a primitive tribesman. But veneration would produce gross religious error if it led to the worship of lightning itself, rather than the *cause* of lightning, the wise and benevolent Creator.[38]

Another example of Howe's attempt to balance intuition and reason comes from closer to home. Howe's experiment with Laura occurred almost simultaneously with another famous exploration into the religious intuitions of children, Bronson Alcott's work at his Temple School in Boston. In a series of structured "conversations," Alcott tried to elicit the naive spiritual wisdom of his charges. When he published a record of his work in 1836, *Conversations with Children on the Gospels,* many Bostonians were outraged. Howe added his voice to this chorus, denouncing Alcott's project as "too absurd for serious notice." "You will hear these mewling-pewling philosophers questioned upon the most abstruse and mystical points of religious belief," he scoffed, "and their answers carefully recorded, to be published for the benefit of our generation which is called on to receive instruction from these babes and sucklings!"[39]

Howe's derision seems odd, coming from a man who so carefully reported the naive observations of his own child prodigy and proclaimed, "What an important mission has (Laura) fulfilled! . . . How much has she taught others!" In a calmer moment some years later, he tried to explain what he considered to be the crucial difference between his theory of religious education and Alcott's. Howe acknowledged that Laura Bridgman, so severely deprived of sensory experience, might have provided an "extraordinary opportunity" to test what he called the transcendentalists' "expectant plan" of education. If someone like Alcott had gotten his hands on Laura, Howe speculated, he might have simply shielded the child from "extraneous influences" and waited for "the spontaneous words of the oracle" to pour forth out of her awakened spirit. According to Howe, this mystical romantic faith in the child's natural instincts would have been rewarded with disaster. The only pure and spontaneous impulses she would have expressed would have been the lower ones, those which humans share with animals, such as lust, anger, and covetousness. In short, if nature was simply allowed to take its course, unaided by a wise teacher, the child would have ended up "little elevated above the brute." Laura had "developed more than the animal," he believed, because he understood that, although human nature is naturally pure, it still requires careful guidance and training in order to mature to its full potential.[40]

Many Bostonians, liberal and orthodox alike, were scandalized by the transcendentalist theory of human nature, which exalted individual intuition at the expense of any external authority. Declaring themselves free of all traditional sources of wisdom and constraint, including the church, the Bible, law, and social convention, these free thinkers seemed to respect only the authority of their own souls. Many observers feared that Emerson and his followers had granted individual whim a godlike power, encouraging a radical subjectivism that could only result in a dangerous threat to social order.

Orthodox Christians, and many conservative Unitarians, were particularly outraged by the transcendentalists' disregard for the authority of Scripture and the clergy. Howe, who had his own qualms about the Bible and clerical authority, had no such misgivings. In temperament, he was as much of an iconoclast as his more mystical neighbors, eager to free the individual from the lifeless institutional authorities of the past. But as his harsh critique of Alcott suggests, Howe felt that the transcendentalists had placed too much faith in individual intuitions. Howe felt that society should look to science, not intuition, for a new source of authority. While Alcott and the transcendentalists listened for the intuitive "oracle of reason," Howe found his own oracle in Baconian science, with its clear, rational, and inductively derived laws of nature.[41]

There was one law of nature that Howe tried to hide from Laura, the fact of death. Before she came to Perkins, the child had been taken to a funeral where, by chance, she happened to pass her inquisitive hands across the face of the corpse. The mystery of this cold, stiff flesh filled her with dread. She had not been at Perkins long before she brought the subject up to her teacher, recounting the experience with a shudder. "I was afraid to feel of dead man before I came here, when I was a very little girl with my mother; I felt of dead head's eyes and nose; I thought it was man's; I did not know." Howe explained to his audience that Laura's fear of death proved that the "attachment to life" was an "innate sense." Yet her fear of death was one natural instinct that he felt might disrupt, rather than aid, her religious development.[42]

Laura wanted her teachers to explain what she had experienced. But Howe saw that any attempt to give the child "a correct idea" of death would entangle him in the subject of religion, raising many more questions in the child's mind, questions which he feared would only confuse her and spoil his experiment. Better, he felt, to delay any discussion of death until "a development of her reason should be attained." But Howe worried, with good reason, that Laura would not be put off so easily, that she would never agree to drop the subject until he deemed her ready for an answer. Her fear was too deep, her curiosity and her instinctive love of life too powerful to be denied—and the combination, he thought, might produce a morbid obsession with death that would warp her moral and religious development. Anticipating this possibility, Howe tried to set her mind at ease by giving her an antidote from natural theology. Hoping to "counterbalance" her "dread of death," he told her about "the germination and growth of plants." This lesson from nature, he hoped, might suggest to her troubled mind "a consoling hope of resurrection."[43]

Laura's fear of death was not so easily laid to rest, and her anxiety was only fueled by the death of Orrin, one of her fellow students, when she was twelve. As Howe broke the news to Laura, she responded with "a contraction of the hands,—a half spasm, and her countenance indicated not exactly grief, but rather pain and amazement." Seeing this reaction, Howe felt that he could no longer avoid trying to explain death to the child, that he had to allay her fears. Yet, just as he had anticipated, the conversation soon carried the child into spiritual waters that Howe considered "beyond her depth." Trying to explain that Orrin's body died but his soul lived on, he struggled to make the child understand the distinction between "material and spiritual operations." Laura only responded with a flurry of questions: "Is breath dead? is blood dead? have flies souls? Why did not God give them souls?" Howe groped for simple words to convey his complex answers. "Alas for the poverty of her language," he later exclaimed, "I could hardly make her understand how much of life and happiness God bestows even upon a little fly!"[44]

Howe tried to make Laura understand that she had "a spiritual existence as separate from her bodily one." But he found that Laura "disliked" the idea. She closed the conversation by flatly insisting, "I shall not die." Howe was relieved to drop the subject for the time being. Yet Laura was extremely curious about what had happened to Orrin, and she quizzed her friends and teachers about it for days. "Why did he die? Why did soul go very quick? Do you want to see Orrin? Why does not God take us? Why did God kill Orrin?"[45]

Because death is a natural event, triggering powerful emotions, one might expect that Howe would have welcomed Laura's reaction as an ideal opportunity to further her religious education. Just as he was thrilled when the child asked questions about the origin of things, a curiosity which he believed would lead her eventually to infer the existence of a Creator, he might have reasoned in similar fashion that Laura's aversion to death was God's way of leading all souls to contemplate their ultimate destiny. One orthodox educator, Dr. Thomas Gallaudet, proposed this very idea, suggesting that if children were made to touch a corpse, this would provide them with a riveting lesson in the mortality of the flesh, one which would heighten their interest in the immortality of the soul.[46]

Howe insisted, to the contrary, that Laura "needs not the fear of death" in order to develop her moral and religious nature. In his view, orthodox ministers used talk of death, the afterlife, and God's judgment of souls as a carrot and stick, manipulating people much the same way orthodox schoolmasters used prizes and whippings to control their students. This approach, he believed, turned the hope of heaven and the fear of hell into degrading substitutes for true piety, calling people to God by appealing to selfish concerns for their own safety rather than by inspiring them to the selfless goal of "doing good for the love of goodness and serving God for the love of God." Divine judgment there was, Howe believed, but it came in the form of earthly "unhappiness" and ill health, a punishment that was not meted out by an angry judge but by the benevolent provisions of God's natural law. Until Laura could understand that law, Howe believed, any talk of God's judgment would only terrorize her needlessly and fuel her unfortunate obsession with matters far beyond her intellectual grasp. For the child's sake, and for the purity of his experiment, he hoped that Laura would drop the subject.[47]

Yet Howe could not keep death at bay, and Laura encountered it several more times in the early years of her education. The death of President Harrison, of Howe's horse, of two other children connected to Perkins, even of the animals that became the meat she ate, all prompted Laura to renew her barrage of questions about mortality, about the soul, and about God's power over the life and death of His creatures. In these instances, the delight that Howe usually took in Laura's desire to know the divine first cause of natural events turned to dread. Laura eagerly used each of these incidents to pry more information about religion from Howe. "Doctor told me about God," she reported proudly to her teacher after one of these sessions. "It was very little say," she had to admit, but added "he told me when I was very tall he would teach me about God much."[48]

🜚 In addition to the abbreviated lessons in theology that Howe was forced to give whenever Laura experienced a death, her contacts with students and visitors provided the child with many more clues. By the time Laura was eleven, her language skills had developed to the point where she could communicate with other blind students and a large circle of acquaintances who had learned the manual alphabet. Although Howe felt that this social interaction was good for Laura's emotional and intellectual development, he worried that it might spoil the purity of his investigation into her religious intuitions. While her teachers tried, they could not entirely shield Laura from religious words and phrases that she learned in conversations with other children and with visitors who were unaware of the doctor's wishes.

One afternoon when Laura was eleven, she explained to her teachers that it was raining because "God is very full." Surprised, her teacher asked who had told her about God. Laura replied evasively, "No one; I think about God." Two days later she confessed that a visitor, Miss Penniman, "was wrong to tell me about *God*," proof that the child had not only begun to learn about religion but also knew that, for a reason unknown to her, the subject was taboo. When asked what Penniman had told her, Laura replied, "She told me I must love God, and that he is *fair*." Her teacher, obeying the doctor's orders, "made no remark upon it."[49]

Laura also stumbled across religion in her reading of various raised-letter books at Perkins. Howe tried to prevent her from reading the Scriptures and the other religious literature that he had prepared for the blind students. But Laura, combing the schoolrooms with her "feelers" ever on the alert, sometimes ran across these books anyway. When she did, these texts provoked a curiosity that her teachers were under orders not to satisfy. For example, when Laura was twelve, her teacher recorded this entry in her journal: "When I came to give her a lesson she brought me a testament and asked me the meaning of Gospel; she wanted me to tell her about the part she had read yesterday; wanted to know 'what is centurion,' & 'who was sick unto death?' Told her she must wait till Dr. had taught her many things."[50]

By the time Laura was twelve, Howe recognized that, if he hoped to maintain the purity of his experiment into the growth and education of her soul, he would have to take a more drastic and very public step to isolate her from these chance encounters with religious ideas. Before announcing his plan, he wrote to the Bridgmans, seeking permission to use his own discretion in Laura's spiritual training. As Baptists, the Bridgmans presumably did not share Howe's liberal theological views, if they understood them. But they were indebted to the man who had done so much for their daughter. Deferring to his wishes, they granted him full control over their child's religious education.[51]

Howe then announced, in his 1843 report, that after long deliberation and careful consideration of the opinions of others, he had decided to claim a monopoly on the child's religious education. Making public a policy that he had pursued privately from the start, he asked Laura's many visitors to refrain from discussing religion with the child. Even more controversially, Howe confessed that, as Laura's sole spiritual mentor, he had no plans to teach her any of the "doctrines of revealed religion." This decision, he admitted, was "diametrically opposite" the opinion of many who had been urging him for several years to teach the child the orthodox path to salvation. "I am aware of the high responsibility of the charge of a soul," he explained. "And the mother who bore her can hardly feel a deeper interest in Laura's welfare than I do; but that very sense of responsibility to God, and that love which I bear to the child, forces me, after seeking for all light from others, finally to rely upon my own judgment."[52]

In his effort to better control Laura's interactions with others, Howe assigned Mary Swift to be the child's full-time instructor and companion. Like the other female teachers at Perkins, Swift was an idealistic young woman who had devoted herself to the education of the blind ever since her arrival at Perkins in 1840. She was one of the first graduates of the state's new normal school in Lexington, an institution that was a cornerstone of Mann's school reform program. There she had been exposed to the latest pedagogical theories, and inspired by the prospect of reforming society through education. Accepting this new assignment, Mary Swift knew that she would now be at Laura's side almost constantly, serving as the child's eyes and ears on the world. And she also understood that Howe expected her to use that power over Laura's mind to shield the child from exposure to religion.

Howe knew that his plan to isolate Laura would earn him "more of human censure than of approbation." Attempting to justify his method, he repeated his claim that her mind was still "not prepared" to understand religious truths. Before she could have any coherent idea about God and the fate of her soul, he argued, her reasoning powers needed to develop further. He repeated his claim that Laura's progress thus far had shown that a child's religious faculties were "the last to develop themselves, and are of tardy growth." In a pointed reference to the orthodox practice of early religious training, Howe conceded that his intelligent and enthusiastic student could be taught to memorize "any dogma or creed, and be made to give as edifying answers, as are recorded of many other wonderful children, to questions on spiritual subjects." But he insisted that, as long as Laura's innate religious sentiments and her reasoning ability were still undeveloped, any religious instruction would be nothing more than a misguided attempt to "force" the growth of her soul through "artificial culture." The result would be "a hot house plant instead of the simple and natural one that is every day putting forth new beauties to our sight."[53]

Prior to his 1843 report, Howe had often justified his decision to delay

8. When Laura was still an adolescent, Howe often boasted that she had become one of the most famous women in the world. (*Courtesy of Perkins School for the Blind, Watertown, Massachusetts*)

Laura's religious education by claiming that the child's unique handicap made it impossible for her to understand the metaphorical language of theology. Deprived of the social context that allowed other children to pick up the meaning of new words almost effortlessly, she had always approached language with a literalness that made it hard for her to grasp abstractions. "None but those who have seen her engaged in the task, and have witnessed the difficulty of teaching her the meaning of such words as *remember, hope, forget, expect,* will conceive the difficulties in her way," Howe explained. If she struggled to grasp the meaning of a simple word like *remember,* he suggested, she surely could make no sense of the lofty metaphorical language of religion.[54]

If Laura was "forced" by those around her to try to understand God prematurely, Howe feared, she would only develop "unworthy" ideas about her Creator, ones that would ultimately impede her religious development. "I should fear that she might personify Him in a way too common with children, who clothe Him with unworthy, and sometimes grotesque attributes, which their subsequently developed reason condemns, but strives in vain to correct." Howe certainly believed that Laura suffered unusual barriers to learning about God. But, as this comment suggests, he also felt that all children were incapable of understanding religious ideas, that all were prone to develop superstitious notions about their Creator that might haunt them into adulthood.[55]

As far as Howe was concerned, orthodox Christians were misled by the same literal understanding of language which had so often confused Laura. Instead of relying on their own mature reason, searching for the underlying spirit of God's will, they bowed in "blind obedience" to the letter of the law. Orthodox parents and teachers then planted these repugnant views of God and man deep within their children's vulnerable souls. People raised with this premature religious training were, in Howe's opinion, locked in a state of spiritual infancy, their moral and spiritual growth forever stunted.

While Howe's critique of orthodox religion and education had been implied in his educational experiment from the start, his attempt in 1843 to justify his monopoly on the child's religious education made these views explicit for the first time. Laura would receive no instruction in religious doctrines, he explained, because he saw "no necessary connection" between "particular" creeds and "a moral and religious life." Theological doctrines, he suggested, were arbitrary fetters on the mind, barriers to a mature spiritual life. At some points, he still seemed to argue that her introduction to the doctrines of Biblical religion should be delayed due to her unique condition. But at other times his readers could not mistake the fact that he believed that such instruction should actually be avoided altogether, not just for her but for all.[56]

The orthodox, of course, disagreed. They considered assent to certain basic gospel truths, especially Christ's message of salvation, a matter of eternal life or death. "It is said continually," Howe wrote, "that this child should be instructed in the doctrines of revealed religion; and some even seem to imagine her eternal welfare will be periled by her remaining in ignorance of religious truths." Few of their worries were relieved by Howe's assurance that, even if Laura should die before learning any of the Christian doctrines, she would still be "taken to the bosom of that Father in heaven, to whom she is every day paying acceptable tribute of thanksgiving and praise, by her glad enjoyment of existence." Laura's immortal soul, Howe suggested, was secure, not because she had a knowledge of God but rather because she lingered in a state of unselfconscious, childlike innocence. She was still in Eden, Howe claimed, and he intended to keep her there as long as possible.[57]

Howe knew that the announcement of his plan to monopolize Laura's religious education would be obnoxious to orthodox Christians, many of whom already felt antagonized by Horace Mann's ongoing crusade to remove Calvinist doctrine from the common schools. Howe was not making a private confession of his faith but a very public experiment, clearly aimed against some cherished principles of Calvinist orthodoxy. He surely realized that by carrying his education of Laura onto this controversial theological ground, he was inviting the very charges of sectarianism which, with the rest of his blind students, he had tried hard to avoid, dragging his student and his institution into the wider controversy over religious education in the common schools. Yet, he could not resist the unique opportunity that Laura seemed to provide—the chance to prove scientifically that humans are born with an instinctual yearning for God, and to demonstrate the best method for developing those religious intuitions into a mature and enlightened faith.

Perhaps inspired by Howe's controversial decision, Horace Mann chose this moment to offer his readers a more openly confrontational interpretation of the meaning of Laura Bridgman's education. In 1843 he began his annual review of Howe's report on her case with a backhanded slap at Boston's Calvinist past, suggesting that if Howe had performed his miracle of education a century and a half earlier, "both teacher and pupil would probably have suffered under the provisions of the statute against witchcraft."[58]

Mann then proceeded to stretch the theological moral of Laura Bridgman's story to its utmost limit. Throwing political caution to the winds, he wrote of a vision that had come to him after long hours of "reflecting upon this unparalleled case." Before his eyes he had seen Mother Nature, "severe, yet radiant with love," standing over Laura's cradle on the eve of the illness that had destroyed her eyes and ears. Then came "a moment of lofty and holy passion." Speaking in the cadences of Elizabethan verse that Mann evidently took for the native dialect of all of God's messengers, Mother Nature cried out, "*Thee* will I save from the follies and vanities that invade the soul, through the eye; *thee* will I save from the contaminations that pour their sweet poison into the heart through the ear; . . . *thee* will I save from the debasements of appetite, by which so many millions are degraded below the brutes." With these words, nature mercifully seared the child's senses forever closed, "as with a red-hot poker."

Lest his readers should miss the theological point of this flight of poetic fancy, Mann concluded by asking:

> When will the time come, in which the renovated condition of society and a perfecting of the art of education will cease to make it a blessing to a child to be deprived of those senses with which it holds communication with the world? We say the "blessing", for though we acknowledge she lost much in being deprived of the outward world, yet we believe she has had a thousand fold compensation in having all that was innocent and pure and lovely, in the inner temple, kept from desecration and sacrilege by that loss. She has been rescued from the corrupting influences of our present social condition.[59]

If there were lessons to be learned about the human soul from Howe's famous experiment, Mann had clearly distorted them beyond recognition, driven by his desire to win polemical advantage against his orthodox foes.[60]

By the end of 1843 some leaders of the orthodox community concluded that Howe and Mann were turning Laura Bridgman's education into a public demonstration of their own decidedly unorthodox ideas about human nature. It seemed clear to them now that Howe was not conducting an impartial psychological investigation but was determined to use Laura's story as a rhetorical battering ram in the service of Mann's educational reforms. Convinced that Howe's experiment was endangering the child's eternal destiny, they prepared to wage a public struggle for Laura Bridgman's soul.

Chapter 8

Crisis

Among the many distinguished guests who paid a visit to the Perkins Institution in 1841 was Julia Ward, the daughter of a wealthy New York banker. Ward was escorted to Perkins by two of Howe's close friends, Charles Sumner and Henry Wadsworth Longfellow. As the trio gazed upon "the face into which Dr. Howe had so recently brought intellectual life," Howe rode up to the school on his black stallion, cutting the figure that had impressed so many young women in Boston. Julia Ward, though eighteen years Howe's junior, was likewise attracted to the handsome philanthropist, the "living heart" of this illustrious enterprise. Howe, who was then forty years old, had sometimes despaired that he would remain a permanent bachelor, but the two soon began an enthusiastic courtship.[1]

While Howe and Julia Ward were brought together by Laura Bridgman, their romance was unsettling to the girl. Sharing Howe's bachelor apartment and his dinner table, in the company of his sister Jeannette, Laura had been treated like an adopted daughter, enjoying the privileged center of this unusual family circle. Now, as Howe's attention and affection was increasingly directed toward winning the hand of Julia Ward, Laura sensed that her own place in her beloved "Doctor's" world was threatened. These fears were only confirmed when, in February 1843, Laura learned that Howe and Julia Ward would be married that spring. As Howe looked forward to a new life, a home and family beyond the walls of the Perkins school, Laura's old life was disintegrating.

Laura's anxiety about this impending change only heightened her already intense attachment to her benefactor, a passion that had been kindled in her first weeks at Perkins. From the start she had been awed by Howe's presence, utterly dependent on his good will and instruction, and nurtured by his affection in a way that she had never fully known from her biological parents, distant in New Hampshire. Howe believed that family life, with its parental affection and influence, was a crucial part of healthy

9. After Julia Ward's first meeting with Howe, she recalled that he "made an impression of unusual force and reserve!" By the early 1840s Howe enjoyed a growing international reputation for his work not only at Perkins but also in the reform of common schools, prisons, and insane asylums. *(Courtesy of Perkins School for the Blind, Watertown, Massachusetts)*

emotional and moral development. He insisted that all of his students should maintain regular correspondence back home and make visits to their families during school vacations. While Howe had come to play a more direct parental role with Laura than with any of his other students, he encouraged her to exchange letters with her mother and arranged for her female guardians to take her home to Hanover for visits several times each year.

As a result of these efforts, Laura maintained a meaningful relationship with her mother, who soon learned enough of the manual alphabet to converse with her child during her visits. But Laura remained distant from her father, even afraid of him. Daniel Bridgman seems to have done little to bridge this emotional gap; Laura complained during one visit home that her father never took the time to take her for walks, as other family members did, and there is no evidence that he ever mastered the manual alphabet or even wrote a letter to his daughter. Much of the love which, under more normal circumstances, Laura might have felt for Daniel Bridgman was given instead to her adopted father and mentor, Dr. Howe.[2]

Laura's obsession with Howe runs like a steady refrain through all of her writings, and through her teachers' journals, during the early years of her education. He was the anchor of her emotional life. Even though he spent little time instructing her each day, delegating this responsibility to her female teachers, Laura duly noted Howe's doings in her daily journal: "Doctor and Martha went to Boston." "Sumner came last night because doctor was very alone." Howe's daughters would later describe Laura's feelings about their father this way: "In the little world in which she lived, he was the supreme power, the last court of appeal, and in the larger realm of her active, hungry thought, his figure dominated all things spiritual and material."[3]

Viewing Howe in this way, Laura had always been troubled by his absences, sometimes caused by his frequent trips to other states in order to win pledges of support for Perkins or to promote the creation of institutions for the blind in other parts of the country. During one such tour, for example, Laura's teacher noted that, "Laura was continually talking about Dr. H. She said, 'I think much about Doctor. I want to see him. I cannot wait till he comes. I am in hurry till Doctor comes. Why did he go? Does he know I want to see him very much? I think Doctor does not love me to go away.'"

Laura's anxiety about Howe's absences and her fears that she might lose his love were no doubt only made worse by his method of moral discipline, his practice of responding to her infractions by withdrawing from her emotionally and sometimes physically. Laura was repeatedly admonished by Howe and her teachers that "Dr. could not love wrong girl." As a result, she was likely to greet any withdrawal of Howe's presence and interest, even one caused simply by physical distance, as a troubling reflection on her standing in his affections.

Thus Laura was deeply disturbed to learn, in the spring of 1843, that not only was the Dr. marrying "Miss Ward," but that the couple would then leave for Europe for a year-long honeymoon. "I am very sad to have Dr. & Mrs. Howe go & stay many months, one year," Laura wrote to a friend, adding, "They will come next Spring, very long."[4]

The presence of Julia Ward, a new and more important love in Howe's life, heightened Laura's anxiety and confusion about his absence. Laura groped to understand how her adopted father's marriage would alter her own place in his affections. "Does Dr. love me like Julia?" she asked her teacher. "No," was the blunt response. When the child then asked if Howe loved God like he loved Julia, her teacher simply answered "yes," a reply that no doubt did as little to console the child as it did to help her understand the new configuration of relationships that was being formed in her midst.[5]

Returning to the subject a few days before the Howes sailed to Europe, Laura told her teacher, "I love Doctor, like Mrs. Howe [does]. I love him very, very much; is he my daughter? He said he was." Her teacher corrected her, suggesting that he must have meant to say that *she* was *his* daughter. Laura then struggled to understand what her relationship with the new Mrs. Howe might be. "Is Mrs. Howe my sister?" she wondered. When her teacher suggested that, since Howe was like a father, Mrs. Howe would be like a mother, Laura quickly interrupted, saying, "No, I cannot love Mrs. Howe [as a mother], because I do not see her often; she is a stranger."[6]

On rare occasions, Laura's resentment of this stranger's intrusion into her life was expressed overtly. "I love [Howe] best of any, why does he not love me?" she demanded to know during one morning lesson. But in spite of her confusion and pangs of jealousy, Laura usually suppressed her fears and remained hopeful about her future with Howe. Anxious to preserve a place in his household, she tried to win his new bride's affections. "When you come home," she wrote to the new Mrs. Howe, "I shall shake your hands & hug & kiss you very hard, because I love you & am your dear friend." Laura was greatly encouraged by the long, friendly letters that Julia wrote in return. She began to refer to Mrs. Howe as her "best friend." But the child's intense and artificial attachment to this woman she hardly knew belies the fact that the child's inner turmoil, her feelings of emotional dislocation and loss, remained.[7]

When Dr. Howe boarded the Atlantic steamer, headed for Europe, he not only left Laura's emotional world in disarray but he also took with him any hope of resolving her growing curiosity about religion. Howe still insisted that the child should set aside her questions about God and death until her intellect had matured to the point where she might be able to develop a sufficiently reasonable and "lofty" concept of the Deity. In short, he wished to postpone her religious education until he deemed her inoculated against the doctrines of orthodox evangelicalism and reasonable enough to be able to conceive of God as a benevolent and abstract spirit, a wise lawgiver, the Unitarian Creator whom he worshipped himself.

Paradoxically, Howe publicly revealed his controversial plan to monopolize Laura's religious education while preparing for his honeymoon. His demand for total control over Laura's spiritual life came just as he was about to lose all contact with her, relinquishing the supervision of her education for a year. Any question that Laura might ask about religion while he was gone, he reminded his teachers, should be gently but firmly deferred until his return. At the same time, Howe enjoined his critics not to tamper with his experiment while he was away: "I would take this opportunity to beseech those friends of hers who differ from me, and who may occasionally converse with her, to reflect that, while the whole responsibility of the case rests upon me, it is unjust in them to do what they may easily do,—instill into her mind notions which might derange the whole plan of her instruction."[8]

What Howe failed to admit was the fact that his whole plan was already showing signs of derangement. Unwilling to isolate the child completely from her fellow students and Perkins visitors, Howe had never been able to shield her entirely from religious language. He admitted as much in his annual report of that year, conceding that she had already asked him questions about God, about death, about the soul. But he continued to believe that these questions were prompted not by the natural development of her mind but by "expressions dropped carelessly by others, as God, heaven, soul, etc." These questions were unfortunate but unavoidable impurities in the test tube of Howe's experiment, but he insisted that they revealed nothing about the true nature of Laura's mental development or her readiness to understand religious ideas.[9]

Yet this public acknowledgement of Laura's religious questions left his readers with the false impression that her questions about religion were casual and haphazard. Laura's teachers, recording her conversations each day in their journals, left ample evidence that her interest in religion was not at all casual but urgent. Prompted by whatever source, her questions were growing more frequent and insistent just as Howe was leaving for Europe. Perhaps distracted by his courtship, perhaps blinded to the facts of Laura's case by his complete faith in his phrenological theory of mental development, Howe ignored ominous signs that his pupil was approaching the point of emotional crisis.

In part, Laura's growing obsession with the mysteries of religion was just another expression of her always keen sense of curiosity. She had approached far more mundane subjects, from the capitols of Europe to the fine points of grammar, with a similar intensity. Once she encountered any word, theological or otherwise, she could not easily be put off until she was satisfied that she understood its meaning.

Ironically, Howe's effort to shield Laura from religion only succeeded in investing all religious words, and all questions about God, with an irresistible aura. A knowledge of God, Laura had been told time and again, was reserved for those who were old enough to understand. Like most adolescents, Laura was eager to grow up, to enjoy the autonomy, the respect, and the confidences that are afforded only to adults. Because she was so dependent on her guardians, she seemed to feel that impulse all the more. A knowledge of God, she came to believe, would be the one sure proof that she had grown up and earned the independence she wanted so badly. When a teacher asked her if she would like to be tall, Laura's immediate reply was, "Yes because I want to learn about many Gods and to wear collar." Laura pleaded with her teacher, "I want to see God. I want Dr. to make me see." Dr. Howe, she was convinced, knew all the answers, but now he was leaving for Europe. Her chance to "see God" would disappear across the Atlantic for at least one long year.[10]

Laura's growing obsession with religion can be explained in part as a symptom of her natural curiosity and as an expression of her desire to become an adult. But it also reveals a more troubled and volatile aspect of her emerging personality, her sense of fear and vulnerability as she tried to make her way through a world she could neither see nor hear. From her earliest years at Perkins, Laura had suffered pangs of anxiety about her physical safety, often expressed through a recurring fear of animals. Animals of all kinds were a threat, unknown and largely unknowable. While Laura was fascinated by creatures, from flies to horses, and was always eager to discuss them with her teachers, her curiosity was in part inspired by this anxiety. She worried that horses might step on her; she dreaded the gentle dog that lived at Perkins; she feared that pigs might walk across her as she slept. She often complained to her teachers about nightmares, dreams that woke her in the night, leaving her breathless and trembling under her sheets. "Something had four legs," she explained to her teacher one morning. "It ran almost over me." Another time, Laura told her teacher about "a number of dreams which frightened her—all were about animals." While fears about animals are not uncommon among all children, Laura's terrors were no doubt amplified by her isolation, her sense of powerlessness before the unseen forces of the world around her.[11]

By the age of twelve, Laura expressed this sense of vulnerability in other ways as well. She worried that she would lose the care and protection of her guardians—that her teacher would die, that she might go "crazy" and have no one to care for her, that she might be forced to leave the school one day and be left with no way to support herself. At the same time, Laura's fear of death became more acute and more personal. One day Mary Swift found her looking "anxious and troubled." The child wondered, "Why did I not die when I was very sick?" This question was the first of many she put to her teacher about the subject of her own mortality. "If I eat fish hooks could I be dead?" "If I do not eat or drink will I be dead?" "If I stopped my breath ten minutes I should die. Would you be sad?" she asked her teacher not long after. "Would you like to have God stop your breath & die to-day?—When God wants you how can he stop your breath?" Swift always did her best to change the subject, mindful of Howe's instructions to avoid the topic, as it was bound to lead to a discussion of the soul's immortality.[12]

Laura's fear of death may have been inspired by her more general feelings of powerlessness and vulnerability. But as her reference to God's power to "stop your breath" suggests, these fears were mingled with fascination, even attraction. She dreaded death, yet—guided by Howe's cryptic remarks and her own gleanings of Christian theology from books—she also began to see heaven as a place where those fears might at last be laid to rest. In their first conversation about the soul, prompted by the death of Orrin, Howe told Laura that when the body dies, the soul lives on, and that "good souls" are invited by God to heaven, a place where all souls are happy. Howe had no desire to carry the matter any further; he only offered this explanation to quiet the child's fears, hoping that she would rest assured and lose interest in the subject. But as usual, Laura latched on to this new word "heaven" with great intensity. "I know about Heaven and God good and going to Heaven when dead," she bragged in a letter to a friend. "How many souls in Heaven?" she wanted to know. "How large is Heaven?" "Is there a *door* to Heaven?"[13]

Laura was particularly anxious to know more about how God decided whom to invite to heaven. Howe, ever on the alert for a way to motivate Laura to be on her best behavior, assured her after Orrin's death that God always invited "the good." This, of course, left unspoken the second half of this cosmic formula, that God would *not* invite the "bad" to heaven, a point Howe was silent on in part because he was ambivalent about this conclusion himself. Fearing that any talk of God's judgment would only terrorize the child and that further mention of heaven would only fuel her unfortunate obsession with matters far beyond her intellectual reach, Howe hoped Laura would not pursue the subject any further. But she would not, *could* not, let the matter rest. She quickly inferred on her own that, if God only chose the good, then those guilty of bad behavior risked not getting an invitation to heaven. Bringing the lesson straight home, Laura worried that "God will not want me if I am not gentle and kind," a prospect that filled her with anxiety. When, she asked her teacher, would she learn to be good enough so that God would want her? Was she "*sure* he will invite us?"[14]

"She has the idea," Mary Swift wrote in her journal, "that all people who die have attained the heights of goodness, & the reason we are not all wanted in heaven as she expresses it is because we are not good enough." This conclusion added a new urgency to Laura's struggle to subdue her passions, to gain the self-control that would at last make her "good enough." Without losing her desire to please Howe, she became increasingly anxious to satisfy a new and more daunting judge.[15]

Laura's occasional, inadvertent encounters with the Scriptures reinforced her conclusion that God's love was conditional, that He was angry with those who failed to be good. During Howe's absence, Laura chanced upon a raised letter Book of Psalms. There, to her horror, she read that "God is angry with the wicked every day." The child immediately applied the passage to her own situation, concluding that her own wickedness—her outbursts and her attempts to deceive her teacher—had brought God's wrath upon her. The thought that God, this mysterious and powerful being whom she had hoped might serve as her protector, was actually angry with her left her "very pale and much excited."[16]

Because of Howe's ban on religious discussion, Laura's ideas remained in flux, a mass of shifting fears and inchoate hopes. Gathering hints from various sources—stray lines of Scripture, casual religious allusions made by her visitors, and Howe's little lessons in natural theology—she welded these disparate parts into an ill-formed whole, held together only by her relentless emotional urgency. The end result of these sacred speculations was not haphazard, however, but a reflection of her own deep internal needs. At a time when Howe was increasingly distant, the God Laura envisioned was much like the Doctor writ large. In fact, the child often used Howe as a point of reference for comprehending the character of God. Does God know as much as Doctor? she wondered. Is He kind and gentle like Doctor? Laura concluded that, like her beloved mentor, God was all powerful. And God, like Howe, was her protector. Yet both were also capable of withdrawing that love, casting her out into the darkest of isolation, if she did anything to incur their displeasure.

Although Laura's image of God merged with her image of Howe, he would scarcely have recognized his own theology in his pupil's religious speculations. He worshipped a God with quite different "attributes," bowing before the author of cause and effect, the unknowable being who decreed the benevolent natural law and then withdrew to let the consequences take their course. Confident of his own intellect, sure of his power of self-control, Howe valued his moral freedom as the Creator's greatest gift. He tried to serve his God through the noble exercise of this freedom, by molding his own character and the practices of his society to conform to the sacred truths revealed in the laws of nature.

Laura, as a female in a society controlled by men, as a child, and as a deaf-blind person, felt her dependence much more strongly than her freedom, her weakness more than her power. She sought safety and acceptance, not the challenge of a moral crusade. Struggling to conquer her passions in order to please those adults who scrutinized her every move, she looked for a God who offered forgiveness, one who would finally release her from this painful inner struggle, one who would relieve her from the guilt she felt over her moral failures. Laura conceived of God as an intimate, personal being, not the distant author of natural law. Taking a fatherly interest in the daily trials of His children, He offered her the promise of protection from the unpredictable forces, the leaping dogs, and sudden deaths of the natural world. No better example of the way Laura's physical vulnerability influenced her search for religious meaning can be found than a dream she described to Mary Swift when she was thirteen: "I dreamed God took my breath away to Heaven . . . I went into a good place that God knew that I could not fall off the edge of the floor."[17]

In April 1843 Howe traveled to New York for his wedding, an event he described to Charles Sumner as "the very central bower of paradise." The next month, the Howes boarded a Boston steamer bound for England, a journey made in the company of Julia's younger sister, Annie, and another pair of illustrious reformer/newlyweds, Horace and Mary Peabody Mann. As he set off for a year-long honeymoon in Europe, Howe entrusted his famous experiment to Mary Swift, a faithful, committed, but clearly overburdened young teacher, only twenty years old.[18]

If Howe harbored any lingering concerns about his experiment with Laura Bridgman, he must have been greatly encouraged by the triumphant reception that he received from England's liberal, reform-minded elite. Aided by the widespread dissemination of Charles Dickens's *American Notes*, published just a year before, Howe arrived in England to discover himself hailed as one of the greatest humanitarians and pedagogical geniuses of the age. Edward Everett, the Massachusetts politician who was then serving as American ambassador to England, wrote that "none of our Countrymen, since I have been here, have excited greater interest,—received more attention,—or left a better impression than the Howes." After reading Dickens's account, one Englishman told Howe, "Never have I read anything which delighted me so much. Never have I seen recorded or heard of Philanthropy like yours, in respect to Laura Bridgman, it is beyond all praise." The reformer Harriet Martineau begged him to visit, writing that she hoped to "indulge in thanking you for my share in the world's benefit from your work in [Laura Bridgman's] case."[19]

The entourage of American reformers had a less successful audience with Thomas Carlyle, the romantic sage who the year before had sent Howe a glowing letter of praise for his work with Laura Bridgman. Howe was kept home by a violent headache, and Mrs. Carlyle fled beforehand lest she be exposed to the "American environment." Consequently, Julia Ward Howe and the Manns spent an uncomfortable afternoon pouring tea for Carlyle, listening to what Julia later described as his "monologue." But, from all other corners, Howe's bride was amazed to find that "London has rung with my husband's praises . . . Everybody comes to see him, and to talk about Laura Bridgman."[20]

Howe was pleased by this reception but also humbled. His very real practical accomplishment, his pioneering work in the education of the deaf-blind, had been achieved because he had spurned Old World precedent and put faith in his own Yankee common sense and ingenuity. But once he had succeeded in teaching her language, he had been suddenly thrust into a far different role; no longer just a practical educator and the administrator of a school, he was now hailed as a great intellectual, the philosophic interpreter of a profound psychological experiment. This was a role that Howe had embraced, to be sure. Squelching any qualms he might have had about his own preparation for such an investigation, he had seized upon the platform afforded by Laura's case and used it to advance the Unitarian agenda of social reform, while at the same time promoting his career and his institution. But six years into his work with Laura Bridgman, his visit to Europe brought him face to face with the discomforting fact that he was actually quite ill- prepared to conduct such a complex inquiry into the hidden recesses of the human mind.

Perhaps recalling the disparity between his theory and Laura's reality, Howe felt chastened by the praise he received from Europe's intellectual elite. He confided these feelings to Sumner, writing that, "I have received very much of undeserved kindness, & felt quite ashamed . . . to find that people had imagined me to be a person of some extraordinary merit."[21] Not long after, Howe again expressed these feelings to Sumner: "One gent writes that he wants to see me more than any other man in Europe. He has published a little book with physiological reflections on privation of senses which he dedicates 'To Dr. Howe—the ingenious & successful teacher of Laura Bridgman.' The man looks up to me, yet it is evident from reading his books he has himself ten fold more talent acquirement & merit than I shall ever have."[22]

In the face of this humbling realization, Howe could only take refuge in a renewed dedication to his career as a servant of humanity. "Every year I live," he wrote to his friend back in Boston, "brings closer home the conviction that we must work for others & not for our own happiness (God will take care of that) alas! that my practice falls so far short of my theory."[23]

꙰ Howe and Mann spent the next several months touring the workhouses, schools, asylums, and prisons of England and the continent, gleaning new ideas for their work back home. Horace and Mary Mann returned to Boston after a six-month tour. The Howes, after learning that Julia was pregnant, moved on to the gentler climate of Rome to await the birth. Laura was ecstatic when she heard the news that Dr. and Mrs. Howe were expecting a baby. Not recognizing that the arrival of this new child would end any chance that she might have had of resuming her place as Howe's "adopted" daughter, Laura told Mrs. Howe, "I love your baby very much . . . I should like to live with you and your husband & dear baby." Laura hastened to add that, "I shall always set [the baby] a good example." The Howes both remained silent about Laura's request.[24]

Howe passed his days in Rome in leisurely fashion. Having asked Sumner to look in on Perkins from time to time, he evidently enjoyed his respite from the daily cares of running the school. Howe made the acquaintance of another Boston traveler, Theodore Parker, the radical Unitarian minister who would serve as a spiritual mentor and companion till Parker's death in 1859. Parker stayed long enough to baptize Howe's child, Julia Romana Howe, in a ceremony that Howe found deeply moving. He also enjoyed an extended visit from his friend and phrenological advisor, George Combe. The two spent many happy hours touring the Vatican's sculpture museums, making phrenological speculations on the great craniums of antiquity.[25]

In the midst of this quiet interlude in Howe's frenetic life of reform, he received a letter from Laura which must have alerted him that all was not well back in Boston. Without preface, Laura picked up her frantic questioning just where she had left off when he had last seen her in Boston. "What can I first say to God when I am wrong?" she pleaded to know. "Would he send me good thoughts & forgive me when I am very sad for doing wrong? Why does he not love wrong people, if they love Him? Would he be very happy to have me think of Him & Heaven very often?" After a dozen similar questions, Laura added, "You must answer me all about it, if you do not I shall be sad." Howe chose not to reply to Laura's letter, a silence which no doubt added to the child's mounting sense of frustration.[26]

Laura had particular reason to be concerned about God's feelings about "wrong people." Since Howe's absence, she had found it more difficult than ever to control her temper and to refrain from the small deceptions and rude acts which her teachers had been trying to banish from her behavior for much of the previous seven years. In a moment of pique, Laura destroyed another child's handiwork; on another occasion she blatantly lied to conceal the fact that she had broken a glass; and she repeatedly refused to acknowledge male visitors to the school, even those she knew well. Even when Laura was not overtly disobedient, Mary Swift fretted that the child was showing an increasing tendency to "submit to proper authority only after much argument."[27]

The darkest moment of this struggle came one February morning, just two days after Laura had sent Howe her plaintive letter, pleading with him to explain why God could not "let wrong people go to live with Him & be happy." As was so often the case, Laura's tantrum erupted quite unexpectedly. Waiting in their classroom for visitors to arrive, Mary Swift asked Laura to put her handkerchief away in her desk. The child ignored her, Swift then insisted, and Laura responded by slamming the lid of her wooden desk, making "such a noise as to startle all in the schoolroom." Swift approached her pupil, who was evidently "getting into a passion," and commanded her to place the handkerchief in her desk again, this time gently. Instead Laura slammed the desk a second time, and then, in Swift's words, she "uttered the most frightful yell I had ever heard," a cry "more like an animal than a human being." Laura stood alone, pale, trembling, and defiant.[28]

The moment was broken by the sound of approaching visitors. Lest these sightseers should find Laura, this reportedly angelic child, seething like an outraged beast, Swift quickly ushered her from the room. She then applied the usual punishment, withdrawing and leaving Laura alone. For almost two days the child sat by herself, unrepentant and aloof. As she waited anxiously through this battle of wills, Swift confided to her journal that she "never felt the need of counsel more."[29]

With tears of contrition, Laura yielded at last, pleading with her teacher for forgiveness. "I was sad and cried this afternoon, and thought I was very wrong," she told Swift. "And I asked God to forgive me and send me good thoughts and to love me." For the time being, the storm had passed, but Laura's "bad feelings," as she called them, would return. In the midst of her anxiety about religious matters, Laura seemed to be intensifying her struggle to gain mastery over her worst impulses. The more she tried to squelch them, however, the more prone she became to fits of uncontrollable anger and frustration. With Howe off in Europe, Swift was left alone with the responsibility of guiding Laura through these dark rages.[30]

While Howe remained silent, Laura continued to press Mary Swift for information about God. "When you look up, do you see Heaven?" she asked. "How can God *help* hearing when I ask him to forgive me?" she wondered. Swift recorded that her only reply was to remind Laura that she "did not want to talk about it until Dr. Howe answered her letters." Once again, Swift "turned to the window to try to change the subject."[31]

Two months later, Laura sent Howe a second letter. This one was less frantic, mingling religious questions with news about geography lessons and sleigh rides. But she closed the letter with a plaintive reminder, "I want you to answer my last letter to you about God & heaven & souls & many questions." Three months after Laura's first letter, Howe relented and sent her a long reply. "You ask me in your letter a great many things about the soul and about God," he wrote, "but, my dear little girl, it would take very much time and very many sheets of paper to tell you all I think about it, and I am very busy with taking care of my dear wife; but I shall try to tell you a little."[32]

Howe tried to explain that "God is a spirit, the spirit of love." As always, he directed Laura's attention to the divine revelation of nature, not the Scriptures. God, he told her, was like a loving father, an image that fit awkwardly with Laura's own experience but was no doubt emotionally compelling. He told Laura to find proof of God's paternal love in the fact that "this great world" was "full of beautiful things"; clearly a loving Creator had provided all that is necessary to make the human family happy, "if they have the mind to be, and if they love one another." "God wants everybody to be happy all the time, every day, Sundays and all," Howe went on, "and if they love one another they will be happy; and when their bodies die, their souls will live on, and be happy, and then they will know more about God." Howe concluded by asking the child to rest content with his brief answer and to "not be afraid." "Your mind is young and weak, and cannot understand hard things," he told her, but he assured her that he would explain it all to her when she was ready.[33]

Laura was delighted to receive the letter, had Swift read it to her twice, but then made no further reference to Howe's long awaited revelation. Swift concluded that, "although she understood each separate word, . . . the argument was beyond her capacity." Swift's conclusion that Howe's simple theological lesson was too difficult for Laura to understand would seem to confirm the doctor's claim that the child was still intellectually unprepared to learn about the challenging subject of religion. But Swift's feelings about Howe's letter, about his entire theory of Laura's religious intuitions, and about her own role in his experiment were far more complex and ambivalent. In the course of her daily, almost constant, interaction with Laura during the year of Howe's absence, Swift had become convinced that her student was quite ready for religious instruction and was even suffering from the lack of it. Howe's ban on these topics was, in her opinion, "disastrous," producing in Laura "an impatience in waiting that extended to other things." In a state of perpetual anxiety over matters of religion, Laura interrupted her lessons on a daily basis, trying to draw the conversation toward the topic of God.[34]

Swift also believed that the frustration Laura felt at always having these questions turned aside by her teachers accounted for much of the child's problem in controlling her temper. One afternoon, for example, Swift chastised Laura for being too critical of those around her. In anguish over yet another moral lapse, the child wanted to know how to ask God for forgiveness and how she might know if He had forgiven her. Receiving her usual short answer, the child retired to a chair and conducted her own silent soliloquy. Most of her thoughts flew on fingertips too rapid to read, but Swift caught these three phrases: "I am very sorry." "Doctor said he preferred to teach me himself." "Why cannot I know?"[35]

Like Howe, Swift believed that most of Laura's initial interest in religion had been sparked by her conversations with the other blind girls at Perkins. But once Laura's curiosity had been aroused, Swift felt that her pupil was then prepared to receive lessons in religious truths. Writing years later, she explained her growing disillusionment with Howe's experiment:

> As soon as [religious] doctrines were mentioned to [Laura], she received them very readily. It was far more difficult to teach her many common things of life than to teach her these truths, which indeed she learned so

easily that we could not determine when and how she obtained knowledge of them. Her soul seemed to be prepared for them, receptive of them . . . She asked Dr. Howe, "What is a soul?" and received the idea at once. Could she not then have received the Biblical doctrines? A girl capable of asking such questions is capable of receiving the replies.[36]

As Mary Swift labored to maintain control over Laura and to guide her through this emotional crisis, she grew to resent her "enforced reticence." Howe's experiment, she concluded, was proving to be positively harmful to the child's welfare. Furthermore, she felt that, even when Howe had been forced to answer some of Laura's questions, the very image of God which he offered her was too abstract and intellectualized for the child to understand, and insufficient to answer Laura's deep emotional need for protection and forgiveness. Swift was an evangelical Christian who did not fully share Howe's liberal views. As she struggled to remain faithful to her employer's instructions, she became increasingly convinced that she was harming the child.

In addition to her private concerns about Laura's welfare, Swift may also have felt public pressure to defy Howe's orders. Enforcing Howe's program of religious censorship placed the young woman in awkward situations, as she interacted with a public that often did not know about, or did not agree with, Howe's attempt to isolate the child from religious language. During one Saturday exhibition while the doctor was away, a man from the crowd asked Swift to ask the child, "What is the condition of the Soul after death?" In her journal, Swift recorded the anxiety she felt when the public's interest conflicted with Howe's theory: "I replied that she knew very little on such subjects & I thought it would be improper to ask her such a question. I was so much taken by surprise that I hardly knew what to say."[37]

Faced with this public pressure, as well as Laura's growing unruliness, Swift seems to have concluded that she should try to satisfy Laura's curiosity, that the child desperately needed to learn about the gospel and take comfort in the message of Christ's atonement. "I was unable to appeal to [Laura's] highest motives," Swift recalled later. "She was living under the old dispensation, and had not even the example of Christ as a model; for until my last month with her, she did not even know his name."[38]

But before Howe returned, Laura had learned Christ's name, and much more. While the actual sequence of events remains unclear, a few weeks before Howe's return from Europe a group of orthodox evangelicals evidently decided to defy Howe's ban. Given Mary Swift's close daily supervision of the child, they probably did so with her knowledge, if not her direct assistance. Coming to Perkins on a sacred mission, they signed into the child's eager hand their own answers to her questions about God's nature and the path to forgiveness and heaven.[39]

When Howe arrived back at Perkins, he was shocked to discover that Laura's religious questions had taken an entirely new turn, as she struggled to absorb the biblical words and evangelical concepts that had just been added to her vocabulary. Howe found the child "perplexed and troubled" because she could not understand why the Lamb of God "should continue so long a lamb, and not grow old like others, and be called a sheep." He knew then that "some persons more zealous than discreet" had broken their "implied promise of not touching upon religious topics." Howe considered this disruption of his plan for Laura's religious education "the greatest disappointment of his life." The unfettered, natural soul that he had dreamed of guiding to lofty heights of religious knowledge had been sidetracked into the empty commonplaces of evangelical religion. "I hardly recognized the Laura I had known," he mourned to his friends. Howe never specified who the offenders were, but Mary Swift left Perkins not long after Howe's return.[40]

In consultation with Horace Mann and other trusted friends, Howe carefully prepared his next public report on Laura, using that platform to condemn those "misguided" proselytizers who had ruined his experiment. Thanks to their "well meaning officiousness," Howe wrote in his 1845 report, Laura's mind was now befuddled with talk of "the Atonement, of the Redeemer, the Lamb of God, and of some very mystical points of mere speculative doctrine." Venting his disappointment over his botched experiment and his exasperation with his orthodox critics, he abandoned the tone of religious neutrality that had constrained him in his prior reports. He declared that the religious concepts Laura now struggled with "were perhaps not farther beyond her comprehension than they were beyond the comprehension of those persons who assumed to talk to her about them; but they . . . troubled her, because, unlike such persons, she wished that every word should be the symbol of some clear and definite idea."[41]

Howe repeated his arguments for delaying Laura's religious education. In another attack on the orthodoxy's practice of early religious training, he wrote, "I might long ago have taught the Scriptures to Laura; she might have learned, as other children do, to repeat line upon line, and precept upon precept; she might have been taught to imitate others in prayer." Howe insisted that, no matter how well she might have learned to mimic the forms of piety, her actual understanding of God would have remained limited by her own severely constricted intellect and the paltry "materials with which her mind had been stored." Once this feeble conception of God was permitted to take root in her mind, Howe argued, no amount of subsequent enlightenment could relieve her of her first misconceptions.[42]

Moving to the attack, Howe claimed that this was a liability that Laura did not struggle against alone: "How vague is the idea which many people attach to some words! and of how much mischief to the world has this vagueness been the source. How long does it take to sever those ties! how many of us go to our graves without ever breaking a fibre of them—without ever having divested words of the crude ideas attached to them in childhood, or contemplated the things with the clear eye of reason."[43]

The orthodox could not fail to miss Howe's point, that he had delayed Laura's religious education not only because of her unique condition but because he felt that early religious education was harmful to *all* children. These "vague words" that Howe considered "mere metaphysical speculation" were in fact the very doctrines which orthodox evangelicals considered to be the core of the Christian faith, the doctrines of the fall, Christ's atonement, and God's final judgment. Up until this point, Howe had been vague enough about his purposes so that the orthodox could charitably assume that he had been shielding Laura from these "Biblical doctrines" because of the unique obstacles to her education caused by her handicap. He now made it clear that he believed that *all* children should be protected from indoctrination into these "superstitions" and that those adults who still believed them had failed to break free from the "crude ideas" of their childhood. Lashing out in anger, Howe argued that the tenets of evangelical Christianity were not something which he hoped Laura Bridgman would eventually grow into as she matured but rather that they were notions he hoped the rest of society would gradually grow out of as it matured.

₰ Until the publication of Howe's 1845 report, orthodox criticism of his religious experiment with Laura Bridgman was remarkably tentative. Howe wrote that he heard "continually" from those who disagreed with his experiment, orthodox men and women who urged him to teach the child the doctrines they considered essential to her salvation. While he may have heard such suggestions privately, few of them have been preserved in his letters, and the orthodox only rarely expressed their concerns in print. In countless articles about the child written for evangelical papers during the early years of Laura's education, no writer failed to praise Howe for his Christian benevolence. Any reservations about his experiment were expressed in an indirect fashion. A writer for the *Christian Observer*, for example, agreed with Howe that the difficulties of teaching the child "revealed truth" were great. "It would be perilous to instill false notions, which are worse than none," this writer admitted, but added, "if true intelligence can be given, it ought not to be withheld."[44]

But Howe's 1845 report opened a floodgate of criticism from orthodox writers. Most of the controversy centered in Boston, where it quickly became entwined with a larger Calvinist counter-assault against Horace Mann's common school reforms. But the first and most thorough attack on Howe's experiment came from an orthodox editor in New York. Not long after Howe's report was published, Dr. George Cheever announced in his *New York Evangelist* that Howe's statements "must awaken the attention of every Christian to the incalculable importance of having truly religious teachers in such an institution, for if the blind lead the blind, both shall fall into the ditch." Cheever denounced Howe's plan of instruction for Laura Bridgman as an attempt to replace the divine revelation of Scripture with the lessons of human reason, an approach that was nothing more than "pure Deism, or Naturalism."

Sounding an argument that orthodox critics would use repeatedly over the next few years, Cheever rejected Howe's claim that the essential doctrines of the Bible were too difficult, too abstract and metaphorical, for Laura, or any other child, to understand. Hadn't Christ ordered his disciples to "Suffer the little children to come unto me?" Cheever asked. While Laura had stumbled temporarily over the metaphor of the Lamb of God, he rejected Howe's conclusion that this proved that the child was incapable of understanding the true meaning of the phrase. "The author of this report can never make us believe that a child whose mind is so quick as hers, and a child that can write such letters as she does, could not have been made to understand the meaning of such a metaphor." Indeed, Laura's insistent complaints about her own feelings of guilt and her questions about the best way to ask God's forgiveness only confirmed that the child was crying out for knowledge of Christ's atonement. Cheever concluded: "Now we hold it to be impossible that a person, whether child or idiot, who is capable of a sense of sin, and of the consciousness of having offended God, should be incapable of the idea of a Savior . . . Poor Laura's situation is indeed critical, if her instructors either will not or cannot direct her anxious mind to the Savior."[45]

Howe learned of the *Evangelist* article through a friend in New York, who wrote to inform him that he had been "pretty severely attacked." But before that news could reach him, the controversy erupted closer to home. A week after the New York article was published, a mouthpiece of Boston orthodoxy, the *New England Puritan,* joined the fray. "We cannot but feel great dissatisfaction with this manner of dealing with immortal minds," its editor lamented. Following the same line of argument as Cheever, the *Puritan* denounced Howe for relegating "information concerning the Redeemer" to the ranks of "mere speculative doctrine." Likewise, this critic rejected Howe's claim that the lessons of the Bible were too difficult for Laura to understand; "We are among those who believe the Scriptures to have been designed by their Divine Author, for all classes, old and young, rich and poor; and that they may be safely left to tell their own story, as soon as the human mind is able to understand truths of any kind."[46] Again following Cheever, the *Puritan* declared that Howe had published ample evidence himself, in Laura's letters and religious comments, proving that the child was hungry for the very thing he had denied her, news of Christ's atonement for her sins. "She is longing after the information which the Scriptures alone can furnish," the *Puritan* lamented, "and yet he thinks it injudicious to introduce her to them."[47]

The *Christian Watchman,* an orthodox paper that once sang in the chorus of Howe's admirers, now expressed nothing but contempt for the doctor's theological speculations. Responding to his observation that Laura, and "most children," are "as pure as Eve was," the *Watchman's* editor wondered sarcastically:

We cannot tell how the Dr. found this out, for we have never seen it laid down in any of the medical books, either homeopathic or allopathic. And as he has come to the knowledge of so important a fact, if it be a fact, we regret that he has not gone further, and told us . . . whether Eve, before she ate the tempting apple, manifested as clear symptoms of depravity as Laura Bridgman; whether she was petulant, inclined to deceit, to anger, &c. At least, he ought to tell us how he came by the knowledge of the relative degree of Eve's purity, for we suppose he makes this statement as a man of fact and science. It is a subject on which we feel considerable interest.[48]

Howe made no direct reply to these attacks. Instead, he took the offensive against his opponents, joining forces with Horace Mann in a bitter campaign against the orthodox schoolmasters of Boston. The conflict began when thirty-one schoolmasters, mostly of orthodox faith, published a 144-page pamphlet that challenged Mann's gloomy assessment of the state's common schools, ridiculed his interest in phrenology, and criticized his theory of moral discipline. By challenging their right to use corporal punishment, the masters claimed, the secretary had undermined the foundation of their "rightful authority," inviting anarchy into the classroom. Mann responded with a sarcastic reply to the schoolmasters, and in the next year two dozen more pamphlets, running to hundreds of pages, were published by partisans of both sides.[49]

In the midst of these rhetorical fireworks, the conflict was finally resolved not through persuasion but through brute political force. In fall 1844, in the aftermath of his disappointment with Laura Bridgman, Howe and several of Mann's other allies made a successful bid to win seats on the city's school board. As a member of the board, Howe used this platform to mercilessly ridicule Boston's old guard teachers and their methods of corporal punishment and rote learning. Leading a committee that conducted citywide examinations of the pupils, he launched a campaign to discredit the schoolmasters as incompetent and brutal hacks and to drive them from their posts.

Even Howe's allies on the school board thought his methods were unfair and vindictive, and few of the old teachers actually lost their jobs. Howe's faction did succeed in eliminating the use of corporal punishment in Boston's classrooms, at least temporarily. But his harsh and uncompromising approach to the orthodox schoolmasters only fueled further resentment against him, inviting a new round of criticism of his work with Laura Bridgman.[50]

The most damaging objection came from Dr. Heman Humphrey, the orthodox president of Amherst College. Humphrey was a moderate man, a leading proponent of child nurture among the orthodox, a supporter of most of Horace Mann's reform program, and one of the important orthodox voices on the State Board of Education. Mann was absolutely dependent on his support, while his Calvinist critics had more than once attempted to draw Humphrey into the controversy on their side, hoping to use his influence to veto the secretary's liberal reforms. Humphrey had remained in Mann's camp, providing him with a crucial vote of confidence.[51]

But in 1846 Humphrey publicly criticized Mann for reprinting one of Howe's reports on Laura Bridgman in the *Common School Journal*. In an anonymous letter to the orthodox *New England Puritan*, Humphrey charged that Howe's claim that Laura was naturally pure might be expected in a journal promoting "Liberal Christianity" but had no place in one "intended for general circulation," one which was supposed to represent a common school movement that claimed to be without sectarian bias.[52]

Reflecting on Howe's suggestion that Laura, or any other child, could be "perfectly holy," Humphrey wrote that:

> It is not our happiness to have any such children as these; and we do not wish Dr. Howe or any other religionist of the same school, to come into our families, by the aid of the *Common School Journal*, and tell them, that they are or ever were "as pure as Eve was." We do not believe it. We have not so read our Bibles. We believe with Paul, that "they are by nature, children of wrath even as the others;" and that however young they may die, they must be renewed by the Holy Spirit and washed in the blood of Christ; or they cannot be saved.[53]

When Mann learned that this letter was written by a member of his own state board, by a man who wielded considerable influence over the fate of his reforms, he was forced to distance himself from Howe's "sectarian" comments. "I hope God will spare my life," he privately assured Howe, "and crown my labors, by enabling me to do something for the direct subversion of Calvinism; but while I hold my present position, it is the concurrent dictate of justice and policy that I should not enter, as a combatant, the theological arena."[54]

Mann then published a disclaimer in his *Journal*, apologizing for the slip and explaining it as an editorial oversight. Blaming the distraction of his considerable responsibilities, he claimed that he had not carefully read Howe's report before printing it and had not noticed the offending comment. The fact that he had not written his usual elaborate preface to Howe's report that year may be taken as supporting evidence for his claim that he did not know the contents of Howe's report. Yet it should be noted that, in previous years, Mann's own writings about Laura Bridgman in the *Journal*—including his extraordinary "vision"—contained numerous comments as extreme as any of Howe's and as obviously aimed against the fundamental tenets of orthodoxy.[55]

Humphrey's relatively mild chastisement seemed to reinvigorate Howe and Mann's orthodox critics, particularly those still angry about the way Howe had humiliated the Boston schoolmasters. In fall 1846, a year after Howe stepped down from the city's school board, an orthodox paper sounded the alarm that the city was being swept by a wave of juvenile delinquency: "Public journals have teemed with recitals of instances of juvenile depravity, and public meetings have been called to extend a salutary alarm." At one of the largest of those meetings, a fiery orthodox minister, the Reverend Matthew Hale Smith, told the concerned citizens gathered at Faneuil Hall that "depraved men were never bolder than now. Murders, robberies, house breaking, are deeds of daily occurrence." Many felt unsafe walking the city's streets after dark. And, "most startling" of all, many of these criminal acts were being perpetrated by "boys and youth." In addition to violent crime, there was shameful evidence of a new spirit of "licentiousness." Students had recently been caught circulating "French pictures," and some "boys and girls" had set up a room, "furnished with all that panders to base and wicked passions," where they met secretly at night.[56]

Smith and his orthodox allies attributed this outbreak of youthful wickedness to the "new kind of influence and teaching" introduced into the schools by Mann and Howe. The city's crime wave, they charged, was the inevitable consequence of the reformers' radical new "no-punishment" doctrine. As one orthodox writer put it, "God is now revealing to us the true nature of that philanthropy, that proposes to exterminate all crime by taking away all penalties and all law—that proposes to heal all disobedience in children, by removing all authority to be obeyed—that proposes to rectify the depravity in man, by throwing the reins upon the neck of every depraved passion . . . What else could have been expected from such diligence in sowing the seeds of mischief?"[57]

While these disgruntled Calvinists directed most of their anger at Horace Mann, the highest lightning rod of the common school movement, they also began to take aim at Mann's vociferous ally. The outbreak of delinquency, the Reverend Smith exclaimed in a widely circulated pamphlet, was all that society could expect when Scriptural injunctions were replaced by newfangled philosophies, when the laws of Moses were ignored in favor of the heresies of Dr. Howe.[58]

While both sides in this "common school controversy" were motivated in part by personal animosities and professional jealousies, there were fundamental issues at stake. Mann and Howe's plan to eliminate corporal punishment and rote learning from the state's common schools challenged not only the reputation of teachers and local school committees but also notions about human nature that had prevailed in New England for two hundred years. Most historians have sympathized with the reformers, describing the debate as an important chapter in a wider struggle between the forces of enlightened democratic liberalism and the reactionary fanaticism of the orthodox.[59] But this explanation obscures the fact that the reform agenda enjoyed the support of a majority of the orthodox citizens of

Massachusetts. In his thorough history of Mann's conflicts with the orthodox, Raymond Culver concluded that the secretary was actually opposed
by a very small, though vocal, group of critics.[60] In fact, none of his reforms would have been possible if he had not enjoyed broad political and
financial support in a state where orthodox Christians greatly outnum-
bered the liberals. Mann knew that he never could have survived the political battles against his Calvinist foes without backing from those he called
"the best among the orthodox."[61]

As this orthodox support for Mann suggests, in the 1840s the nation was
undergoing a revolution in attitudes about child-rearing. Popular magazines preached romantic ideas about childhood to their middle-class audiences, and orthodox and liberal alike took an interest in what Horace
Bushnell called the "Christian nurture" of children. At both ends of the
theological spectrum, the nurture movement preached that children are at
least potentially good, that adults are responsible for promoting this potential through the development of their children's "character," and that
the best way to do this was not through stern authority but through affection, moral example, and a careful attention to the child's environment.[62]

As this broad consensus about the value of child nurture suggests, by the
mid-nineteenth century, Calvinism was a waning force in American culture. In a society that was becoming increasingly egalitarian, optimistic,
and materialistic, the view that humans are inherently sinful and that God
has saved only a predetermined elect seemed irrational and outmoded.
While most antebellum Americans did not abandon their belief in the per-
vasiveness of human sin and God's threat of eternal punishment, many
tempered this with a new faith in the remedial powers of parental nurture
and public education. From this broad historical perspective, the decline
of Calvinism was caused neither by Mann and Howe's frenzied attacks on
the Boston schoolmasters and their allies nor by Howe's experiment with
Laura Bridgman but by the inexorable forces of urbanization, democrati-
zation, evangelical revivalism, and consumer capitalism.[63]

But in the 1840s, these profound social changes were only dimly perceived by both the reformers and their adversaries.[64] Howe and Mann continued to believe that orthodoxy was a powerful, monolithic, and implaca-
ble foe bent on reversing their reforms. As far as they were concerned, the
orthodox cause was personified by men like the Reverend A. W. McClure,
an influential Boston minister who thunderously denounced his society's
new infatuation with the "Heresy of Love" and called on his followers to
restore the sterner faith of their Pilgrim fathers.[65]

In 1847 the Reverend McClure used the pages of his monthly journal, the *Christian Observatory*, to launch the most thorough attack yet against Howe and his experiment with Laura Bridgman. Like others before him, McClure warned that Howe was recklessly gambling with a child's soul. "He has not only embraced a theological system for himself," McClure warned, "but he has also embarked another spirit with his own upon it, that they may together seek their eternal destinies." "The one grand doctrine," McClure explained to his readers, "which Dr. Howe has labored to prove from the case of Laura Bridgman is, that man is by nature holy. On this controverted Pelagian ground, his Institution takes its stand. Annually it gives us instruction on this doctrine as illustrated, and, in its view confirmed, by Laura Bridgman's history." McClure declared that such views contradicted the Bible and were therefore "of an infidel character."[66]

After reviewing all of Howe's previous reports on Laura Bridgman, McClure also argued that Howe's claim that the child was naturally honest, obedient, and "pure as Eve" was not only unscriptural but also unfactual, contradicted by Howe's own public writings on Laura's case. In his reports, Howe had related a few stories about the child's small lies, her attempts to impose her will on other children, and her resistance to some lessons. Howe, of course, presented these stories only to illustrate the effectiveness of his approach to pedagogy and discipline. He excused her misdeeds as momentary aberrations which in no way contradicted his claim that her moral instincts were pure and reliable. But Calvinists like McClure drew a quite different moral from the same stories, finding in them confirmation that Laura's soul was born in rebellion against God. McClure wondered, "How reconcile Laura's unsullied purity of heart with her deception, her anger, her unrelenting impenitence, her delight in inflicting pain; instances of all which are related?" Howe's brief mention of Laura's moral "lapses" in his earlier public reports had come back to haunt him.[67]

Having established to his satisfaction that Howe's speculations on Laura Bridgman were justified neither by observation nor by scriptural revelation, the angry reverend went on to attack him at his most vulnerable political pressure point. McClure conceded that, since Howe had the permission of Laura's parents, he had the right to instruct her in any way he chose. But he took exception to the fact that, as director of the Perkins School, Howe had transformed his annual reports into a public platform from which to promote his infidel theories. Perkins, though funded in part by taxpayers of all denominations, was, according to the *Observatory*, a "sectarian institution." Furthermore, McClure chided Howe for maintaining an "illiberal" monopoly on the child's education. As a "public officer," Howe had been entrusted with the child's education, "but not responsible to represent only Pelagianism in his Institution, and to stand as door-keeper to shut out the views and sentiments of thousands of his fellow-citizens."[68]

Some journals came to Howe's defense. An editorialist for the *Christian Register*, a leading voice of liberal Christianity in Boston, wrote that "it mortifies and grieves us to read these [McClure's] narrow, captious charges, which are so entirely without foundation." A contributor to the *North American Review* applauded Howe's denunciation of the "injudicious ardor of some religious zealots." "It is to be lamented," this author wrote, "that, in such a peculiar case, the right purposes of piety should have been guided by so wrong a judgement."[69]

In spite of these gestures of support, McClure's criticisms hit their mark. Howe was not, as McClure had suggested, a "public officer," since Perkins was a private institution. Still, the school relied on the state's good will for its charter of incorporation and for much of its yearly operating funds. The danger of alienating state lawmakers, the majority of whom were orthodox, must have loomed particularly large in the mid-1840s, because the school had run into embarrassing financial difficulties, caused by a reduction in state support and by Howe's policy of not refusing any likely student, regardless of his or her ability to pay tuition.[70]

Anxious to protect the nonsectarian reputation and financial well-being of their school, the trustees tried to distance the institution from its director's controversial religious speculations. In the next annual report, published soon after the *Observatory*'s attack, they made it clear that Howe had made his remarks on Laura Bridgman only in his capacity as a doctor and private citizen, not as the official spokesman for the school.[71]

As always, Howe's comments on Laura's progress for that year were relegated to an appendix. In this portion of his 1847 report, he attempted for the first time to answer what he called the "unjust and injurious" charge that he had been exerting "sectarian influence" in his school. Such a criticism, he wrote, threatened the "general interests" of the entire institution. Howe explained that the misunderstanding arose because some uncharitable observers misunderstood the nature of his writings on Laura Bridgman. "They are special Reports, made by me, and for which I alone am responsible. They do not pretend to give the views of the Trustees or officers of the Institution."[72]

Howe entertained no illusions that this explanation would satisfy his most vehement orthodox critics, but he was anxious to assure the rest of the public, whose good will and donations were so crucial to the school, that he was not a religious radical who was trying to impose his unorthodox theological ideas on the impressionable minds of his blind students. Laura Bridgman, he explained, was a "peculiar case." Her condition offered scientists an unprecedented chance to plumb the depths of human nature. Anxious not to squander this opportunity, Howe had chosen in this one instance to depart from the strict standards of nonsectarianism that governed all other aspects of the school's operation.[73]

Howe had done this because he thought that Laura Bridgman's education could provide the world with scientific evidence which would prove the liberal theory of human nature. But now he was forced to admit that his experiment was a failure, that it had proven nothing. Placing humanitarian concerns over scientific ones, he had never been willing to isolate her completely from the human community. As a result, he explained, the child had been exposed to "ignorant and selfish persons" whose harmful influences had disrupted the natural course of her development. Addressing himself to the many philosophers, scientists, and educators around the world who "looked upon her case as an interesting experiment for ascertaining the natural character and tendencies of the human heart," Howe confessed that he had never been able to "conduct the experiment of her education in an entirely satisfactory manner."[74]

This was an anticlimactic end to a story that had inspired poets and intrigued philosophers for a decade. The experiment that had made Howe into one of the most admired American philanthropists of his day was now over, its result inconclusive. Howe was saddened and angered by the lost opportunity, considering it one of the greatest disappointments of his life. His only task now, he believed, was to try to repair the damage done by those who had chosen to destroy what they could not understand.

Chapter 9

Disillusionment

When Mary Swift departed from Perkins in May 1845, Laura Bridgman was left without a daily companion and instructor. That summer she received no lessons and little supervision. Laura spent her days wandering around the school, conversing with teachers, visitors, and blind girls who could speak her manual language. Fearing that Laura's new freedom was exposing her to all of those influences from which he had always tried to protect her, Howe was anxious to find a replacement for Swift. At the end of August he enlisted Sarah Wight, an instructor of the blind girls at Perkins, to become Laura's new "constant companion."[1]

Like her predecessor, Wight was in her early twenties, an intelligent and idealistic young woman committed to the cause of educational reform. Unlike Swift, she was a liberal Christian, more sympathetic to Howe's beliefs. While Howe maintained a supervisory role in Laura's education, he again entrusted daily responsibility for the child to her female companion.

Just as Laura had feared when she first learned about his marriage plans, her relationship with Howe was changing. After returning from their honeymoon, the newlyweds had moved into Howe's old apartment at Perkins. Though struggling with her new maternal duties, Julia welcomed Laura into their household. Within a year, however, the Howe's were expecting the second of their six children. They left Perkins for a home not far from the school, leaving Laura behind to live in her own room in the female dormitory. She became a welcome guest, but no longer truly a member, of her beloved Doctor's family.[2]

Once again placed under a teacher's watchful eye, Laura returned to a state of semi-isolation, spending nearly every hour of the day with Wight. Their solitude was interrupted only by a daily visit from Howe and by meetings with important visitors and two or three carefully selected blind girls. "By this means," Mary Swift later wrote, perhaps with some lingering bitterness, "Laura was prevented from receiving any new ideas, except through the medium which he approved."[3]

Laura was nearing her fifteenth birthday as Wight began her duties. Howe felt that his student was approaching a critical juncture, a time that he had "always looked forward to . . . with great anxiety." Laura was passing from a child into a woman, raising troubling questions for Howe about how best to respond to her emerging sexuality. Howe made no mention of this in public, but privately he confessed his fears to a few close friends.

Laura had always avoided physical contact with men, and Howe told Francis Lieber that he was sure that she was still entirely naive about sex, innocent of even "the slightest conception of what difference in gender consists in." Convinced that Laura's sexuality was "slumbering," Howe hoped to keep it that way. As a phrenologist, he believed that the sexual drive is a normal and healthy human instinct, God's way of ensuring "the perpetuity of the race." But when those desires could not, or should not, be acted upon, he believed that God had wisely given *women* the capacity "for subjecting entirely the sexual appetite . . . when the necessity for it exists."[4]

All of Laura's friends and mentors agreed with Howe that marriage was out of the question. She showed no sign of becoming emotionally mature enough to marry, and it seemed evident that she could not properly care for children and a husband. The best course, the British travel writer Harriet Martineau advised Howe in a "confidential" letter, was to "preserve [Laura's] ignorance of the whole truth," avoiding anything that might awaken "a consciousness of her instincts."[5]

But Howe also feared that, if Laura's sexual feelings *were* aroused and if they were denied the conventional outlet of marriage, she might be drawn into a homosexual relationship. Growing up in the female wing of the Perkins school, Laura had often tried to share a bed with her female guardian or with girlfriends she had made among the blind students. Howe had always directed Laura's teachers to discourage this practice, though their journals suggest that they had only limited success.[6]

Now, as Laura reached adolescence, Howe believed that this kind of intimate physical contact could be the "spark" that would ignite an explosion of sexual passion. "Should she pass a single night with a girl of her own age," he confided to Lieber, "or of any age indeed beyond infancy, I should feel as uneasy & watch for the subsequent symptoms almost as I should if she had been bitten by a rabid dog."[7]

Though no clear "symptoms" of Laura's sexual life were ever reported, she clearly began to think about marriage at this time. Sarah Wight reported that one day Laura came to her "blushing and laughing." She asked her new friend, "Do you think I shall ever be married with a gentleman whom I love best & most?" Wight tried to convince her that this was impossible, though Laura resisted the argument that she was incapable of keeping a house. "I can sweep & fix things very nicely," she insisted. Wight and Howe attributed Laura's interest in marriage to some "foolish talk" she had been having with the blind girls, and they vowed to watch her more carefully.[8]

Although Howe fretted over Laura's sexuality, in other respects he was optimistic about her adolescence. Laura was beginning to assert a new independence, he sensed, straining to break free from "the obligations of unconditional obedience" that he had imposed on her up to that point. This "aspiring spirit of the young," he believed, was a natural and healthy stage in any young person's emotional and moral development, but also one that would put his entire theory of moral education to a crucial test.

Howe felt that a wise teacher should not try to squelch an adolescent's emerging sense of "individualism" but, within limits, should actually encourage it. However, he believed that people of Laura's age should only be granted new freedoms commensurate with their powers of self-control. If Laura were allowed to cast aside parental authority before she was capable of replacing it with self-government, she would squander her freedom in the indulgence of childish whim. The result, Howe believed, would be moral and emotional chaos that would make both Laura and her friends miserable. He felt that Laura could only grow into a happy and independent adult if he could teach her to always obey a "new monitor and master—the conscience."[9]

Of course, Howe and his assistants had been trying to develop the child's moral sense from the start, reading her stories with pointed moral lessons, modeling noble and selfless behavior, and pressing the child to pass judgment on her own conduct. Laura had responded enthusiastically to this strict moral regime and had always taken a keen interest in moral questions. But as she entered adolescence, Howe suggested that much of her good behavior up to that point had only been a product of "mere habit and blind obedience." The time was fast approaching when the world would find out if she was capable of replacing the unreflective obedience of a child with the rational self-government of an adult, an internalized commitment to "conscious duty and stern principle."[10]

Sensing that Laura had already entered this "critical period," Howe instructed Wight to give her a crash course in conscientiousness. While Laura had always been closely monitored and forced into a state of constant moral introspection by her guardians, Wight brought a new intensity to this task. During her first day with Laura, she instructed her pupil that "we must try always to do perfectly right every day, & then we should grow better & better." Toward that end, Wight made it a "rule" never to allow "the slightest fault to pass without some notice." Each morning the two began their lessons by reviewing Laura's conduct of the day before. For example, Wight launched a vigorous but unsuccessful campaign to check Laura's interest in fashionable clothes. And she calmly but firmly pressed Laura to suppress her physical exuberance and the loud and unpleasant "noises" she sometimes used to express emotion. In all ways, Wight told Laura, she must learn to grow "still and gentle."[11]

Wight monitored not only her student's acts but also her thoughts and emotions. She urged Laura to conquer all "bad feelings" of impatience and anger and to scrutinize herself, probing and purifying her motivations. Whenever Wight suspected that Laura was doing worthy acts for unworthy reasons, being kind or cooperative or generous just to win approval, she called the child's attention to her apparent hypocrisy. Laura was shamed by these exposures and on rare occasions offered her physical handicaps as an excuse for her moral failings. "I want to do right," she explained. "But I cannot hear with my ears what everybody says about it; what they think is right and best to do."[12]

But Laura's excuses were few and her shame was always temporary, soon giving way to fresh resolve. "I have meditated upon my bad conduct & I shall not do such a wrong thing again," she reported more than once. Like Swift before her, Wight was surprised to find that no subject interested Laura more than matters of right and wrong. After a lesson on "motives," Wight reported, "during the whole lesson [Laura] was very thoughtful, pressing my fingers closely, so that no letter should escape her." After another conversation about motives, she wrote, "In conversations of this kind I think Laura takes a deeper interest than in anything else." Laura even asked her teacher for a special notebook so she could preserve a permanent record of her daily "conduct."[13]

While most of Laura's infractions were small, she continued to struggle against what Wight called her "besetting sin of anger." Her outbursts were less frequent than in earlier years, but Laura still suffered bouts of intense anxiety, frustration, and rage. Serving on the front lines of this battle to conquer Laura's passions, Wight was a regular casualty. Laura twisted her arm, slapped her, tried to bite her, and locked her in what Wight called "one of her most violent embraces."

Just as Mary Swift had done, Wight responded to these attacks by withdrawing, leaving the child alone so that she would feel the full force of her pangs of guilt. But Wight was particularly adept at this form of emotional manipulation. Swift had always been firm with Laura, ordering her to her room and making it clear that she was being punished. Wight, described by her peers as a sensitive and brooding personality, avoided such direct confrontation. She responded to a slap or a bite not with anger but with sympathetic disappointment over Laura's moral failing. Instead of marching Laura to her room, she would often withdraw to her own, complaining of a headache or fever caused, she said, by the "sad thoughts" that Laura had provoked in her.[14]

Laura was remarkably intuitive; her companions often marveled at her ability to judge character and to sense subtle changes of mood among her friends. She sometimes did this by running her fingertips across faces, reading feelings in their contours; other times she deciphered less tangible clues—a handshake, a touch of the arm, the posture of her companions, the vibrations as people moved about the room. Laura was so attuned to this seismic language that her teachers often joked that she was clairvoyant. There was no person whose moods Laura was more attuned to than her teacher, the woman with whom she spent nearly every hour of every day. Thus she never failed to notice when Wight felt, as Laura put it, "exhausted of trying to correct my faults."[15]

Laura had developed intense bonds of affection with both of her teachers, but her attachment to Mary Swift had always been tempered by feelings of resentment and defiance. Because Swift had been more strict and confrontational, Laura had responded to this show of power by making small bids for emotional independence. Under the care of Sarah Wight, the unequal power relationship of teacher and student was still present but more artfully veiled. Wight returned Laura's anger with sorrow, and even small acts of kindness.

On one occasion, for example, Laura shook her teacher's arm violently. Wight retreated but returned soon after to give Laura a sock she had mended. "Why do you do good things to such a wrong girl?" Laura asked, bewildered to find her teacher more wounded than angered by her assault. Perhaps for this reason, Laura grew to love Wight unreservedly, describing her as "my beloved W" and "my pious and excellent teacher." Each time Wight withdrew, expressing sadness or pain over Laura's behavior, Laura sensed the change almost immediately, suffered the stings of remorse, and soon begged her "beloved dove" for forgiveness.[16] "I shall never strike you again. I am so earnest to have my excellent teacher happy always." "I wish you would not talk so mournful; try to be as happy as usual. I cannot help loving you dearly." Other times, she poured out a heartfelt confession in her journal: "An impatient feeling in my heart made me wring my poor teacher's delicate hand." After another incident, she admitted, "I was a very wrong and unjust scholar to hurt [Wight] so much."[17]

In this way, Wight tried to motivate Laura "to control herself perfectly" by appealing to her strong feelings of affection. Rather than attempting to root out the child's bad impulses, Wight felt she was nurturing the child's good ones. "The true way to improve character," she explained, "is to cultivate and develop that which is good and beautiful in the character which will itself gradually overpower and destroy the bad."[18]

Laura's moral setbacks continued, but Howe and Wight both felt that this new technique was working. Howe was pleased to inform his readers that his student was showing "considerable capacity" for self-government. Her violent outbursts came less frequently. More and more, she controlled her emotions and wayward impulses. Howe was convinced that she was doing this not just to please her teachers but out of a growing respect for the authority of her own conscience. Laura agreed that, more than ever before, her most painful punishments were now self-inflicted. She sensed that she had come under the sway of a new and awesome judge from within. "I am too old to be reproved," she informed Wight, but added, "My mind can reprove me."[19]

In some respects, the strong conscience that Howe had cultivated within Laura closely resembled his own. No less than her mentor, Laura became puritanical, tolerating no compromise with evil, the world's or her own. Growing up under the guidance of one of antebellum Boston's most aggressive moral crusaders, Laura learned to respond to tales of others' wickedness with exasperation, quick judgment, and a call for immediate action to right the wrong. Her understanding of public affairs was extremely vague but decidedly Whiggish. She developed a passionate hatred of "drunkards" and slaveholders, concluded from her history lessons that all monarchs were moral monsters, and even scolded the governor of Massachusetts for sending his soldiers to fight in the wicked Mexican War.[20]

Also like Howe, Laura learned to turn that moral searchlight within, probing the minute details of her own actions and motivations. While her occasional lies and outbursts of anger continued through her teenage years, these moral lapses only heightened her interest in problems of right and wrong. Just as Howe's drive to do good was sometimes spurred on by anxious self-criticism about his feelings of ambition, Laura's own struggle with her petty moral failures drove her to make stronger efforts to examine and subdue her rebellious impulses.

In spite of these similarities in their powers of conscientiousness—their moral absolutism and their self-critical introspection—there were important differences. Howe's moral criticism was most often projected outward, while Laura, of necessity, was forced to look within. Howe was an educated male, a combative personality, and a distinguished member of the reforming elite in a city that considered itself a beacon of progress for the rest of the world. As such he spent a great deal of his time correcting and perfecting all "Humanity," using correspondingly less of his vast reserves of moral energy to dwell on his own imperfections. But Laura, whose scope of activity was constricted by her gender and social station as well as by her deafness and blindness, was forced to expend most of her moral zeal attempting to reform her own self. Howe operated on a grand scale, waging war on sin and ignorance throughout society, placing himself at the vanguard of a movement that confidently assumed it was advancing toward nothing less than the gradual perfection of the human race. But Laura could scarce comprehend, let alone participate in, moral issues at this level of complexity and abstraction. Instead, she became a microcosm of the reforming crusade, attempting to stamp out sin not throughout all of society but within her own soul and in those immediately around her.

Lacking a wider field of action, the spirit of perfectionism that Howe nurtured in his student turned her into something of a pedant, obsessively concerned with preserving the moral order of the institution. The routine of daily life at Perkins, where each measured hour was imbued with the mandates of health and hard work, gave her great satisfaction, imposing a grid of purpose on a consciousness that might have otherwise languished in the alienation of silent darkness. Laura's teachers found that the child was best able to control her own self when her environment remained "very uniform." "Departure from her usual habits causes excitement," Howe explained, "which is sometimes excessive, and leaves unpleasant consequences."[21]

By creating order and routine at Perkins, Howe attempted to habituate goodness in all of his students. But this approach ultimately turned Laura into a guardian of small virtues. Each morning she combed her room, ensuring that all was in perfect order. "Not a scrap of paper, not a particle of dirt, escapes her notice," Howe wrote. She expected a similar fastidiousness from others at the institution; she roused late sleepers out of bed, inspected younger children's' hands for cleanliness, and eagerly sought out young blind pupils whom she might instruct and correct.[22]

Laura also developed the habit of offering unsolicited moral advice to her friends and correspondents. She was determined to set a good example for her brothers and sisters back in Hanover and sent them regular letters designed to "make them more wise." In these she chided her brothers for hunting, advised the whole family about matters of hygiene and diet, and exhorted them to "love God very much always, who supplies us with such beautiful flowers & many other things in the world." When the noted reformer Eliza Farnham resigned her job as the matron at Perkins, setting off to California on a humanitarian mission, Laura gave her these words of parting advice: "I hope you will be very happy and useful and loving and kind always; also that you will have reverence and respect for all human beings." Howe noted that Laura often gave such admonitions to her friends, oblivious to the fact that they were usually "in every way her superiors in mind."[23]

While Laura demanded order in her own life and in others', she was never a dour scold. Her puritanical conscience was balanced by a remarkable, and to some even disconcerting, "disposition to mirthfulness." Howe thought there were "few persons so light-hearted, so cheery, so full of mirth, so ready at any moment to laugh at a joke, or join in a game of romps, as Laura Bridgman."[24] In the early years of her education, Laura struggled to understand imaginative language. By her teens, she learned to take great delight in word play, amusing herself by making exaggerated comparisons or satirizing the words of others. "I have had many very pleasant and comical thoughts today," Laura recorded in her journal. Christmas was approaching, and she had spent the afternoon imagining an extravagant party that she might throw for "one hundred of my friends." After providing her guests with an elaborate feast, she dreamed of capping the evening off by amusing them all "very heartily by my most comical remarks." With so many guests and so few beds, Laura daydreamed that her friends would spend an uncomfortable night sleeping in her "bathing closet" and on her shelves. "I am enjoying this castle in the air very much," she concluded.[25]

On some occasions, Laura used her sense of humor to gain some perspective on her own situation. Stumbling over an unanticipated piece of furniture, she would laugh and call herself "very blind." When a rat stole an apple from her room, she used the incident to satirize the intense moral scrutiny which was a way of life at Perkins. "I think that the rat ought to be imprisoned," she joked to herself in her journal. "He ought to have a conscience on purpose to reprove himself very much. I must ask W. to please teach him about doing right & wrong & [being] honest in the night. He would love her very much for her good influence."[26]

Howe often remarked on Laura's cheerful disposition and considered it an invaluable compensation to one who had so many reasons to feel sad and alienated by her predicament. But he found Laura's cheerfulness a mixed blessing. She was well on her way to becoming a grown woman, yet he fretted that her character remained childish. Her love of "romps" and silly jokes betrayed a failure to mature, to become more reflective and sober. Many who knew Laura shared this opinion.

In part because of Laura's apparent immaturity, Howe remained convinced that she was still not intellectually prepared to understand religious ideas. Though she was now in her mid-teens, he felt that her language skills and her intellectual powers still lagged far behind, making her unable to decipher the deeper meanings of biblical metaphor. However, in the aftermath of his controversy with the orthodox over his ruined experiment, Howe felt pressured to begin the child's religious training. Anxious not to alienate "Laura's friends," those people whose good will and donations were so crucial to the school, he assured his readers that they had no cause to be "alarmed" about Laura's spiritual destiny. He would soon begin her religious training and planned to teach this beloved child a broad-minded and "charitable" faith. "It will be charity and good-will to men,—love and obedience to God. I shall explain to her the Bible as I understand it; I shall try to make her believe, as I do, that it contains a revelation of God's attributes, and that it points out to us all the way to happiness through the path of duty."[27]

In public, Howe assumed an air of confidence about his plans for Laura's religious education. Privately, he was less sure, feeling intimidated by the task before him. This, he believed, was the critical final stage of Laura's education; all that had come before was in preparation for the development of the religious sentiments, the noblest and most important dimension of human character. Howe had once dreamed that these would emerge spontaneously, a manifestation of Laura's maturing mind that would provide scientific insight into the nature of the soul. Now he had to console himself with a more limited demonstration of the value of a liberal approach to religious education. On the heels of his clash with the orthodox, he knew that many were still watching him carefully. Before embarking on this new course of instruction, he first sought the advice of some of his trusted allies in reform.

George Combe, not surprisingly, told Howe that the best religious training he could give Laura would be an introduction to phrenology. A knowledge of "the organs and their functions, with their uses & abuses" would provide her with an unshakable foundation on which to build her faith. But he acknowledged that using this curriculum would expose Howe to more public criticism from orthodox Christians. In light of this, Combe could only defer to Howe's greater experience in the matter. "The religious instruction is a great puzzle for you to work out."[28]

Maria Edgeworth, the Irish author and reformer, also deferred to Howe's better judgment but offered a few suggestions. She warned him that young women Laura's age experience a profound change, their minds and their "sensations" transformed by new powers of imagination. In a normal child, this "fancy" was a good thing, often inspiring young women to write poetry and pursue other "inventions of Genius." But, since Laura suffered from a "half-informed imperfectly organized mind," Edgeworth expected that the fruits of her imagination were likely to be "grotesque, disproportioned, monstrous and perhaps terrific." The solution, she suggested, was to keep Laura's imagination in check by keeping her busy with academic study. Edgeworth also advised Howe not to confuse the child with explanations of "the nature of original sin and of atonement and justification by faith, etc. etc." She agreed with him that such matters were beyond the child's intellectual reach and that a reasonable God could not have made a belief in them "necessary to her salvation." She suggested that Howe should concentrate instead on teaching Laura God's moral commandments, keeping these lessons "as simple, as clear, as hopeful and as firm as possible."[29]

Like Howe's other advisers, the English writer Harriet Martineau prefaced her remarks with a disclaimer: telling him how to teach Laura, she suggested, was like giving Shakespeare a lesson in drama. But Martineau felt that, because she also suffered from sensory handicaps, she might be able to provide Howe with some useful insight into Laura's future. Martineau was severely deaf and also lacked a sense of taste. Writing confidentially, she told Howe that these handicaps had rendered life "very oppressive," often leading her to contemplate suicide. While Laura enjoyed life "very intensely" for the time being, Martineau was convinced that "this is owing to the very small development of her intellectual part." As she grew older, Martineau predicted, she would grow more aware of her condition, and the realization would likely drive her first to despair and then to an early grave.

Martineau urged Howe to begin Laura's religious training right away, giving the child spiritual strength and comfort as an antidote to her impending wretchedness. Like Combe and Edgeworth, she felt Laura should be taught a religion of "pure gladness," unmarred by any mention of "divine wrath" and "the relentless and unintelligible conditions of salvation." Laura should be told that she was a cherished member of God's "human family," an insight which Martineau felt would console the child once she realized that she would never be married and have a family of her own. Once Laura learned to think of herself as a member of the vast family of Humanity, Martineau urged Howe to explain to her that a truly religious life consists of "spiritual service" to others. If Laura could learn to care for others, Martineau explained, she might be rescued from the dangerous spiritual consequences of her sensory isolation and receive some compensation for the fact that she would never marry.[30]

These letters from across the Atlantic confirmed what Howe already believed and must have provided him with a vote of confidence as he began Laura's first, long-awaited lessons in religion. As might be expected, he began Laura's instruction by resuming her lessons in natural theology. He had once hoped that, as she came to understand the laws of nature, she would infer the existence of a Creator on her own. He remained convinced that she had been well on her way to this realization when his experiment had been disrupted by orthodox meddlers. But now Howe decided that he should make the lessons of natural theology more explicit, pointing out to Laura the many ways that nature proved the existence of a wise and benevolent God. Laura was appropriately impressed. Returning to Wight after one of these lessons, she exclaimed, "How industrious God is!"

While Howe emphasized the book of nature, he also introduced Laura to the Bible, concentrating on the New Testament, particularly the moral teachings of Jesus. Just as his advisers had suggested, he kept these lessons simple, optimistic, and Unitarian. Avoiding all mention of the orthodox

10. Laura's autograph was a coveted keepsake for Perkins visitors. Once Howe began to teach her about Christianity, she often added a spiritual sentiment to go along with her signature. (Courtesy of Dartmouth College Library)

doctrine of Christ's atonement, he explained to her that Jesus was a perfect man who was sent by God to show all human beings how to be as good as possible. Laura was deeply impressed by Christ's moral example and embraced the idea of his perfection. When Wight told her the story of Satan's temptation of Jesus in the wilderness, she exclaimed, "Christ was never tempted to do wrong! It is not true, I cannot credit it."[31]

Howe assigned Wight the job of introducing Laura to the Old Testament, a daunting task for a liberal Christian. No less than Howe, Wight had serious qualms about Jehovah's character. "Yesterday commenced teaching Laura a Bible History," she recorded in her journal. "It will be exceedingly difficult to give her an idea of the History recorded in the Old Testament without confusing all her ideas of right & wrong, justice & humanity." Laura was delighted to at last be learning the sacred secrets of religion. In her letters and conversations, she referred time and again to these lessons, turning over in her mind this exciting new information about God.[32]

But Laura's religious training had hardly begun when it had to be suspended for almost a year. In the first months of 1846 her health began to fail. Howe reported that "her appetite has become impaired, she has lost some flesh, and has grown feeble." The first symptoms of illness were bouts of intense "nervousness," a chronic problem for Laura that seemed to grow worse. Howe and Wight concluded that her health was being impaired by the great "excitement" she was feeling about religion. While Laura obviously relished her lessons, Howe decided that her struggle to overcome her linguistic handicap and to understand abstract ideas about God had caused her to expend an "excess" of mental energy. "Excess in anything is injurious," he explained as he canceled her classes and sent her on a trip to Philadelphia, hoping that a change of location would distract her from her religious obsession and revive her health. When she continued to grow more feeble, Howe next sent her home to Hanover, thinking that there might be medicinal qualities in "her native air." Still Laura's health deteriorated, bringing her to what Howe called "a fearful crisis." Invoking a metaphor of spiritualized illness common in the nineteenth century, he told his readers that, "as she grew thinner and paler and weaker, she appeared to be laying aside the garments of the flesh, and her spirit shone out brighter through its transparent veil."[33]

In fall 1846, as Laura neared her seventeenth birthday, her health revived. Howe attributed her recovery to a strict regimen of sea bathing and horseback riding, aided by Laura's strong constitution. Howe was in the midst of a failed campaign for Congress that year. Perhaps for that reason,

Wight took over full control of Laura's religious education when her lessons resumed. Laura's journals from this time are studded with short summaries of the gospel texts: "My dear teacher Wight read to me from the Bible about the sermon of Christ to the people about being anxious about food & the creatures & the flowers & many other things. We are of much more value than the flowers but they are dressed more beautifully than we are." Though Laura often struggled to make sense of these lessons, she was always "exceedingly interested" in them.[34]

Laura was particularly eager to learn more about Jesus, announcing, "I love to think of him so very much better than anything else." Howe and Wight gave Laura a liberal explanation of Jesus' mission, making no mention of the orthodox doctrines of Christ's atonement for sins and his physical resurrection from the dead. Laura summarized these lessons succinctly: Jesus, she had been told, was "very religious to command the people to do right, & to do so much good to all." Laura spent long hours meditating on Christ's "good example," and began to direct her prayers to him, seeking his help as she struggled to control her small sins of impatience and anger. Many times she reported to Wight that she had been troubled by "bad feelings" but had overcome them through prayer. "I thought quickly about Jesus Christ, how good he was, and then my good feelings came again."[35]

In addition to learning Bible stories, Laura constantly probed her teacher for answers to the religious mysteries that had puzzled her for years, questions about the nature of death, the afterlife, and God's judgment. Several times a day she asked Wight about heaven. How large is heaven? she wondered. How could people know that God would invite them there? When would she become good enough to go to heaven? The orthodox Christians who had visited her while Howe was away had given her a great deal of information about this sacred refuge. Now Laura wanted Wight to confirm what she had heard: "Do you know about it?" she asked.[36]

As a Unitarian, Wight was as uncomfortable with these questions as Howe had been and struggled each time to give Laura a liberal understanding of God's judgment and the afterlife. She told Laura that she did not know, and could not know, very much about a Heaven elsewhere, but that she trusted that "God was kind and good to every one." God, she signed into Laura's eager hand, wanted everyone to be good; if people obeyed His commands then they would be happy, not just after they died but right away, here on earth. "If we were good we should be happy anywhere," Wight explained. In spite of repeated efforts to replace Laura's orthodox ideas about an afterlife in heaven with this more reasonable and liberal ideal of earthly happiness, Wight was dismayed to find that Laura "clings to this idea of a place of habitation for happy spirits."[37]

Laura struggled to reconcile the promise of heaven offered by the orthodox—a large and beautiful place where the truly good would be protected by a loving God—with the vision of an earthly quest for personal perfection offered by Howe and Wight. During one such conversation, Laura resolved the issue, "with great apparent satisfaction," by announcing that "[God] is our *Father.*" She soon began to use this affectionate and personal term as a matter of course. Any delicate or beautiful thing would put her in mind of "our kind Father in heaven."[38]

While Wight was providing Laura with most of her religious instruction, Howe monitored his student's progress by reading Wight's daily journal and by visiting with Laura any day that he was at Perkins. As Wight struggled to guide Laura toward a liberal understanding of God, Howe grew increasingly dissatisfied with the results. Though he left no record of his specific complaints, some of his concerns may be inferred from the general direction of Laura's thinking. Her decision to personalize God as a loving "Father" must have sounded, in Howe's ears, too much like evangelical sentimentalism. Howe thought of God not as a father but as a sublime and magnificent Creator who spoke to humankind through the laws of nature. He could not have recognized the more intimate and personal deity that Laura described when she wrote, "I feel in my own heart that [God] is coming to see me from heaven, when I am thinking so earnestly of him."[39]

Howe probably found Laura's adoration of Jesus disturbing for the same reason. While he wanted Laura to respect Jesus as a great moral teacher, he must have found her fervent prayers to him unsettling. Increasingly, she referred to Jesus as God's "only beloved son," deifying him in a manner that a liberal Unitarian like Howe would have found problematic.[40]

Howe also must have been frustrated by Laura's obsession with heaven. As often as Wight tried to direct the child's attention away from the topic of death and God's judgment, Laura always returned to these matters. "It is very solemn to think soberly about Death & how very good we ought to be," she insisted, ignoring all of Wight's efforts to set these concerns to rest.[41]

Howe's concern about Laura's religious development grew until, in May 1847, he decided to take full control of her theological training once again. Like Swift before her, Wight was told not to speak with Laura about religious matters and to refer all such questions to him. Howe started Laura on a new course of daily instruction, determined to guide her to a liberal faith. Although no detailed record of these lessons has survived, the general tone of them may be deduced from Laura's comment as she returned from her first class. Laura informed Wight, "Doctor says I must remember when I read the Bible that there are many mistakes in it."[42]

Howe maintained his monopoly on Laura's religious instruction for the next two months. Like Mary Swift before her, Sarah Wight was now forced to ignore or evade Laura's stream of religious questions, "instead of talking freely and naturally as formerly with her." While Laura was not informed of the change, she sensed it immediately and was troubled. Wight noticed that her student grew increasingly nervous and attributed this "uncomfortable state of mind" to the barrier of silence that Howe had placed between the two women. In a journal entry that Howe was certain to read, Wight wrote, "I am sure that Dr. Howe can teach her infinitely better than I can, yet important as his instructions may be to her, they cannot take the place of the words that she craves daily and hourly from a friend who is constantly with her."[43]

Howe must have read Wight's comment and agreed that his plan was doing more harm than good. The next day he lifted the ban and turned responsibility for Laura's religious education back to Wight, telling her to "answer her questions upon all subjects, and not try to avoid conversing with her on any."[44]

For the next two years Howe remained silent about Laura's education. In his annual reports for 1847 and 1848 he made no mention of his most famous pupil, the first time he had done so since she had arrived at Perkins a decade before. Many who read Howe's reports hoping to follow the latest chapter in Laura's life were disappointed. One reviewer spoke for many of Howe's readers when he noted, "The public will miss the usual representations of Laura Bridgman's case—not a word is said of her."[45]

Howe justified his silence by suggesting that there was little new to report. Laura was making steady progress, but her education was simply moving along the same lines that he had already discussed in earlier reports. "Besides," he wrote, perhaps nostalgically, "the great point of interest was the beginning of the process."[46]

Howe's decision to discontinue his yearly updates on Laura's life may also be explained by the fact that he was distracted by a new slate of reform projects. In the last two years of the 1840s, he spent much of his time successfully rallying public support for a new educational reform, the creation of a school for the mentally handicapped. In addition, the conclusion of the Mexican War inspired him, and many other New England reformers, to take a more active role in the abolitionist cause. In these years, Howe presided over the Boston Vigilance Committee, created to rouse public concern for the fate of fugitive slaves caught in Boston, and he helped Horace Mann make a successful bid for Congress.[47]

In the midst of these crusades, Howe was also distracted by health problems, probably due to a relapse of the malaria that he had contracted during his service in the Greek Revolution. Some of his friends blamed his illness on an excess expenditure of humanitarian energy. Urging Howe to take a vacation from his labors, a friend advised, "Philanthropy is well enough for a man with strong nerves & strong stomach, but it is a decided nuisance to a man who does not eat or sleep. It was never intended that we should perpetually live in a church yard, that we might be reminded of our mortality or that we should forever embitter our existence by ransacking creation for something to make us miserable." Howe eventually took this advice, seeking a hydropathic cure at a water spa.[48]

Howe's cure and his new crusades took him away from Perkins for months at a time in 1848 and 1849. Yet in spite of all of these distractions, he continued to monitor Laura's progress. Whenever he was at Perkins, he paid her brief daily visits and reviewed the journals that she and Wight were keeping. Both filled him with a mounting sense of frustration. As he prepared his annual report at the end of 1849, he decided at last to voice his concerns.

Many of those who had seen Laura in the past two years, Howe wrote, were delighted to find that she was now openly and eagerly discussing religion. "This may satisfy her friends and the public," he complained, "but it does not satisfy me." He wanted his readers to know that "her present beliefs and notions are not mine." Far from being impressed by Laura's new expressions of piety, Howe considered her constant talk about "God, the Saviour, salvation &c" to be empty chatter. He remained convinced that she was only mimicking clichés she could not possibly understand.[49]

Five years after his experiment had been disrupted, Howe attempted for the last time to justify his controversial investigation into Laura's religious nature. In the first exciting years of her education, he reminisced, "it was a touching and beautiful sight to see this young soul, that had lain so long in utter darkness and stillness, as soon as the obstacles were cleared from its path, begin to move forward and upward, to seek and to own its Creator, God!" He had planned to watch her ideas about God ripen slowly, as the culmination of her intellectual and emotional development. But "circumstances" had forced him to "confide her care to others" who had allowed the natural growth of the child's soul to be stunted by premature exposure to "sectarian shibboleths."[50]

Since then, Howe lamented, he had tried in vain to counteract the damage that had been done but was forced to watch Laura gradually adopt her society's conventional notions about God. He believed that Laura had not become orthodox; her faith, though vague and ill formed, was still liberal. Yet he cringed to find her using the "pestilent catchwords" of evangelical Christianity. Instead of developing her own natural and unbiased understanding of her Creator, she now seemed sidetracked into the worship of empty abstractions. Others were delighted to hear Laura's fervent conversations about God, but Howe thought she was only clinging to a faith that would "cheat the religious tendencies and aspirations of the soul with semblance rather than substance, and satisfy its longings to realize an ideal, which ought not to be satisfied, but be ever receding and rising as we make greater effort to bring ourselves up to it."[51]

If there is a tragic dimension to Howe's work with Laura Bridgman, it lies in his inability to accept and respect her unique and heartfelt religious experience, her yearnings for a personal God that would offer her earthly protection and heavenly salvation. Howe's strength as a reformer lay in his absolute commitment to the principles of liberal Christianity and phrenological science, a faith that gave him the single-minded confidence to persevere in his pioneering work with the deaf and blind and mentally handicapped. His was indeed a faith that inspired a life of moral activism, filling him with a restless longing to "realize an ideal."

However, once Laura's linguistic isolation was overcome and her personality began to emerge, Howe's strength of conviction became a handicap. Thoroughly convinced by his own theories and entranced by his vision of a pure and spotless humanity, he was unable to accept—perhaps even to see—Laura Bridgman as the individual that she was. Feeling isolated and vulnerable, Laura sought the protection of a heavenly "father," one who would take a personal interest in her safety, one who could forgive her for the small sins that she struggled so hard to conquer, one who would relieve her of her constant dread of isolation.

At times Laura expressed these spiritual yearnings with touching originality. "I dreamed I wrote a letter to God," she told Wight one morning, "and tried very hard to get some one to carry it." Other times she drew on the language of evangelical Christianity, which provided ample metaphors to express her search for a personal and forgiving God. In either case, her desire to know God, to understand death and her place in the universe, seemed to come from deep within. Inevitably, these spiritual yearnings were often expressed in a very personal and original way, shaped by her experiences as a deaf and blind person. Yet Howe was convinced that the child was only mimicking evangelical platitudes that she had picked up from chats with "careless" acquaintances or insidious proselytizers. He had hoped to find in Laura strong, natural religious feelings and intuitions. He found them; yet when they did not match his own convictions, he dismissed them with contempt.[52]

In the early years of his experiment, believing that Laura's soul and mind were innately pure and uniquely vulnerable to his influence, Howe had dreamed of developing her into an angel incarnate. She would be his showcase, proving what could be accomplished when enlightened educational practices were brought to bear on the pure and healthy impulses of human nature. In the first six years of her education, Howe and many others had transformed her into a symbol of human possibility. As late as 1846, Wight shared Howe's dream that they might turn Laura into "an almost perfect character."[53]

However, as Laura's adult personality started to emerge in the mid-1840s, Howe could no longer ignore what he considered to be her flaws and eccentricities. Her accomplishments against incredible adversity were remarkable, to be sure, but her character remained quite recognizably human. As his great experiment in education came to a close, Howe found much to admire in Laura but also much to regret. She was happy but also strangely childish. She was industrious and conscientious but also pedantic and naive, more preachy than profound. Though almost an adult, she still suffered occasional paroxysms of rage. And in spite of all he had done to avoid it, he felt that her understanding of God amounted to little more than a string of conventional pieties. For a decade Howe had been inspired by a vision of who Laura *could* become, and now this ideal was contradicted by who she actually was. Surveying the results of his thirteen-year experiment, Howe conceded that "my hopes of Laura have, in some respects been disappointed, but that is clearly because they were unreasonable."[54]

Chapter 10

A New Theory
of Human Nature

In the late 1840s, as Laura's personality developed in directions Howe had neither anticipated nor encouraged, he concluded that he must have overlooked "some important considerations" which had doomed his experiment from the start. When Laura first overcame her sensory handicaps, he had hailed this as proof that the mind is superior to the body. He had proceeded with her education guided by the same assumption—that the child's deafness and blindness had not significantly altered her mental and moral faculties. Sensory handicaps, he thought then, posed only a physical barrier to communication. Once this obstacle was overcome, he expected to find her to be, in all other respects, "normal."

But a decade after Laura's arrival at Perkins, Howe decided that her physical handicaps did have mental and moral consequences. Laura's mind and soul, he now believed, had been fundamentally damaged when she lost the use of her eyes and ears. For ten years he had used her case to prove the innate reliability of the mental faculties and the power of the soul over the body. But now his thinking took a new turn toward biological determinism. After years of portraying Laura as the prototype of pure human nature, he announced that she was actually the victim of "a deranged constitution."

Howe's understanding of human nature was changing. Yet his new formulation of the relationship of the mind and body was not as radical a departure from his original premises as might appear. The idea that the mind and body are intertwined had always been a central tenet of phrenology. Because phrenologists located the mental, moral, and spiritual faculties in the material lobes of the brain, they claimed that the qualities of each individual's mind and soul are determined by the health of the body. For this very reason, phrenologists spent much of their time defending themselves against the charge that they were atheistic materialists who denied the existence of an immortal soul.

In his public lectures on phrenology, Howe had always rejected the charge of materialism with contempt but never engaged the issue in a serious way. Likewise, in the early years of his work with Laura Bridgman, he applied many of the ideas of phrenology but used them to arrive at conclusions that contradicted the materialistic implications of the new science. Phrenology, he felt, provided a practical guide to education, one that was more scientific than any other. But haggling over the philosophical implications of its doctrines, he believed, was a waste of time, a distraction from the more important job of applying its insights to the actual improvement of social life.

While other phrenologists shared Howe's belief that the science provided a new foundation for social reform, some were more cautious than he about the prospect for rapid individual improvement. A fundamental axiom of the new science was the idea that mental and moral progress had to be based on physical improvement, marked by actual changes in the size and shape of the brain. Those phrenologists who allowed their hopes to be constrained by observable evidence tended to agree that these changes, measured in the skull, came slowly at best. Through a proper routine of physical and mental exercise, they believed, any individual could expand and invigorate the lobes of his or her brain and reap the mental or moral benefits—but only in small measure. Observation had shown that the body imposed strict biological limits on these powers of self-improvement. To a large extent each person was destined to live within the confines of the constitution acquired at birth.

Because individual progress was slow, these more cautious proponents of phrenology tended to take the long view, expecting significant improvement only over the course of many generations. In this era before the introduction of Mendel's theory of genetics, they shared the common scientific view that offspring inherit whatever physical or behavioral characteristics their parents acquired over the course of their lifetimes. From this premise they reasoned that, if society could learn to obey the laws of health, each small improvement in health made by individuals would serve as a legacy to future generations. If society's institutions were reformed so that all lived according to the light of phrenological laws, then gradually, over the course of many generations, physical and moral ailments could be entirely eliminated.[1]

At the start of his work as an educator, Howe rejected the materialistic implications of phrenology and the limits it imposed on progress, even as he embraced all other aspects of the new science. Like many other American liberals in the early 1830s, he was convinced that the application of science, particularly in the field of education, was about to produce profound and rapid improvements in society. "It is too much the fashion to ridicule the notion of the perfectibility of man," he lectured his fellow phrenologists in 1835. "I cannot conceive that God has implanted in the breast of man those longings after improvement and perfection, those aspirations after early purity, which do exist there, and at the same time, fixed a barrier, beyond which he cannot go, long he never so much to go . . . I know the difficulties are great, but I do not believe they are insuperable."[2]

Speaking this way at the start of his career, Howe had arrived at this hopeful conclusion not on the basis of experimental evidence or practical experience. Rather, he was inspired by a set of political and religious ideals that were shared by many Americans in the Jacksonian period, ideals that infused the culture with a faith in progress and even the anticipation of a democratic millennium. In trying to account for this great mood of optimism felt by many 1830s reformers, historians identify several mutually reinforcing strands of thought that converged at this time. The Enlightenment tradition, filtering down to the middle classes through popular education and the press, helped give antebellum Americans a faith in the possibility of progress through science and technology. The legacy of the American Revolution and the triumph of Jacksonian democracy convinced many that America was destined to become a utopia of the common man. And the tradition of militant Protestantism, reinvigorated by the Second Great Awakening, added to this mix the ancient dream of realizing the biblical prophecy of a future millennium, a thousand-year reign of peace and good will.

Howe's decision to dedicate himself to a career of reform had been inspired, to varying degrees, by all three of these strands of thought. Buoyed by the optimism that was so pervasive throughout his society, he had embarked on his work at Perkins with very high hopes for the blind, expecting not only to improve their difficult lot in life but to vault them into a place of full economic, social, and political equality within a few years. At Perkins, he predicted in his earliest public reports, the ancient curse of blindness was about to be conquered by a powerful new synthesis of Christian benevolence, democratic respect for the individual, and Enlightenment science. Fully developed in body, mind, and soul by a common school education, his students would be transformed from "mere objects of pity" into self-sufficient citizens of the republic.

By the end of his first decade at Perkins, this noble ideal had been dashed on the rocks of experience. The first graduating class of blind scholars, many of them hand-picked for their intelligence and enthusiasm, had more than met his expectations. One young man went on to study mathematics at Harvard, and several male students took jobs, arranged by

Howe, as teachers or directors at some of the new schools for the blind that were being created around the country. But, as the school expanded to serve a much larger number of students, Howe found himself working with children who had less intellectual potential and ambition. For many of them, blindness was only one of several serious liabilities. Some had behavioral problems, others also had mental handicaps, while others suffered from various physical illnesses often related to their blindness.[3]

Trusting in the redemptive power of the common school curriculum, Howe continued to teach all of his students as many of the "common branches of instruction" as they could handle. He also continued to give every student some musical training. Experience soon taught him that very few had talent enough to ever earn a living as musicians, but he decided that a musical education was a good way to "elevate the sentiments and cultivate the moral nature" of the blind.[4]

For the majority of students who did not show a strong aptitude for scholarship or music, the school provided extra training in manual labor, specifically in the crafts of mattress and upholstery sewing and mat-making. The goal, Howe explained, was to prepare these children for "that kind of mechanical labor which must in almost every case be their business and their means of support in after life." Academic and musical training would round out the moral and intellectual nature of the blind, making them enlightened citizens; training in manual skills would elevate them from paupers into self-reliant mechanics and artisans.[5]

From the start, however, graduates from Perkins had trouble earning a living with these skills. Howe watched many of his students leave the school proud and optimistic, only to become humiliated and defeated. By the late 1830s, he received dozens of letters each year from his former students, many pleading for permission to return to the institution. "When I left you requested me to inform you of the result of my efforts here & said that should they prove unsuccessful you would then decide about employing me in institution," one male graduate wrote to Howe. "I earnestly request that I may be so employed otherwise I know not what will become of me—I shall have no alternative but to go to the poor house the thoughts of which is very distressing to me." A female graduate beseeched Howe: "I thought in my happy days when I was a pupil at the Institution that I should be able to help myself through the world. But now as I have been cut off from it I must be entirely dependent on my poor parents for in truth they are poor . . . Dear sir you were a friend to me before and I hope you will be a friend to me now."[6]

Confronted by these desperate letters from his former students, Howe

11. Laura was a diligent worker and an accomplished seamstress. Deeply interested in women's fashions, she made most of her own clothes. Laura showed "good taste," Mary Swift noted, "by choosing for herself both material and style which are appropriate." *(Courtesy of Perkins School for the Blind, Watertown, Massachusetts)*

was forced to reevaluate the purpose of his institution. He still believed that the education he provided was making these blind children more skilled, confident, and self-reliant. But he gradually realized that other social forces beyond his control were undermining his efforts to help the blind become economically independent. Eastern Massachusetts was undergoing an industrial revolution in the 1840s. In many industries, the slow-paced and simple workshop of the artisan was being replaced by the frenzied production of the factory. The simple manual skills that students learned at Perkins were now being done by machines, in a setting that was inhospitable and even dangerous to the blind. If any job was "simple enough for the blind to do," Howe had discovered, "a man of wood and iron, who wants neither food nor wages, has been made expressly to perform it." And those machines were designed to be operated by "men with all their senses." There was no place for a blind man in the modern factory, with its whirring iron shuttles and lathes and its bustling workers. In short, while philanthropists like Howe had done much to prepare the blind to become productive members of their society, industrialization had proven an even more potent force that fast outstripped any gains made by education.[7]

By 1840 Howe spent a growing amount of his time at Perkins trying to help his graduates—writing to prospective employers, consoling and encouraging his students when their prospects looked dim, and often arranging for them to return to the school to work. Over the course of the next decade, he adapted his institution to meet their needs and prospects as he now understood them. The cornerstone of his new approach was the creation of a permanent, publicly subsidized "Work Department" to employ adult blind workers. By 1845 this workshop employed twenty blind men and seven blind women, who sewed mattresses, cushions, and mats that were sold at a school-owned store. Proceeds from these sales paid for raw materials and for a shop supervisor and provided each worker with a modest wage. The only subsidy provided by the school was free board. Howe looked forward to the day when even this small measure of public charity could be eliminated. He felt that, once the workers became more practiced at their crafts and the public learned to accept the idea that the blind could produce top-quality goods at fair market prices, then his former students could enjoy "the unmitigated satisfaction of supporting themselves entirely." But even under the present arrangement Howe felt that each worker could take pride in the fact that they were not charity cases but were earning a "well deserved" income. If these blind men and women could not become entirely self-reliant, he felt that they should at least be given the chance to become as independent as possible.[8]

Historians have observed that many antebellum reformers began with high expectations in the 1830s, only to become disillusioned by the middle of the century when experience taught them that human nature was not as perfectible as they had hoped. Howe's work as an educator of the blind fits this pattern. But his workshop idea also shows that, in his case at least, disillusionment did not produce discouragement. He abandoned his ideals without abandoning the blind. The extravagant hopes of the 1830s gave way in the mid-1840s to goals that were more limited but also more attainable. The changes that Howe implemented at Perkins in the middle decades of the century suggest an evolutionary link from the romantic moral perfectionism of the 1830s reformers to the pragmatic solutions offered by the social scientists and social workers of the late nineteenth century.[9]

Historians have also noted that antebellum reformers often explained dependence as a personal moral problem, produced by laziness, intemperance, and other sins rather than by impersonal economic and social forces. Again anticipating later social welfare thought, Howe generally believed that his students returned to Perkins not because they lacked character and motivation but because they confronted a changing economy that had little use for their skills. In this, the blind became Howe's teachers, eloquently describing for him the disadvantages faced by handicapped laborers in an industrial economy. When Howe wrote to one of his graduates, advising her that she was selling her hand-sewn articles too cheaply, the woman replied, "I think so too, but there is so much competition in every thing I have ever found it useless for people the blind especially to expect a fair compensation for their labor."[10]

Howe was also learning that, contrary to his hopes, the barriers of social prejudice against the blind did not fall easily. While he had successfully manipulated the public's sympathies when raising funds for his school, those same feelings of pity sometimes created a barrier that kept the blind out of public view. The starkest example came when a local church hired the Perkins choir to sing on a regular basis, then thought better of the decision because of "the unpleasant feelings arising on the minds of many, on acct. of the knowledge of their unfortunate situation." Rather than "subject any of the Society to unpleasant emotions" caused by looking at blind children, the church decided instead to "dispense with their services."[11]

Although Howe realized that the blind struggled against disadvantages far beyond their control, he never completely broke with his society's prevailing view that social problems were caused by a failure of individual initiative and morality. At the outset of his work, he had claimed that the blind were intellectually and morally no different from sighted people and were distinguished only by the accidental disadvantage of their handicap. But in the mid-1840s, during the same years that he was rethinking his conclusions about Laura Bridgman, he decided that the blind *were* different, that their sensory deprivation had serious physical, intellectual, and moral consequences.

Because movement is difficult for blind people, he concluded, most were lazy. Experience had taught him that they could not resist "the temptation of the lolling-chair." Their lack of exercise, he added, made them less physically attractive. They often had poor posture, underdeveloped muscles, and nervous tics. "If a person should compare the cadets at a good military academy with the boys who have just entered a school for the blind," Howe wrote, "he would almost conclude that they were two distinct races of being." Based on crude statistics that he had gathered from blind schools around the country, Howe concluded that this physical inferiority made the blind more vulnerable to disease and early death.[12]

Struggling to understand the blind's physical deficiencies and their economic failures, Howe reconsidered his ideas about the link between body and mind. He had always believed that a healthy body was an important foundation for a strong mind, but now he derived a new conclusion from this principle. In his 1847 report, he announced that experience forced him to admit that the physical limitations of the blind also seemed to cause their mental inferiority. "The brain and nervous system are generally of the same character as the rest of the bodily organization," he explained, "and the consequence is, not only a want of that spontaneous activity which causes what is usually called natural quickness and intelligence, but also a want of mental power." Because the blind had weak bodies, they usually suffered from a "listless and profitless mood of mind."[13]

To this physiological explanation for the mental inferiority of the blind Howe added an epistemological one. Their intellectual development was retarded, he suggested, because their minds lacked the crucial "stimulus" provided by sight. "Blindness . . . always and necessarily cuts off some of the means by which alone certain intellectual faculties are developed and some mental qualities are formed," he explained in 1848.[14]

By making this claim that the sensations provided by sight are an essential ingredient in mental development, Howe contradicted the epistemological principle he once thought he had proven in his experiment with Laura Bridgman. Laura, he had once claimed, refuted the doctrine of materialism by proving that the mind is active and whole, even when deprived of sight and sound. A decade later, with his experiment in disarray and the blind returning to his care, he arrived at a very different understanding of the relationship between mind and matter, sense impressions and thought.

Howe also decided that the mental deficiencies of the blind affected their moral nature. Giving his favorite argument from design a strange new twist, he suggested that the idea that the blind could be morally equal to the sighted was a slight on the Creator's skills as the architect of humanity: "To suppose there can be a full and harmonious development of character without sight is to suppose that God gave us that noble sense quite superfluously." The experience of sight, he now reasoned, was an essential stimulant to intellectual development and activated "several faculties in particular." One of these was the aesthetic sense. Since the blind could not appreciate light and color, Howe reasoned, their sense of beauty must be incompletely developed. Again reversing an opinion which had guided him to that point, Howe suggested that the religious nature of the blind was therefore stunted by their handicap, since "contemplation of the beauties and glories" of Creation was one of the most important sources of religious feeling.[15]

Studying the effect of blindness on his students, Howe concluded that not all of them suffered from these physical, mental, and moral shortcomings. He divided the blind into two categories—those blinded by chance circumstances and those for whom blindness was a manifestation of a deeper constitutional weakness. In the former group he included those who lost their sight because of an accident and some who were blinded as a result of "violent disease." These, he found, represented a cross-section of human potential. Among his pupils at Perkins, they were of average or above average intelligence and made rapid progress in their studies.[16]

But in Howe's experience, the second group was much larger, those whose blindness was not accidental but congenital, caused by a constitutional flaw inherited from their parents. These children either were born blind or were, in Howe's phrase, "born to become blind"—destined to lose their eyesight in early childhood due to an inherited predisposition to disease. Howe thought that congenital blindness could be passed from parent to child in two different ways. His simple statistical surveys had confirmed that, if one or more of the parents was blind, some or all of their children would also be blind, through the workings of a stark and unavoidable law of hereditary transmission. But Howe believed that, even if the parents' vision was intact, they could still pass the affliction to their children if they failed to respect the laws of health. While the parents' specific infractions were often hard to pinpoint, Howe thought that many cases of blindness could be attributed to paternal intemperance, sexual excess, intermarriage between family members, or the physical exhaustion brought on by the frantic pursuit of wealth.[17]

Throughout history, Christians had explained blindness as one of God's ways of punishing "sin." Since his first days at Perkins, Howe had attacked this idea as a dark superstition. Yet as he formulated his own theory about the cause of blindness, he simply naturalized the traditional explanation, dressing it up in the terminology of science. He replaced the idea that God blinded people because of their sin with the idea that blindness was caused by the violation of one of the Creator's natural laws of health. This attempt to provide a more scientific explanation for blindness, based on a naturalized moral law, had little effect on the specific content of that law. No less than the more traditional Christians, Howe cataloged a predictable list of the moral infractions that resulted in the punishments of blindness, deafness, insanity, and imbecility. Whether God's moral law was handed down to Moses or derived from the anatomical models of phrenology, the rules of right living remained the same.

But Howe's attempt to provide a scientific explanation for the causes of blindness and of the intellectual and moral frailties of the blind did lead him to articulate a view of human nature and social reform that was quite different from the optimistic ideas which had guided him through the first fifteen years of his work as a reformer. When he began to teach the blind, Howe had believed that human nature was essentially good, or at least neutral, and could be molded by a careful attention to environment. However, by the mid-1840s he concluded that education alone would not improve society but that it had to be combined with a new attention to the laws of heredity.

Howe developed his ideas about the laws of heredity in a series of public reports in the late 1840s, first on congenital blindness and then on the causes of "idiocy." These writings were widely disseminated, making him the nation's most influential proponent of hereditarian thought in the decade before Darwin published his *Origin of Species* (1859). Howe's enthusiasm for the subject was shared by a number of other reformers, including many phrenologists, mesmerists, the writers of popular health and marriage guides, and the utopian followers of John Humphrey Noyes. Each of these movements dreamed of harnessing the forces of heredity to serve the cause of social progress. Yet, like Howe, none of them abandoned their respect for the influence of the environment on human character and continued to look to education as a vital mechanism of social progress. Grappling with the nature of inheritance without a knowledge of Mendelian genetics, their ideas were fluid, merging the categories of "nature" and "nurture" that we now tend to keep distinct. All of these reformers shared Howe's belief that acquired characteristics are inherited. Children do not simply receive an immutable set of biologically determined traits from their parents but also inherit the accumulated effects of their vices and virtues.[18]

Following this line of thought, Howe concluded that many of the children at Perkins had inherited the affliction of blindness from parents who had violated God's natural law. "It will be seen that the wit of man cannot devise a way of escape from the penalty of a violated law of nature; that not a single debauch, not a single excess, not a single abuse of any animal propensity, ever was or ever can be committed without more or less evil consequences; that sins of this kind are not and cannot be forgiven." Parents who break these laws, Howe often suggested, were blinding their own children "as much as though they gouged their eyes out after they were born."[19]

Because Howe was a champion of liberal Christianity, one might expect him to be deeply troubled by the evident injustice of this arrangement. The laws of heredity that he described bore an ironic resemblance to Calvin's doctrine of original sin. In both cases, the burden of human sin was inherited, its punishments imposed on apparently innocent children from the moment of their birth.

Yet Howe insisted, to the contrary, that the hereditary transmission of blindness only proved God's "kindness and love." Far from locking humans into a rigid biological determinism, he felt that the laws of heredity affirmed human freedom and the possibility of social progress. The calamities of blindness, deafness, and disease, he maintained, were God's way of instructing human beings in the lessons of nature, showing them rules of right living which they were free to use to promote their own happiness. Howe did not accept the idea that God blinded people out of anger, seeking personal vengeance against sinners. But he did believe that God blinded people indirectly, through the secondary causes of His "stern and inexorable" laws. God sent "outward ailments" like blindness and deafness as "signs of inward infirmities." These handicaps were, in other words, physical chastisements meant to remind human beings of their moral failures.[20]

According to Howe's new theory, God instituted the law of heredity not to seek vengeance against the wicked but as a motivational tool to guide his wayward creatures back into compliance with the laws of health and morality. When men and women realized that the price for their sins would one day be exacted against their children, even "to the third and fourth generation," this would serve as a powerful incentive for them to tame their immoral impulses. If only their own safety was involved, people might be willing to risk God's wrath in order to satisfy their "sensual pleasures,"

Howe explained. "But there will appear in the far-off and shadowy future the beseeching forms of little children,—some halt, or lame, or blind, or deformed, or decrepit,—crying, in speechless accents, 'Forbear, for our sakes; for the arrows that turn aside from you are rankling in our flesh.'"[21]

As scientists discovered these natural laws and promoted them through education, Howe looked forward to the day when blindness, deafness, and other handicaps could be eliminated. Just as God had always intended, human beings would follow His laws upward to new heights of "health and vigor," culminating in the perfection of human nature.

Although Howe never claimed that his students were personally responsible for their condition, his hereditarian ideas had the effect of turning blindness into a mark of moral failure. "The child is blind that the sin may be avoided," he claimed, "and no other blind children be begotten." In the early 1830s he had rejected the popular notion that the blind were fundamentally different from the sighted. He had defined blindness as a superficial and accidental trait and called for the seeing members of society to drop their prejudices and to adapt their institutions in order to accommodate the blind as equals. Now he confessed that he had been too optimistic and that "the inequality between [the blind] and other persons is greater, even, than at first appears." Blindness, he suggested, was a symptom of social immorality, an unnecessary evil to be eliminated.[22]

While Howe's hereditarian explanations for blindness seemed to change the moral status and social expectations of the blind, his commitment to their education and welfare never wavered. He had once argued that the blind were due a full education because they were equal to the sighted; now he claimed that their inferiority made them even more deserving of help and compassion. Grouping the blind and deaf with the insane, the criminal, and the dependent, Howe looked forward to the day when all of "those unfortunates" would no longer "encumber the march of humanity." But until the distant day when none suffered from these maladies, he urged, "Let none of them be lost; let none of them be uncared for; but whenever the signal is given of a man in distress—no matter how deformed, how vicious, how loathsome, even, he may be; let it be regarded as a call to help a brother." In short, although Howe's conception of human nature had changed, his commitment to humanitarianism remained.[23]

Howe was revising his ideas about the cause of blindness and the capabilities of the blind at the same time that he was reevaluating his conclusions about the meaning of his experiment with Laura Bridgman. His disappointment with the person she had become and the disillusionment he felt about the talents and prospects of his other blind students were mutually reinforcing. In both cases, he concluded that his students had not fulfilled his expectations because he had not accounted for the effect that their handicaps would have on their minds and souls. Though he had once claimed that Laura Bridgman's pure and reliable mental faculties had triumphed over her physical limitations, he now confessed that "I do not believe that Laura Bridgman is so happily organized as many other children."[24]

Again Howe used Laura's case as a stage from which to promote his latest theories about human nature. In 1845 he began to openly discuss Laura's difficulties, developing a hereditarian explanation for her apparent character flaws. Her nervous and volatile disposition and her imperfect health, he now wrote, were symptoms of deeper "constitutional disturbing forces" which she had inherited from her parents. Tactfully, Howe did not try to identify the origin of these inherited flaws, refusing to speculate about which natural laws the Bridgman family may have transgressed. He insisted, to the contrary, that both of the Bridgmans were "of good moral character." But he did note that Laura's father had a "small brain," while Harmony Bridgman's, though active, was not much bigger. In addition to a small brain, the Bridgmans also passed on to their daughter a nervous temperament, with a "dash" of the "scrofulous." This combination of inherited traits was what made Laura high strung, "very liable to derangement," and predisposed to contract the disease that had ultimately destroyed her eyes and ears.[25]

The Bridgmans, quite understandably, took offense at the suggestion that their brains were undersized. Perhaps anxious not to dwell on these delicate matters, Howe spent more time developing his epistemological explanation for Laura's character deficiencies. The mind and the soul need sensory stimulation in order to develop properly. Because, in Laura's case, "three of the great avenues of sense had been blocked up," Howe believed now that her physical, mental, and moral development were inevitably distorted. "The beautiful harmony between the macrocosm and the microcosm—between the world without and the world within her, is broken." When Laura lost her eyes and ears, she also lost any hope of developing a fully balanced, harmonious character.[26]

Through the lens of this new theory of human nature, Howe reinterpreted the "facts" of Laura's case. For example, he revised his explanation of Laura's struggle to master her temper. For ten years he had treated her outbursts as momentary aberrations, which he blamed on the harmful outside influences that had temporarily disturbed the child's naturally cheerful disposition. But in the late 1840s he decided that Laura's temper was actually the expression of an internal flaw which he called a "constitutional disposition to irritability." No longer minimizing the importance of these incidents, Howe freely confessed that his student had often experienced "a sudden paroxysm, and an irrepressible nervous explosion." These moments of moral frailty, Howe now believed, could be traced to a physical cause. They were, he explained, "never disconnected with some derangement of her physical health."[27]

As with the blind, Howe's hereditarian explanation of Laura's shortcomings stopped short of complete biological determinism; he still insisted that education had an important role to play, partially compensating for the effects of her inherited weaknesses. While Laura's nervous temperament made her volatile and predisposed to anger, for example, Howe believed that her teachers had done much to subdue this impulse and cultivate the child's gentler qualities. Laura may not have become the perfect individual he had once hoped for, but he insisted that, with her teachers' help, she had learned to be calm, considerate, and affectionate most of the time. Only on occasion did the darker impulses of her nature break through.[28]

Yet Howe had to confess that there were limits to what education could accomplish when working with flawed human material. Experience had taught him that the "disturbing forces" which had marred Laura's character could never be entirely overcome. Her character, he conceded, would always be constricted by the "mental peculiarities" she had inherited. The great lesson to be learned from Laura's case, he now claimed, was that "native dispositions, and tendencies, and peculiarities may never be eradicated or entirely changed."[29]

Chapter 11

My Sunny Home

Laura's formal education ended in 1850, when she was twenty years old. As she entered adulthood, Howe expected that she would fade from public view, her story no longer an object of public fascination and scientific speculation. Perhaps with some feelings of nostalgia, he wrote that "the great point of interest was the beginning of the process. With her it was the first step that was the most difficult and most interesting." Howe's friends noticed a change in his attitude toward his experiment. Francis Lieber, the political philosopher, spent many days at Perkins making an in-depth study of Laura Bridgman's "vocal sounds" for the Smithsonian. After trying without success to engage Howe in further discussion about Laura's case, Lieber confided to their mutual friend Dorothea Dix, "Do you know that I fear Howe has lost a great deal of interest in Laura?"[1]

That spring Sarah Wight resigned from her post as Laura's teacher and companion. Five years of almost constant attention to Laura's needs had left her physically exhausted. After a few months of recuperation, Wight told Laura that she planned to marry a Unitarian missionary, George Bond. The news came as a double blow to Laura, who had misinterpreted Bond's regular visits to Perkins as a sign that he had been courting *her*. Laura's closest friend soon set sail to join her new husband at a missionary outpost in the Sandwich Islands. "I miss you very much incessantly," Laura wrote to Wight the first winter she was gone.[2]

With Wight's departure, Laura's life at the school changed drastically. She no longer had new lessons to master and no longer enjoyed the company of a "constant friend." Howe arranged for a few blind girls to visit Laura each week, and he continued to pay her a daily visit whenever his other reform interests did not carry him away from the school. Laura spent the rest of her day roaming the halls of the Perkins Institution looking for someone to talk with, or working alone in her room. "The time seems to me very tedious," she complained to Wight.[3]

Aided by her buoyant personality, Laura soon recovered her enthusiasm for life. "I am such a mirthful child toward you today," she wrote to Wight. "I wish to puzzle you out by letting you take the glances of this comical style of my writing. I think it is most likely that you may consider I am so dressy with such a new & original language." Laura took pleasure in a variety of new friendships, becoming particularly close to her old teacher, Mary Swift, who had since married and still lived in the Boston area. Their old conflicts now forgotten, Laura came to think of Swift as a second mother.[4]

Laura also settled into a busy work routine, spending many hours of each day knitting, sewing, and crocheting. Because the purses, lace collars, and embroidered handkerchiefs she produced were not only of excellent quality but also a novelty, she always found a ready market for them among her acquaintances and visitors to the school. Laura used the money she earned—about a hundred dollars a year—to buy small gifts for her friends and occasional articles of fashion for herself. She also took great pleasure in using some of the money to help the poor. Often, as she walked with her friends along the streets of Boston, she would give a few coins to her companions, asking them to pass them on to anyone who seemed to be in need.[5]

This experience of providing for herself and for others gave Laura the feeling of maturity and self-reliance that she had been longing for since adolescence. Belatedly, she declared her new spirit of independence from Sarah Wight, now thousands of miles away in the Sandwich Islands. She playfully informed her former teacher, "I am not the slightest afraid of having you censure your old pupil Laura because I love to indulge myself in working more than it is right or best. I enjoy myself so much more than I can realize."[6]

Laura's feeling of economic independence was, of course, an illusion. The money she earned as a seamstress could never cover her living expenses nor pay for the institutional support that she enjoyed at Perkins. As both Howe and her parents recognized, Laura was destined to be dependent on others for the rest of her life. Someone would have to provide her not only with food, clothing and shelter but also with long hours of patient companionship. Laura would always need others to talk to, to take her for walks, to stimulate her mind and serve as her eyes and ears on the world.

In 1852 Howe concluded that the best place for Laura to find this support was back in Hanover with her family. At his insistence, she had been making regular visits to New Hampshire ever since she arrived at Perkins. Now he arranged for her to leave the institution for good and to take up

12. Laura's knitting and crocheting found a ready market among visitors to Perkins and provided her with a modest annual income. She used that money to buy gifts for her friends, and she enjoyed giving some away to the poor. *(Courtesy of Dartmouth College Library)*

permanent residence in the Bridgman farmhouse. There were practical economic reasons for this decision. Perkins, as Howe often insisted, was a school, not an asylum; it received public funding to support young scholars, not permanent adult residents. While the Bridgmans could not afford to pay the full cost of maintaining their daughter at the institution, they were quite willing and able to provide for her at their home.[7]

But for Howe, money was always a secondary concern; his decision to send Laura to Hanover was determined more by ideology than by economics. After two decades as the director of Perkins, Howe concluded that institutions for the blind, including his own, were at best a necessary evil. A temporary stay at a school like Perkins, he felt, was useful for blind children, offering them specialized instruction that was not yet available in the regular common schools. He also still believed that blind children could gain more confidence in their own abilities when they were not forced to compete with sighted children.

But Howe decided that, in the long run, institutionalization harmed the blind, encouraging their sense of isolation from the rest of society and amplifying their worst characteristics. Because Perkins's residents spent most of their time interacting only with other blind people, Howe noticed, they became more "clannish." Surrounded by others who suffered from the same faults, they were more likely to become lazy and vain, traits that Howe now believed were particularly common among the blind. Howe also decided that the strict routine and same-sex living that were an unavoidable part of institutional life were unnatural, and therefore harmful.[8]

To counteract these ill effects, Howe began to explore various schemes for deinstitutionalizing care for the blind. At his suggestion, the blind adults who toiled in the workshop were now encouraged to make their own living arrangements outside the institution. He proposed that the older blind students might also be better off living away from the school, rooming with "normal" families of sighted people in the surrounding area. Howe hoped that this would force them to become more self-reliant and teach them to interact with the world of the sighted majority. This new arrangement, he also believed, would expose them to the more balanced and natural social environment of family living.[9]

For the same reasons, Howe thought that Laura would be better off with her family. But he decided that she should first make a trial of the new arrangement. To the Bridgmans he wrote, "I wish her to have an opportunity of trying how she likes living at Hanover, & making up her own mind. She must understand however that she is perfectly free to come here if she elects to do so." Howe was attempting one final experiment with Laura Bridgman, but—perhaps chastened by past experience—he made no dogmatic predictions about the outcome. Writing to Laura in Hanover, he always assured her: "I still keep your room for I do not know but you may want it."[10]

At first, Laura seemed to enjoy her new life in Hanover. "I am most delighted to reign at H. with my blessed family," she wrote to Mary Swift. Laura had always been close to her mother, and she was now able to develop a relationship with some of her younger brothers and sisters. Her oldest sister Mary sometimes took her for walks, and she became particularly affectionate with her brother Addison, a young man who was preparing to study medicine. She proudly informed Swift that her brother was "so fa[i]rly delighted to have me at home . . . He mentioned to me a short time ago that he thinks of me the most of any one else in the immence earth."[11]

But from the start Laura felt homesick for Boston. "I love and respect all of my friends the more & farther I appreciate them in my absence." Laura's feelings of loneliness grew worse over time because none in the busy Bridgman household could afford to spend a great deal of time providing her with the companionship and mental stimulation that she had enjoyed at Perkins. Deprived of the conversation that was her crucial link to the world around her, Laura's health began to deteriorate. As winter approached, Harmony Bridgman wrote to Howe, alarmed by the fact that her daughter had almost stopped eating. "She won't probably live many years unless her health is better," she fretted.[12]

Although Laura insisted that she was still happy, she grew weaker. Convinced that this experiment had failed, Howe arranged for an assistant, Mary Paddock, to bring Laura back to Perkins. When Paddock arrived at the Bridgman farmhouse, she found that Laura had grown so weak that she could not leave her bed. Revived a bit by the thought of returning to Boston, Laura agreed to eat some solid food. The next day she rallied enough strength to attempt the journey. Delayed first by snowdrifts, the trip back to Perkins came to a halt when Laura fainted from fatigue. After several days of rest, the two resumed the journey. Stretched out on a couch in the railroad car, Laura repeatedly signed the same two questions into Paddock's hand: "Would doctor meet them? Was he glad she was coming?" By the time Laura was carried to her old room at Perkins, her friends assumed that she would not live. However, after months of nursing, her health gradually revived.[13]

Recognizing that Laura needed the stimulation and support of the institution, Howe and Dorothea Dix raised an endowment that guaranteed Laura a permanent place in the school that she now called her "sunny home." Laura continued to visit her family during the school's summer vacations, but during the rest of the year she was an active member of the Perkins community. While no crowds lined up to see her as in former days, she satisfied a steady demand for autographs and maintained a broad correspondence with friends and well-wishers.[14]

Laura had a quiet but happy life at Perkins, grounded in the regular rhythms of institutional routine. She always rose early, dressed neatly, and combed her room with her delicate fingers, making sure that all was spotlessly clean and in order. The rest of her day was spent visiting with the matron of the school, attending writing classes with the blind children, and working on her own knitting and needlework. She also did light housework and often helped the blind girls in their sewing classes. One graduate of the school remembered Laura as a patient but demanding instructor. Guided by the sensitive tip of her tongue, she threaded needles for the young blind girls. But many of them dreaded the prospect of having her examine their work, for she never tolerated shoddy workmanship and often ripped out anything that did not meet her high standards.[15]

Laura also continued to write each day, maintaining a wide correspondence, keeping a regular journal, and even preparing several brief "autobiographies," based on recollections of her childhood in New Hampshire. While most of her writings contain a mundane record of her daily activities, at times they offer a window into the person Laura had become. "I have had numerous very pleasant ideas during this day," she recorded in her journal when she was twenty. "Many ideas were extremely apparent and comical to my little heart. Several of those subjects seemed as if they wished to suggest to me that my sensitive brain could recall them . . . I love to have such ideas keep recurring towards my tiny brain so well."[16]

Laura's writings confirm what her friends often noted about her personality, that she was a playful, energetic, imaginative, and generous spirit, but also a bit eccentric and childlike. "Little pleasures," one family friend noted, were always welcomed by Laura "with the enthusiasm of a child." Even as an old woman, an acquaintance from Hanover recalled, Laura enjoyed twirling donuts on her fingers.[17]

As she grew into adulthood, Laura remained fascinated by the subject of religion and spent long hours reading her raised-letter Bible. While she continued to revere Howe and look forward to his visits, he was only a distant influence in her life now, his attentions increasingly absorbed by politics and the impending Civil War. Conversing freely with blind girls and visitors, Laura was exposed to a wide variety of religious opinions and continued to express ideas that Howe found too conventional and too evangelical.

In the early 1860s, when Laura was in her early thirties, she experienced a profound spiritual conversion, one which confirmed and amplified her lifelong attraction to the doctrines of evangelical Christianity. In 1860 the matron at Perkins brought her the news that her oldest sister Mary had died suddenly. Laura was devastated by the loss. "I burst into a bad cry," she later recalled. "My heart ached so painfully; it was broken with a great crush . . . I could hardly spell a word with my fingers for many hours. My soul was cumbered and cast down." In her anger and despair, Laura rejected God. "She continued for months to cherish bitter feelings," Swift remembered, "and to shun conversations on religious topics, which had previously been her delight."[18]

By the time Laura returned to Hanover for her summer vacation, however, Harmony Bridgman noticed a "marked change" in her daughter. The two spent long hours discussing matters of religion. Laura then sought out the local pastor's wife and began to teach her manual sign language. "It was soon evident why she had been so anxious that I should learn to talk," the woman later recalled, "as she began to tell me of her feelings upon the subject of religion." Using this woman as a translator, Laura explained to the pastor that she had experienced a "change of heart," a profound spiritual experience that she called being "baptized with the Holy Ghost." She wanted the minister to confirm her conversion experience by also baptizing her in water.[19]

Laura had to leave New Hampshire before the ceremony could be arranged, but she returned in the summer of 1863 and again requested to be baptized. After the pastor's wife interpreted Laura's testimony before the congregation, members voted to accept her as a member of their church. On a July afternoon, they accompanied her to the bank of a nearby brook so that she could be baptized. Laura had been terrified at the prospect of being plunged under water, fearing she might drown, but as she waded into the brook she was filled with peace. "My soul was overwhelmed with spiritual joy and light," Laura recalled. "A glorious light shone in my head. My soul was cast into the hand of my dear Saviour by faith."[20]

Laura's family and friends in New Hampshire were deeply moved by her calm, earnest profession of faith. Back in Boston, Howe was "shocked and pained" by the news and disgusted when he saw an "extraordinary change" in Laura's personality. The first indication he received about Laura's conversion may have come in one of her letters. Innocent of the theological gulf that now separated her from Howe, Laura wrote to him from New Hampshire, anxious to share the news of her baptism with her mentor. "I am most happy to draw a portion of time to address you this holy day," she greeted him. "I hope that you are very happy in Jesus & God. I pray & praise him day & night. I am so happy that I am buried with the Redeemer in baptism. I shall meet you in a most blissful world when we are called by the mercy of God to live with him & Jesus Christ & the Holy Angels."[21]

Howe surely cringed as he read these words, realizing that, after all he had done to direct Laura's soul down the path of liberal Christianity, she had chosen instead to become an ardent evangelical Baptist. He was deeply disappointed, and often told his friends that he could no longer recognize "the girl whose clearness and simplicity of mind had so fascinated him in this conventional and professing sectarian."[22]

Laura probably saw very little of Howe over the next decade. Howe's biographer suggests that, although he stayed on as director of Perkins, he visited the school only "occasionally . . . during lulls in his fight against slavery." Laura may have spent more time with Howe's wife and children in these years. Julia was quite preoccupied, struggling to hold together a stormy and unhappy marriage while trying, against her husband's wishes, to launch a career as a writer, lecturer, and suffragist. Still, she made an effort to cultivate her friendship with Laura and to include her in the Howe family circle. In the early 1870s the task of running the school passed on to the Howes' oldest daughter, Julia Romana Howe, and her husband, Michael Anagnos. After the war Howe was often drawn away from Boston by his work for the Freedmen's Bureau, and later as a member of a presidential commission studying the prospect of U.S. annexation of Santo Domingo.[23]

Though busy with new schemes almost to the last, Howe's health grew fragile in the early 1870s. On a January morning in 1876, as he prepared to walk to Perkins for a visit, he collapsed and fell into a coma from which he never recovered. As the hour of his death drew near, Laura was brought to his bedside. Julia Ward Howe watched as Laura ran her fingers across Howe's face for the last time. She recalled that "a little agonized sound, scarcely audible, alone broke the silence of the solemn scene. All who were present deeply felt the significance of this farewell."[24]

Though Howe had been a distant figure in Laura's life for many years, she was deeply affected by the death of the man she still thought of as her adopted father. A couple of weeks after the funeral, she told Mary Swift, "It pains my feelings in thought of never meeting & grasping my best & noble Friend Dr. Howe on earth. The path seems so desolate & void without sight of him to us all." But Laura did not feel entirely abandoned, finding consolation in her faith. She concluded her letter by adding that "Jesus is all & in all."[25]

In the decades that followed his failed experiment, Howe had taken little interest in making further scientific speculations about Laura Bridgman's case. At the urging of others, he had tried to summarize his observations in a single manuscript but eventually abandoned the project. Other intellectuals, however, continued to discuss Howe's famous experiment well into the late nineteenth century. As late as 1879, the young scientist G. Stanley Hall wrote that "comparatively few comprehensive treatises in any department of mental or moral philosophy or psychology written in Europe or America during the last quarter century can be found without the mention of her name."[26]

Hall, who became one of the nation's leading psychologists and president of Clark University, was the last scientist to make direct observations of Laura. Two years after Howe's death, Hall spent several weeks at Perkins, running her through a battery of psychological tests. He peered into her eye sockets and ears to precisely note the damage done by fever more than forty-five years earlier; he spun her on a swing to test her response to dizziness, shouted into her ear through a pasteboard trumpet, sent "electrical irritations" to "various parts of the brain," and vibrated tuning forks against her false teeth. He even sneaked up on her while she was napping to see if she would be startled awake by the light touch of a thread on her skin. She was.[27]

Whatever the significance of Hall's findings, the kinds of questions he thought to ask reflect a profound change during the nineteenth century in the way scientists thought about the brain. Hall considered the issues that stirred Howe's antebellum audiences to be dated and somewhat quaint. For Hall's contemporaries in the last decades of the century, speculations about Laura's religious sentiments were now replaced by an interest in the responses of her nerve endings. Ancient questions about how much of human personality is innate and how much is learned remained unanswered, but intellectuals in Europe and America moved on to new concerns.

One reason for this shift was the rapid progress that had been made in neurological research, as European scientists developed new laboratory techniques for investigating the brain and central nervous system. In the course of this research, Howe's beloved science of phrenology had been largely discredited. By the 1870s, scientists accepted phrenology's once controversial claim that the brain is the seat of the mind. And most adopted its theory of the localization of brain functions, though in a much more cautious form. But experiments had refuted most of phrenology's other key claims, particularly the theory that the brain is a collection of distinct organs or faculties and that these are reflected in the shape of the skull. By the time of Howe's death, the reading of skulls had gone the way of alchemy, ridiculed by the academic establishment as a pseudo-science.[28]

For Howe, phrenology's map of the mental faculties had provided the link between Laura's brain and her character, giving science its insights into those branches of human activity that he considered most important—morality and religion. But the scientists of Hall's generation concluded that human behaviors were far too complex to be caused by single, neatly identifiable regions of the brain. Concentrating on what they could measure in their laboratories, they viewed the brain as a mechanism that interpreted the sensations of outside stimuli and sent appropriate responses to the motor system. Ethical impulses and spiritual intuitions, they found, were an unpromising field for empirical investigation. Though Darwin made passing references to Laura's case in his own work, his theory of evolution further marginalized the discussion of religion in scientific circles in the last decades of the nineteenth century. Thus, to Hall's peers, Laura Bridgman's sense of balance became far more interesting than her sense of right and wrong. Hall noted in 1879 that, while Howe's reports on Laura Bridgman could be considered "almost classic" texts in the field of psychology, most were out of print.[29]

In the last years of her life, Laura's faith remained strong, a recurring interest in all of her conversations and her correspondence. Most often, she expressed her religious ideas in the evangelical cliches of the period. But at other times she found a voice that was uniquely her own, one that not only expressed her Christian faith but also her unique experience of the world as a deaf and blind person. For example, near the end of her life she wrote several poems. In one of them, which she titled "Holy Home," Laura described her vision of Heaven.

> I pass this dark home toward light home.
> Earthly home shall perish,
> But holy home shall endure forever.
> Earthly home is wintery.
> Hard it is for us to appreciate the radiance of holy
> home because of the blindness of our minds.
> How glorious holy home is, and still more than a beam of sun![30]

Chapter 12

Legacy

After a brief illness, Laura Bridgman died in 1889, at the age of fifty-nine. Even then, she remained in the service of science. An autopsy was performed, and her brain was removed for examination, though no important neurological insights were apparently gleaned from it. A plaster cast of the brain was placed in the archives of the Perkins School for posterity.[1]

Laura's funeral was held in the central hall of the Perkins Institution, the place that her achievements had transformed into one of the most celebrated schools of the nineteenth century. At the head of her casket, mourners placed a bust of her beloved Dr. Howe. In the minds of many who gathered for the funeral, the identities of the two, teacher and pupil, were inextricably linked. Howe was, they felt, Laura's spiritual father, the one who had granted her a second life. Speakers told the story of their mutual accomplishment one more time, recapturing for a moment the sense of wonder which so many felt more than fifty years before, when they first heard that a deaf and blind girl had learned to talk with her fingers.[2]

Yet, even then, Laura Bridgman's story was passing out of the collective memory of American public life, eclipsed by the accomplishments of another deaf and blind woman, Helen Keller. Keller was one of the many deaf-blind children who benefited from the pioneering work done at Perkins by Howe and Laura Bridgman. Keller's parents first realized that their own daughter could be taught when they read an account of Laura's education. In 1887 they wrote to Howe's successor at the Perkins School, Dr. Michael Anagnos, to enlist a private tutor for their daughter. Anagnos recruited one of Perkins's instructors, Annie Sullivan. Before leaving for Alabama, Sullivan read all of Howe's reports on Laura Bridgman and got Laura's advice as well.[3]

When Annie Sullivan guided her pupil to language, she retraced the steps first marked by Howe and his protégé a half century earlier. But Keller's breakthrough came much more quickly. She accomplished in three lessons what Laura had taken three months to understand. Reading accounts of her progress sent back to Boston by Annie Sullivan, Anagnos soon concluded that "history presents no case like hers." In interest and "vivacity" this "second Laura Bridgman" was at least her predecessor's equal, while in "quickness of perception, grasp of ideas, breadth of comprehension, insatiate thirst for knowledge, self-reliance and sweetness of disposition she certainly excels her prototype."[4]

Ironically, Helen Keller seemed to be everything that Howe had hoped for from Laura. She was, like Laura, an eager student. But her language skills surpassed anything that Laura had ever attained, and she showed herself capable of a much deeper level of understanding about the world around her. As she matured into adulthood, she proved to be wise, compassionate, and liberal in faith, the very embodiment of Howe's most optimistic ideas about human nature.

A couple of years after the start of her education, Helen Keller came to Boston to live at the Perkins School for a time. There she met Laura Bridgman, then an elderly woman. At their first meeting, Laura shunned

13. Laura never appeared in public without concealing her damaged eyeballs behind glasses or a green velvet ribbon. This is a rare image of her without such a covering. (*Courtesy of Dartmouth College Library*)

the young scholar when she discovered that she did not have tidy hands, and later scolded her for not being "very gentle." "In my eagerness to kiss her good-bye," Keller wrote years later, "I trod on her toes, which greatly annoyed her, and made me feel like the bad little girl of the Sunday school books." This encounter, though anticlimactic, is suggestive of the difference between the two women. Laura demanded a strict moral order within the narrow confines of her world at the institution, while Keller grew up to become a remarkably worldly person, an articulate champion of much broader causes. Laura scrutinized fingernails, while Keller wrote treatises on socialism and Swedenborgian religion.[5]

William James, the last American philosopher to take a passing interest in Laura Bridgman's story, noted the gulf that separated these two women. In 1903 he wrote a review of a book about Laura's education that had been written by two of Howe's daughters. Looking over the details of Laura's case, James found her to be "just a little anemic by contrast" to Keller. Each of the women, he felt, symbolized the interests and characteristics of their times. From the perspective of the more secular twentieth century, Laura's personality seemed "intensely moral,—almost morbidly so." She was a creature from a distant world, a time and place where everything bore the "stamp of conscience." From James's more modern point of view, the controversies over her moral and religious education that had once absorbed so many intellectuals in Boston and around the world all seemed rather quaint. Laura Bridgman's entire story, he thought, wore "a white veil of primness."[6]

James found Helen Keller, by contrast, to be a perfect symbol of the restless, enthusiastic energy of the early twentieth century. While Laura was "almost a theological phenomenon," Keller was "primarily a phenomenon of vital exuberance. Life for her is a series of adventures, rushed at with enthusiasm and fun. For Laura it was more like a series of such careful indoor steps as a convalescent makes when the bed days are over." Applying his theory of pragmatism to the matter, James concluded that Keller's superiority over Laura Bridgman was a sign of evolutionary progress. Laura's "decidedly attenuated personality" had given way to the "untrammeled soarings" of Helen Keller. Bridgman's most important legacy, James concluded, was the fact that her accomplishment set the stage for the superior performance of her successor. "We cannot forget that there never could have been a Helen Keller if there had not been a Laura Bridgman."[7]

Helen Keller, for one, did not forget. In 1937 a group of blind girls from Perkins traveled to New Hampshire to place a granite marker on the grounds of the Bridgman farmhouse and to hold a ceremony commemo-

14. At Perkins, Howe printed dozens of raised-letter books for the blind, including treatises on moral philosophy, English novels, and geometry texts. Laura's favorite book was the Bible. *(Courtesy of Dartmouth College Library)*

rating the 100th anniversary of Laura Bridgman's breakthrough into language. Keller was invited as the guest of honor. Hospitalized by illness, she was unable to attend, but sent a letter to be read at the ceremony:

> With ever new gratitude I bless Dr. Samuel Gridley Howe who believed, and therefore was able to raise that child soul from a death-in-life existence to knowledge and joy. The remembrance fills me afresh of the first deaf-blind person in the world to be taught whom I met in the first days of my own glad awakening. Again I feel the dainty lace lengthen as her lovely hands ply the needles. I dwell on her deliverance so radiant with Christ's Teaching that faith is might to save and to bless.[8]

Like Laura Bridgman before her, Helen Keller had done a great deal to promote the cause of education for the deaf-blind. As news of her accomplishments spread, an international audience was once more inspired by a profound story of intellectual resurrection, their sympathies again turned toward those who suffer the isolation of a double sensory handicap. Unlike her more sheltered predecessor, Keller seized the opportunity that her fame afforded her to play an active public role, writing and organizing on behalf of those whom she called "the loneliest people in the world."[9]

For Helen Keller, the anniversary celebration at the Bridgman farmhouse was a reminder of a noble work that remained unfinished. "Sadly I wonder," she reflected in her letter, "why since that inspiring event so few doubly handicapped children have been sought out and led back to the sunshine of human intercourse." This call for more attention to the needs of the deaf-blind was well founded. Although Howe's reports on Laura Bridgman had inspired other educators to find and help these children, a systematic program to educate them was long deferred. In the 1950s Perkins founded one of the first training programs to help teachers deal with the formidable obstacles faced by those with double sensory handicaps. But at the close of that decade, a full century after Laura Bridgman had signed her first words, a majority of the nation's deaf-blind children received no education at all. [10]

A rubella epidemic in the early 1960s caused a surge in the number of deaf-blind children and again focused the public's attention on their plight. As part of a wider movement to improve special education, the federal government created a network of regional centers to support the deaf-blind in 1968. Today, almost half of the nation's deaf-blind children are integrated in some fashion into mainstream public schools, while the rest are served in more specialized institutions. Although only a fraction of deaf-blind adults are able to find employment, a number have successfully integrated into family and community life, aided in many cases by recent improvements in teaching methods and communication technology. [11]

In spite of these modest successes, the presence of deaf-blind people in our society is scarcely noticed; no person with this double sensory handicap has engaged the public the way Laura Bridgman did in the nineteenth century. Few people today would dream of spending a Saturday afternoon at an institution for the blind or the deaf, observing and interrogating its residents about their grasp of the physical world and their intuitions about the spiritual realm. Modern audiences, however, have found other, less intrusive ways to approach people whose sensory and linguistic experiences are drastically different from their own and to ask them some of the same questions.

A number of recent popular books have offered case studies of people with sensory disabilities, compelling stories that allow us to think about many of the same questions Laura Bridgman raised in her own time— questions about the way language creates mind, about what life might be like without light or sound or words. A young girl tied for most of her life to a bed, deprived of almost all sensory stimulation, a blind man who suddenly gained his sight later in life but never learned to interpret much of what he saw, a deaf man who reached middle-age with no knowledge of language—each of these cases are only the latest variations on a quest begun three centuries ago by Enlightenment thinkers, to both teach and learn from people with sensory handicaps. Just as Laura Bridgman's story did for her contemporaries, the experiences of these men and women entice us because they promise to illuminate something profound about the human mind, offering an insight that might otherwise elude scientific investigation.[12]

In the end, these attempts to resolve age-old questions about human nature by probing the experience of a single handicapped individual seem doomed to failure. A sampling pool of one person, struggling against severe liabilities, can hardly be used to draw meaningful conclusions about all of humanity. And, as Howe realized, our moral responsibility to help the disabled imposes sharp limits on this line of research, protecting people who desperately need the stimulation of social interaction, not the further isolation of a laboratory.

Although Howe's experiment was a scientific failure, it did teach his society some important lessons. Laura Bridgman's dramatic story drew the public's attention to the wider reform movement that was transforming the lives of many disabled people in nineteenth-century America. Howe and other educators invented teaching tools, experimented with curriculum, and built new institutions that helped thousands of people with sensory handicaps to overcome the physical barriers that had always deprived them of an education. The faith these humanitarians placed in the potential of the blind and the deaf was fully confirmed by their students, who eagerly seized this opportunity to claim a greater measure of dignity and autonomy in their lives. Their academic accomplishments and their courage in the face of imposing obstacles forced many Americans to rethink their ideas about the very meaning of disability. Chipping away at centuries of accumulated prejudice and misunderstanding, these students and their teachers began to dismantle one of the greatest barriers faced by the blind and the deaf, the deep-rooted misconception that people with sensory handicaps are unreachable and somehow less than fully human. In the crucial early years of this important reform movement, no person did more to challenge those assumptions and inspire a new respect for the disabled than Laura Bridgman.

As Howe began his work at Perkins, he predicted that the rift which had always divided the disabled from their fellow human beings was about to be closed. Education would soon empower the blind, the deaf, and even the deaf-blind to claim their democratic birthright as moral, social, and economic equals in their society. This radical vision ran counter to all of human history, but in the nineteenth century the realization that a deaf and blind girl could talk and play and work made anything seem possible. Since then, generations of disabled people and their allies have worked toward that same goal, trying to ensure that no member of society is marginalized because of a physical or mental disability.[13]

Observing the centennial of Laura Bridgman's breakthrough into language, Helen Keller concluded that this ongoing rescue mission was Laura's greatest legacy. "It is well for us to rejoice together in Laura Bridgman's triumph over a cruel fate," Keller wrote. "But in a true sense her anniversary cannot be celebrated until the hundreds of beseeching, broken lives of which hers was one are healed with renewing love and the power of the mind. Each one rescued is a witness to truth, justice and fair dealing. Each one neglected is a denial of the right of every human being to education and opportunity."

Abbreviations

AR   Annual Report

BPP   Laura Bridgman Papers, Perkins

HPH   Howe Papers, Houghton

HPP   Howe Papers, Perkins

LP   Lamson Papers, MHS

MHS   Massachusetts Historical Society

TJ   Teachers' Journals, BPP

Notes

An earlier version of portions of the Introduction and Chapter 4 appeared in the *History of Education Quarterly* (Fall 1974) under the title "'More Important than a Rabble of Common Kings': Dr. Howe's Education of Laura Bridgman.'"

Introduction

1. "Our Country and the London Fair," *Evening Transcript*, 14 June 1851; John Allwood, *The Great Exhibitions* (London, 1977), 22.
2. "Our Country and the London Fair," *Evening Transcript*, 14 June 1851; Maude Howe Elliott and Florence Howe Hall, *Laura Bridgman: Dr. Howe's Famous Pupil and What He Taught Her* (Boston, 1903); Mary Swift Lamson, *Life and Education of Laura Dewey Bridgman* (Boston, 1881; New York: Arno Press, 1975); Harold Schwartz, *Samuel Gridley Howe: Social Reformer* (Cambridge, 1956), ch. 6.
3. "Our Country and the London Fair," *Evening Transcript*, 14 June 1851.
4. Roger Shattuck, *The Forbidden Experiment: The Story of the Wild Boy of Aveyron* (New York, 1994); Harlan Lane, *The Wild Boy of Aveyron* (Cambridge, 1976); Roger Batra, *The Artificial Savage: Modern Myths of the Wild Man* (Ann Arbor, 1997).

1. In Quest of His Prize

1. Lord Byron, "On This Day I Complete My Thirty-Sixth Year" (1824), cited in *Byron and Greece*, ed. Harold Spender (London, 1924). Byron met his sought-after soldier's death not long afterward. Howe's daughter, Laura Richards, reported that Byron was her father's favorite poet. "I have sometimes wondered whether, had it not been for Byron, he would ever have seen those isles and hills which he was to know so well." Laura Richards, *The Letters and Journals of Samuel Gridley Howe*, ed. Laura Richards, 2 vols. (Boston, 1906), 2:21.
2. Edward Everett, "Review of Coray's Aristotle," *North American Review*, Oct. 1823, 401, 417–418. See also Harold Schwartz, *Samuel Gridley Howe: Social Reformer, 1801–1876* (Cambridge, 1956), 8. Jefferson cited in E. M. Earle, "American Interest in the Greek Cause, 1821–1827," *American Historical Review*, Oct. 1927, 44–63; Edward Everett, "Review," 316–318. Earle suggests that only the national leadership's

traditional antebellum fear of "entangling alliances" in Europe prevented President Monroe from taking direct action in support of the Greeks.

3. Years later, Howe downplayed his decision to aid the Greek cause, suggesting to Horace Mann that, "lacking prudence & calculation, I followed an adventurous spirit." Howe to Horace Mann, 1857, p. 7, Howe Papers, Houghton (hereafter HPH). Howe's biographer, Harold Schwartz, also suggests the possibility that Howe left for Greece out of "boyish petulance" when he was unable to afford to marry a woman that he loved. Schwartz, *Samuel Gridley Howe*, 10. E. M. Earle seems to have expressed it best when he suggested that "philhellenism was an emotion rather than a reasoned conviction." Earle, "American Interest," 61.

4. Howe cited in Schwartz, *Samuel Gridley Howe*, 18.

5. E. M. Earle suggests that Howe was one of the few "philhellenes" who was fair enough to admit that the Turks often fought heroically, while the Greeks were fully as capable of cruel and selfish acts as their opponents. Earle sums up the Greek Revolution this way: "The truth is that by both Greeks and Turks the war was waged as a war of extermination, accompanied by the most obscene and barbarous cruelty" (62). It is interesting to note that Howe, the young idealist, was at the very outset of his career exposed to some of the most horrific scenes of human cruelty, folly, and selfishness imaginable, yet managed to retain his faith in the goodness and improvability of human nature. In short, the optimistic views of human nature that he expressed throughout his adult life were not simply the product of a sheltered existence in well-mannered Unitarian Boston.

6. Howe to Mann, 1857, HPH; Schwartz, *Samuel Gridley Howe*, 33–38. Howe's "Washingtonia" might be considered one of the first, most exotic, and least well known of a long line of utopian agricultural experiments that were undertaken by New England idealists in this period. Howe later took an interest in the theories of Fourier, the French utopian whose ideas about community were applied by early American socialists. There is no evidence, however, that Howe took an active part in the planned agricultural communities of the Fourierists, Owenites, and transcendentalists once he had returned to Boston. A full account of Howe's experiences in Greece can be found in Samuel Gridley Howe, *Letters and Journals*, ed. Laura E. Richards (Boston, 1909; rpt. New York, 1973), vol. 1.

7. Howe's appearance was recounted by Mrs. William Greene and quoted in Laura Richards, *Samuel Gridley Howe* (New York, 1935), 71; S. G. Howe to William Sampson, 19 April 1831, in *Letters and Journals*, ed. Laura Richards, 2:382.

8. Schwartz, *Samuel Gridley Howe*, 41; Howe, *Letters and Journals*, 2:386.

9. Boston's school for the blind was the first to receive a state charter, in 1829. However, because of the two-year delay in starting the school, the first school for the blind in operation was in New York. The school there opened its doors in March of 1832, several months before Boston accepted its first pupils. Berthold Lowenfeld, M.D., *The Changing Status of the Blind: From Separation to Integration* (Springfield, 1975), 87.

10. Schwartz, *Samuel Gridley Howe*, 42; John L. Thomas, "Romantic Reform in America," *American Quarterly* (Winter 1965): 663.

11. Lowenfield, 65–68; Denis Diderot, "Letter on the Blind," *Diderot's Early Philosophical Works*, trans. Margaret Jourdain (Chicago, 1916), 117. While Howe suggested that Diderot's speculations on blindness displayed "more ingenuity than observation," he thought enough of Diderot's "Letter on the Blind" to translate it himself and print an English edition in raised letters for the blind.

12. William R. Paulson, *Enlightenment, Romanticism, and the Blind in France* (Princeton, 1987), ch. 4.

13. Samuel Gridley Howe, "Education of the Blind," *North American Review*, July 1833, 58, 34.

14. Ibid., 58. Although Howe is generally credited with these innovations, many of them were actually developed by a Boston inventor, Stephen P. Ruggles, perhaps working under Howe's supervision. "What Invention Has Done for the Blind," *Scientific American*, 5 March 1864, pp. 149–150.

15. Howe, "Education of the Blind," 36, 47.

16. Ibid., 56, 21.

17. Samuel Gridley Howe, *Address of the Trustees of the New England Institution for the Education of the Blind to the Public* (Boston, 1833), 6.

18. Howe, "Education of the Blind," 20–21.

19. Howe, *Address of the Trustees*, 11, 13.

20. Lowenfield, 85–86, 89. Lowenfield suggests that, following in the footsteps of Samuel Gridley Howe, American society has continued to favor integration of the blind into the mainstream of society more than European countries have. Lowenfield adds, however, that the blind still face many barriers to full integration.

21. Howe, "Education of the Blind," 56.

22. Harmony Bridgman to Howe, 1838, Howe Papers, Perkins (hereafter HPP).

23. Harmony Bridgman to Howe, 1 Feb. 1841, HPP.

24. Mary Swift Lamson, *Life and Education of Laura Bridgman* (Boston, 1881; New York, 1975), 2–3.

25. Schwartz, *Samuel Gridley Howe*, 52; Richards, *Samuel Gridley Howe*, 72–73; Julia Ward Howe, *Memoir of Dr. Samuel Gridley Howe* (Boston, 1876), 17. In a letter to an unidentified town official from this time period, Howe writes, "We are desirous of procuring the most promising ones [students] for this purpose." Howe to ?, 23 July 1832, HPP.

26. "Exhibition of the Blind," *Christian Watchman*, 29 March 1833.

27. Ibid.; "Exhibition of the Blind," unidentified clipping in Laura Bridgman Papers, Perkins (hereafter BPP).

28. "Exhibition of the Blind," *Christian Watchman*, 29 March 1833. The bill supporting the New England Asylum for the Blind is reprinted in the *Boston Weekly Messenger and Massachusetts Journal*, 14 March 1833.

29. "Exhibition of the Blind," *Juvenile Rambler*, 27 March 1833, 10 April 1833; Howe, *Annual Report of the Trustees of the New England Institution for the Education of the Blind* (Boston, 1834), 6; Schwartz, *Samuel Gridley Howe*, 53.

30. Maud Howe Elliott and Florence Howe Hall, *Laura Bridgman: Dr. Howe's Famous Pupil and What He Taught Her* (Boston, 1904), 1–27; Schwartz, *Samuel Gridley*

Howe, 53–54; Edward Everett Hale cited in Richards, *Samuel Gridley, Howe*, 76; Julia Ward Howe, *Memoir*, 18–19.

31. E. C. Sanford, "The Writings of Laura Bridgman," *Overland Monthly*, 1887, 12.

32. Laura Bridgman, from the "Autobiography Read at the First Picnic on the Kindergarten Grounds," 1885, unpublished manuscript in BPP.

33. Harmony Bridgman to Howe, 1838, HPP; Laura Bridgman, autobiography, 1885.

34. James Barrett to Howe, 11 July 1837, HPP; Dr. Reuben Mussey to American Asylum of Hartford, cited in Lamson, *Life and Education*, vii; Laura Bridgman, autobiography, 1885, BPP; Laura Bridgman, "Earliest Autobiography," 1849, BPP.

35. Harmony Bridgman to Maude Howe Elliott, 7 Jan. 1890, BPP.

36. Laura Bridgman, autobiography, 1885; autobiography, 1849.

37. S. G. Howe to Dr. Dixon, Charleston, SC, 4 July 1841, HPP.

38. Howe, *Nineteenth Annual Report* (Cambridge, 1851), 18–19.

39. Sumner cited in Schwartz, *Samuel Gridley Howe*, 107.

40. David Donald, "Toward a Reconsideration of Abolitionists," *Lincoln Reconsidered* (New York, 1961). Donald evidently includes Howe in his composite portrait of New England abolitionists.

41. Richards, *Samuel Gridley Howe*, 1–2. This claim that Howe did not think of himself as a member of an established family, whose authority was being eroded by newcomers, seems confirmed by Laura Richards. She recalled that her father was "little inclined to talk about his forbears; his concern was with tomorrow, not with yesterday."

42. Schwartz, *Samuel Gridley Howe*, 1–3.

43. Howe to Horace Mann, 1857, HPH; Howe cited in Schwartz, *Samuel Gridley Howe*, 41.

44. Howe's record on the "labor question"—his denunciation of Jacksonian labor unions as a symptom of workers' greed—has led some historians to characterize him as an economic conservative fearful of the masses. But Howe's writings suggest that he was little concerned with the issue one way or another. Like most antebellum Americans, particularly those outside the working class, he distrusted unions as unfair combinations. Yet he was much more likely to denounce the wealthy for their lack of civic spirit and compassion than he was to dwell on the dangers of ignorant and greedy workers. Donald, "Toward A Reconsideration of Abolitionists," 30.

45. Ronald G. Walters, *American Reformers, 1815–1860* (New York, 1997), 210–213. Walters singles out Howe's work at Perkins as evidence that, at least in a limited number of cases, "human sympathy toward disadvantaged 'others' was very much a part of asylum building" (211). The most influential works which have taken this view of Jacksonian reform institutions are David Rothman, *The Discovery of the Asylum* (Boston, 1971; rev. 1990), and Michael Katz, *The Irony of Early School Reform: Educational Innovation in Mid-Nineteenth Century Massachusetts* (Cambridge, 1968). For critical reviews of the "social control" interpretation of New England reformers, see Lawrence Frederick Kohl, "The Concept of Social Control and the History of Jacksonian America," *Journal of the Early Republic* 5 (Spring

1985), and Conrad E. Wright, *The Transformation of Charity in Postrevolutionary New England* (Boston, 1992), appendix 1.

46. S. G. Howe, "Education of the Blind," *Literary and Theological Review* 3 (June 1836): 270. Because he assumes that reformers were motivated primarily by "fear," Walters (*American Reformers*, 207) concedes that the great efforts made to build asylums for the insane is "far more surprising than their willingness to invest in prisons." The average Jacksonian taxpayer, he suggests, could not have believed that there was much to fear from this small group of people. My argument here is that schools for the blind and the deaf, built in dozens of states in the 1830s and 40s, present a similar anomaly for those who emphasize that antebellum reformers were motivated primarily by a fear of social unrest. This evidence does not overturn the social-control thesis but qualifies it—something which some proponents of the idea have already done. See David Rothman, "Social Control: The Uses and Abuses of the Concept in the History of Incarceration," in *Social Control and the State: Historical and Comparative Essays*, ed. Stanley Cohen and Andrew Scull (Oxford, 1983), 106–117.

47. John L. Thomas, "Romantic Reform in America, 1815–1865," *American Quarterly* 17, no. 4 (Winter 1965): 656–681. Thomas's view of the pre-1830s reformers, one shared by many historians of the social-control school, is effectively challenged by Lois Banner, "Religious Benevolence," and by Conrad E. Wright, *The Transformation of Charity in Postrevolutionary New England* (Boston, 1992). For a balanced approach to the social control question, see Steven Mintz, *Moralists and Modernizers: America's Pre-Civil War Reformers* (Baltimore, 1995), xvi-xvii.

48. Howe, *Fifth Annual Report* (Boston, 1837), 11.

49. Wright, *Transformation of Charity*, passim.

50. In her account of her husband's career, Julia Ward Howe explained, "The romance of charity easily interests the public. Its laborious details and duties repel and weary the many and find fitting ministers only in a few spirits of rare and untiring benevolence. Dr. Howe, after the laurels and roses of victory, had to deal with the thorny ways of a profession, tedious, difficult, and exceptional . . . He was also obliged to keep the infant Institution fresh in the interest and good will of the public, and to give it a place among the recognized benefactions of the Commonwealth." Julia Ward Howe, *Memoir*, 19–20.

51. Studies which reach similar conclusions about the social standing and middle class ambitions of the antebellum reformers include Paul Boyer, *Urban Masses and Moral Order in America, 1820–1920* (Cambridge, 1978), 60–64; Lois Banner, "Religious Benevolence as Social Control: A Critique of an Interpretation," *Journal of American History* 60 (June 1973); Jonathan Messerli, *Horace Mann: A Biography* (New York, 1972), ch. 4; Walters, *American Reformers*, 13–14. Howe quoted in Schwartz, *Samuel Gridley Howe*, 41.

52. "Asylum for the Blind," *Boston Weekly Messenger*, 24 Jan. 1833; "Exhibition of the Blind," *Christian Watchman*, 29 March 1833; Elizabeth Peabody to Julia Ward Howe, 9 Feb. 1876, *Letters of Elizabeth Palmer Peabody, American Renaissance Woman*, ed. Bruce A. Ronda (Middletown, CN, 1984), 377; Howe, *Letters and Jour-*

nals, 2:16; Messerli, *Horace Mann,* 233–234, contains an account of Horace Mann's very similar reactions to a visit to Perkins.

53. William Awl, Columbus, OH, to S. G. Howe, 13 Aug. 1836, HPP; Joseph Phillips, Monticello, GA, to S. G. Howe, 4 June 1838, HPP.

54. *North American Review,* April 1841, 486.

55. Howe, *Address of the Trustees* (1833), 11; *Annual Report* (1834), 5.

56. S. G. Howe to Mr. Erbin, 27 Jan. 1841 (masturbation); Howe to L. M. Brown, 30 Dec. 1844 (discipline); Howe to Rev. Thayer, 26 Dec. 1844 (book funds); Howe to A. Dewitt, 28 Sept. 1841 (flannels), HPP.

57. Charles Goff to S. G. Howe, 18 Oct. 1848, HPP; Howe to Horace Mann, 17 May (?), HPP. This letter is likely from the mid 1840s, a period after Howe's discovery and work with Laura Bridgman. As a result, it does not prove Howe's feelings during the mid-30s, before finding Laura Bridgman. Rather, it is cited to show an enduring characteristic of Howe's motivation as a reformer, a spirit of restlessness that led him into numerous causes over the next four decades.

58. Edward Parks, "Introduction," in Lamson, *Life and Education,* xxiii. Contrary to Howe's opinion and to popular perceptions to this day, those who suffer the loss of one of their senses are not able to compensate for the loss by developing greater sensitivity of their remaining senses. Julia Brace's sense of smell, for example, was no greater than it would have been if she had not lost her ability to see and hear. However, people in this condition may develop a greater ability to interpret the sensory input they receive, making better use of sensory information that a "normal" person rarely notices. See Michael Monbeck, *The Meaning of Blindness: Attitudes toward Blindness and Blind People* (Bloomington, 1973), 17–18.

59. Howe, "Laura Bridgman," *Barnard's American Journal of Education,* Dec. 1857, 388.

60. Elliott and Hall, *Laura Bridgman,* 39. Evidence that Dr. Mussey was also corresponding with the director of the American Asylum for the Deaf in Hartford about the Bridgman case is found in James Barrett to S. G. Howe, 11 July 1837, HPP.

61. S. G. Howe, *Ninth Annual Report* (Boston, 1841), 25.

62. Elliott and Hall, *Laura Bridgman,* 41–43; S. G. Howe, "Laura Bridgman," *Barnard's American Journal of Education,* Dec. 1857, 389–390. Howe's accounts of the meeting suggest that he initiated the idea of sending Laura Bridgman to an institution, but a letter to Howe by a Dartmouth student, sent before Howe arrived in Hanover, suggests that the Bridgmans "have intended to send her to some suitable Institution, when they should get able." James Barrett to Howe, 11 July 1837, HPP.

63. Samuel Eliot quoted in Elliott and Hall, *Laura Bridgman,* 39.

64. S. G. Howe, *Sixth Annual Report* (Boston, 1838), 6.

2. Mind over Matter

1. Mary Swift Lamson, *Life and Education of Laura Bridgman* (Boston, 1881; New York, 1975), 5; Laura Bridgman, "Earliest Autobiography," 1849, Laura Bridgman Papers, Perkins (hereafter BPP).

2. William Ingalls, M.D., *A Lecture on the Subject of Phrenology Not Opposed to the Principles of Religion; Nor the Precepts of Christianity* (Boston, 1839), 10. Howe never publicly mentioned using force, however mild, to win Laura's submission.

3. Samuel Gridley Howe, *The Education of Laura Bridgman*, ed. Julia Ward Howe (Boston, 189?), 4. The extent of the novelty of the Laura Bridgman experiment is exaggerated by Julia Ward Howe's description and her husband's own public interpretation of Laura's education. In the previous century a great deal of attention had been paid to similar cases of deaf-blindness, most notably the case of James Mitchell, a Scottish boy born deaf and blind. While those cases excited a great deal of philosophical interest, there was little doubt that James Mitchell was, in spite of his handicaps, "capable of reflexion and reasoning." Likewise, Laura Bridgman's own behavior prior to meeting Howe clearly suggested that she contained active powers of reasoning. Perhaps the drama of the Laura Bridgman experiment was heightened by more immediate comparison with the case of Julia Brace at the American Asylum in Hartford, whose physical infirmities were accompanied by apparent mental ones.

4. Maude Howe Elliott and Florence Howe Hall, *Laura Bridgman: Dr. Howe's Famous Pupil and What He Taught Her* (Boston, 1904), 157.

5. For general works on the influence of Scottish philosophy in America see Sydney E. Ahlstrom, "The Scottish Philosophy and American Theology," *Church History* 24 (1955): 257–272. Daniel Walker Howe, *The Unitarian Conscience: Harvard Moral Philosophy, 1805–1861* (Cambridge, 1970); Donald Myer, *The Instructed Conscience* (Philadelphia, 1972); Richard Petersen, *Scottish Common Sense in America, 1768–1850* (Washington, DC, 1963).

6. Daniel Walker Howe, *Unitarian Conscience*, passim; Ahlstrom, "Scottish Philosophy and American Theology," 257–269.

7. Samuel Gridley Howe, *An Address Delivered at the Anniversary Celebration of the Boston Phrenological Society* (Boston, 1836), 18.

8. For a fuller discussion of the tenets of phrenology see John D. Davies, *Phrenology, Fad and Science: A Nineteenth-Century Crusade* (New Haven, 1955); David Gustino, *Conquest of Mind: Phrenology and Victorian Social Thought* (London, 1975); and Robert M. Young, *Mind, Brain and Adaptation in the Nineteenth Century* (Oxford, 1970).

9. Howe to Horace Mann, 1857, Howe Papers, Houghton; typescript copy in Howe Papers, Perkins (hereafter HPP).

10. Dr. J. C. Warren to Dr. J. Stevenson, 11 Nov. 1832, vol. 46, Joseph Warren Papers, Massachusetts Historical Society (hereafter MHS); Jonathan Barber, *An Address Delivered before the Boston Phrenological Society, on the Evening of Its Organization* (Boston, 1833); Howe, *Address*.

11. Howe, *Address*, 18. On the central role of phrenology on nineteenth-century discussions of psychology see Young, *Mind, Brain and Adaptation in the Nineteenth Century*, passim.

12. George Combe, *The Constitution of Man Considered in Relation to External Objects*

(Boston: Allen and Ticknor, 1834: rpt. Delmar, NY: Scholars' Facsimile Press, 1974); see Alfred Young, ch. 4, for a discussion of nineteenth-century ideas about the link between the brain and language ability.

13. Howe, *Ninth Annual Report* (Boston, 1841) (hereafter *Ninth AR*), 24.

14. Ibid., 25. Howe's conclusion that Laura's own language of gestures, no matter how well developed, would have restricted her intellectual range seems supported by modern research on the linguistic development of the deaf. Most deaf children who are not taught a form of Sign or oral language will instinctively improvise a symbolic system of their own. These self-made languages, researchers have found, are never able to attain the complexity and power of more abstract symbolic language—either signed or spoken. "The deaf mute who has not been taught to speak," one study concluded, "does not possess all those forms of reflection which are realized through speech . . . [He] indicates objects or actions with a gesture; he is unable to form abstract concepts, to systematize the phenomena of the external world with the aid of abstract signals furnished by language but which are not natural to visual, practically acquired experience." A. R. Luria and F. Yudovich cited in Oliver Sacks, *Seeing Voices: A Journey into the World of the Deaf* (Los Angeles, 1989), 43.

15. "Julia Brace," *Religious Magazine and Family Miscellany,* Aug. 1847, 347–355. The instructors at the Hartford asylum had, in fact, attempted to teach Julia Brace the use of the alphabet, in the hopes of eventually teaching her "moral and religious truth." Their own efforts largely parallel the technique later used by Howe, although Howe never publicly acknowledged this fact. Guided by carved wooden letters, Julia did learn to form the letters of "a few simple words." But, one writer reported, this cumbersome process of communication "soon became uninteresting to her," and apparently to her teachers as well, who abandoned the project as hopeless. After Howe's success with Laura Bridgman, Julia Brace was invited to come to Perkins to see if she might be able to learn to use the alphabet under Howe's instruction. The experiment produced a similar disappointing result, and Julia returned to Hartford. Howe claimed that this failure was probably due to the fact that she had passed the age when she could easily learn language. Considering that she did not enter the Hartford asylum until the age of eighteen, this seems like a likely reason why her initial language training in Hartford failed as well. Julia Brace's experience points to the importance of Laura Bridgman's young age as a crucial factor in the ultimate success of Howe's educational efforts.

16. Thomas Reid, *An Inquiry into the Human Mind on the Principles of Common Sense,* in *Thomas Reid's Inquiry and Essays,* ed. Ronald E. Beanblossom and Keith Lehrer (Indianapolis, 1983), 31–35. As educators of the deaf now point out, this scheme which divides language into a primitive system of manual gestures and a "higher" spoken language leaves out a third possibility: that a manual sign language may become as sophisticated, as capable of expressing abstract thought, as a spoken language. Because Howe accepted Reid's view of manual gestures, he became a leading proponent of teaching deaf children to speak and banning sign language from schools for the deaf. Historians of deaf culture now suggest that this "reform," fully

realized a few years after Howe's death, set deaf education back for almost a century. Sacks, *Seeing Voices*, 27–28; Douglas C. Baynton, "'Savages and Deaf-Mutes': Evolutionary Theory and the Campaign against Sign Language in the Nineteenth Century," *Deaf History Unveiled*, ed. John Vickrey Van Cleve (Washington, DC, 1993), 92–112.

17. Dugald Stewart, "Of Language," *Collected Works* (Edinburgh, 1854), 4:9.

18. Howe, *Tenth Annual Report* (Boston, 1842), 21.

19. Denis Diderot, *The Letter on the Blind,* trans. Margaret Jourdain, in *Diderot's Early Philosophical Works* (Chicago, 1916), 89.

20. Sacks, *Seeing Voices*, 15–17.

21. Wright's description in Lamson, *Life and Education,* 5–6; *Ninth AR,* 25.

22. *Ninth AR,* 26.

23. In his book on the experience of deafness, Oliver Sacks cites several historic cases that seem to parallel Howe's 1841 observation that Laura's understanding of the symbolic power of language was learned quite rapidly and that it had a profound transformative effect on her mind and spirit. Reviewing the story of Massieu, Sicard's famous deaf pupil who learned sign language at the age of fourteen, Sacks writes that, "in this way, at the age of fourteen, he entered into the human estate, could know the world as home, the world as his 'domain' in a way he had never known before." Sacks describes the experience of Kaspar Hauser in similar terms. Hauser was a German man who grew to maturity without learning any language, because his abusive guardians had locked him in a dark room for most of his childhood. When he emerged and learned language, Sacks writes, "this awakening to the world of shared meanings, of language, led to a sudden and brilliant awakening of his whole mind and soul." Sacks, *Seeing Voices,* 48, 52.

24. Howe, *Sixth Annual Report* (Boston, 1838) (hereafter *Sixth AR*), 11–12.

25. Ibid.

26. Lamson, *Life and Education,* 7.

27. *Sixth AR,* 6.

28. *Sixth AR,* 6–7.

29. Howe to "Sec. of State of Maine," 18 Oct. 1837, HPP.

30. Michael J. Morgan, *Molyneux's Question: Vision, Touch and the Philosophy of Perception* (Cambridge, 1977), 82, 96–97; John Yolton, *John Locke: An Introduction* (New York, 1985), 134–135; *Condillac's Treatise on the Sensations,* trans. Geraldine Carr (Los Angeles, 1930), xxii; S. G. Howe, *Seventh Annual Report* (Boston, 1839) (hereafter *Seventh AR*), 9–10.

31. S. G. Howe, "Atheism in New England, I," *New England Magazine,* Dec. 1834; S. G. Howe, "Atheism in New England, II," *New England Magazine,* Jan. 1835.

32. Howe, "Atheism in New-England, I," 505–506, 509; "Atheism in New-England, II," 56–57.

33. Howe, "Atheism in New-England, II," 60.

34. Sir William Blackstone, *Commentaries on the Laws of England* (Philadelphia, 1771) I, book I, 304; S. G. Howe, *Education of Laura Bridgman,* 212–213. In the Public Eye

35. Lamson, *Life and Education,* 8.

36. Howe to Harriet Martineau, 27 Apr. 1838, HPP.

37. Drew in Lamson, *Life and Education*, 7.

38. *Seventh AR*, 9–10.

39. Howe, "Notes on Laura Bridgman," in S. G. Howe, *Education of Laura Bridgman*, 213.

40. "Massachusetts Asylum for the Blind," *Godey's Lady's Book*, Sept. 1842, 156.

41. Dr. John Kitto, *The Lost Senses* (New York, 1852), 210; Ingalls, "A Lecture on the Subject of Phrenology," 10.

42. L. Minot, "Review of *Eighth Annual Report*," *Christian Examiner and General Review*, July 1840, 373.

43. Ibid., 367.

44. Ibid., 370.

45. *Ninth AR*, 24. Also quoted in Kitto, *Lost Senses*, 207. Kitto, in one of the few contemporary accounts that treats Howe's account with a modest measure of skepticism, commented, "This is perhaps too highly colored."

46. Howe quoted in Mary Howitt, "Laura Bridgman," *Howitt's Journal*, 9 Oct. 1847.

47. *Ninth AR*, 36; S. G. Howe, *Education of Laura Bridgman*, 386.

48. Howe, *Eleventh Annual Report* (Boston, 1843), 27; Howe, *Education of Laura Bridgman*, 386.

49. Douglas L. Geenens, "Neurobiological Development and Cognition in the Deafblind," in *A Guide to Planning and Support for Individuals Who Are Deafblind* (Toronto, 1999), 152–153.

50. G. Stanley Hall, "Laura Bridgman," *Mind* 14 (Apr. 1879), 152–153.

51. Steven Jay Gould, *The Mismeasure of Man* (New York, 1981), 22.

52. For a general summary of the phrenologists' attack on the method of introspection, see "On the Comparative Merits of Phrenology and the Philosophy of Reid and Stewart," *American Phrenological Journal and Miscellany* 3 (1 Sept. 1841).

53. Howe, *Address*, 11–12.

3. In the Public Eye

1. Harmony Bridgman to Howe, 1 Feb. 1841; Harmony Bridgman to Mrs. Smith, 15 March 1838, Laura Bridgman Papers, Perkins (hereafter BPP).

2. S. G. Howe to Mr. and Mrs. Bridgman, 30 March 1838, Howe Papers, Perkins (hereafter HPP).

3. S. G. Howe, *Ninth Annual Report* (Boston, 1841) (hereafter *Ninth AR*), 28.

4. Ibid.

5. Ibid., 29.

6. *The Emancipator*, 1 April 1841; *Ladie's Pearl and Literary Gleaner*, April 1841; L. Minot, "The Perkins Institution," *Christian Examiner and General Review*, July 1840, 359; "Laura Bridgman; the Deaf, Dumb, and Blind Child," *North American Review*, April 1841, 469.

7. *Boston Recorder*, 1 July 1842. Writing at the end of the century, William Dean Howells wrote that Laura's story "early went over the world, and everywhere stirred

the springs of humanity." William Dean Howells, "An Immortal of Boston," undated magazine clipping in BPP.

8. Howe, *Ninth AR*, 23.
9. Howe to Ramon De La Sagua, n.d., 1838; Howe to Baron Degerando, 13 May 1842,
   HPP.
10. Howe to Dr. Julius, Sept. 1839; Prof. Burdach to Howe, 5 Apr. 1842, HPP.
11. Ellen W. Healy to Howe, 3 Nov. 1838, HPP.
12. G. Stanley Hall, "Laura Bridgman," *Mind* 14 (April 1879): 151; George Combe to
    Howe, 30 Nov. 1842, HPP; George Sumner to Howe, 2 Aug. 1845, typescript copy
    in HPP; Harold Schwartz, *Samuel Gridley Howe: Social Reformer, 1801–1876* (Cam-
    bridge, 1956), 88.
13. Howe sent copies of his reports to the directors of the various schools and asy-
    lums in England and Scotland and to noted reformers such as Harriet Martineau.
    Martineau, herself partially deaf, had visited Perkins the year before Laura's arrival
    and had already provided her countrymen with a glowing account of the Doctor's
    work in her *Retrospect of Western Travel* (1838). Howe's reports, she wrote there,
    breathed "a more exhilarating spirit of hopefulness, a finer tone of meek triumph,"
    than any other work in American literature.
14. Combe cited in Maude Howe Elliott and Florence Howe Hall, *Laura Bridgman: Dr.
    Howe's Famous Pupil and What He Taught Her* (Boston, 1904), 80–81.
15. Charles Dickens, *American Notes* (1842; rpt. New York, 1961).
16. Rogers, Teachers' Journal (hereafter TJ), 29 Jan. 1842, BPP.
17. Charles Dickens, Cincinnati, OH, to Howe, 4 April 1842, HPP.
18. Howe to Horace Mann, n.d., Mann Papers, Massachustts Historical Society.
19. Elisabeth A. Gitter, "Laura Bridgman and Little Nell," *Dickens Quarterly,* June 1991,
    75–79.
20. Howe, *Sixth Annual Report* (Boston, 1838), 6; Dickens, *American Notes,* 47.
21. John F. Sears, *Sacred Places: American Tourist Attractions in the Nineteenth Century*
    (New York, 1989), 222–223.
22. Dr. Sam Henry Dickson, S. Carolina, to Howe, 14 Dec. 1844, HPP; *Christian Watch-
    man,* 11 July 1845.
23. Mary Swift Lamson, *Life and Education of Laura Bridgman* (Boston, 1881; rpt. New
    York, 1975), 46–47.
24. *Ladies' Repository,* June 1845, 454; "Visit to the Blind Asylum at South Boston, Mas-
    sachusetts," *Youth's Magazine or Evangelical Miscellany,* June 1841, 207; Lady Em-
    meline Stuart Wortley, *Travels in the United States* (New York, 1851), 68–69.
25. "Laura Bridgman," *Ladies' Repository,* June 1845, 454; *American Family Magazine of
    Useful and Entertaining Knowledge,* April 1839; "'I Want to See,'" *Youth's Magazine;
    or Evangelical Miscellany,* July 1843, clippings in BPP.
26. "Laura Bridgman," *Mother's Monthly Journal* 7 (Jan. 1842), 27; Rev. W. K. Tweedie,
    The Early Choice: A Book for Daughters (Philadelphia, 1857), 41; S. H. Jenks, Bos-
    ton, to Lucy C. Jenks, Nantucket, 9 Feb. 1840, copy in BPP.
27. Schwartz, *Samuel Gridley Howe,* 89–90; Nelly Bly, "Deaf, Dumb and Blind," *The
    World,* 17 Feb. 1889, clipping in BPP.

28. Dickens, *American Notes,* 47; Wortley, *Travels in the United States,* 68–69.

29. Karen Halttunen, *Confidence Men and Painted Women: A Study of Middle-Class Culture in America, 1830–1870* (New Haven, 1982), passim; John F. Kasson, *Rudeness and Civility: Manners in Nineteenth-Century Urban America* (New York, 1990), ch. 3; Steven Mintz, *Moralists and Modernizers* (Baltimore, 1995), 3–15; Anne C. Rose, *Voices of the Marketplace: American Thought and Culture, 1830–1860* (New York, 1995), 60–72.

30. Howe, *Ninth AR,* 37.

31. Howe, *Eighth Annual Report,* 14–15; *Ninth AR,* 34–37; Swift, TJ, 1 Feb. 184.

32. Laura's teacher Mary Swift explained: "No one, who has not attempted it, can fully understand the difficulty of commencing a new subject with Laura—After thinking it over & over again I feel sure that my sentences are so worded that she will have no difficulty in understanding the words—when perhaps one word may be used in a little different sense from that to which she is accustomed, as for instance this morning, after explaining the word vapor—I said "it *turns* the water into vapor"— She thought a moment & said "do you mean turns round?"—She had never chanced to hear the word turns used to mean change—& of course all her attention was centered upon that one word- & the new truth which I wished her to take was lost." Swift, TJ, 21 Nov. 1843.

33. Rogers, TJ, 14 Nov. 1843; S. G. Howe, *Tenth Annual Report* (Boston, 1842) (hereafter *Tenth AR*), 25.

34. *Tenth AR,* 25; Thomas Carlyle to Howe, 23 Oct. 1842, typescript copy, Howe Papers, Houghton (hereafter HPH).

35. Thomas Carlyle to Howe, 23 Oct. 1842, typescript copy, HPH.

36. Howe, *Eleventh Annual Report* (Boston, 1843), 36–37.

37. Swift, TJ, 4 Sept. 1843; Lamson, *Life and Education,* 142–143; Drew, TJ, 3 July 1841.

38. Drew, TJ, 25 Aug. 1841. Other examples include Drew, 23 June 1841, 3 July 1841, 27 Sept. 1841.

39. Wight, TJ, 23 Dec. 45; Lamson, *Life and Education,* 159; Swift, TJ, 15 June 1844; Howe, *Tenth AR,* 25.

40. Schwartz, *Samuel Gridley Howe,* 76–83.

41. Howe, *Eighteenth Annual Report* (Cambridge, 1850), 48; *Tenth AR,* 19.

42. Lamson, *Life and Education,* 342–343;

43. This possibility is discussed and rejected in Howe, *Tenth AR,* 27.

44. Howe to Mr. Reed, Vermont, 12 June 1842, HPP.

45. Howe, *Eighteenth AR,* 48; Mary Howitt, "Laura Bridgman," *Howitt's Journal,* 9 Oct. 1847.

46. Howitt, "Laura Bridgman."

4. Body and Mind

1. The complete list of the Boston Phrenological Society's collection was published in *A Catalogue of Phrenological Specimens Belonging to the Boston Phrenological Society*

(Boston, 1835). Information about the collection and Howe's role in maintaining it can be found in Howe's letters to J. C. Warren, Warren Papers, Massachusetts Historical Society (MHS).

2. S. G. Howe, *A Discourse on the Social Relations of Man; Delivered before the Boston Phrenological Society, at the Close of Their Course of Lectures* (Boston, 1837), 7–8.

3. Howe, *Discourse on Social Relations,* 8.

4. Ibid., 8.

5. S. G. Howe, "Transcendentalism," *Education of Laura Bridgman,* ed. Julia Ward Howe (Boston, 189?), 217–218.

6. Howe, *Discourse on Social Relations,* 7. Although the tenets of phrenology suggested to Howe that he would have to be patient before he could expect the manifestations of her moral nature to become evident, he could hardly wait. In his first report he could not resist noting that she already exhibited some sense of "right and wrong" and that her moral faculties appeared to be in full working order. But he postponed making any definite conclusions about the child's "moral nature" for the first few years. Howe, *Sixth Annual Report* (Boston, 1837) (hereafter *Sixth AR*), 6–7.

7. Laura Bridgman to Sarah Wight, 29 Dec. 1850, Laura Bridgman Papers, Perkins (hereafter BPP).

8. Howe to L. M. Brown, 30 Dec. 1844, Howe Papers, Perkins (hereafter HPP); Howe, *Eighth Annual Report* (Boston, 1840) (hereafter *Eighth AR*), 19. Howe noted: "On the whole she seems to care less for eating than most children of her age."

9. Howe to Mr. Reed, 12 June 1842, HPP.

10. Laura Bridgman to Harmony Bridgman, 11 Oct. 1846, BPP.

11. Howe, *Fifth Annual Report* (Boston, 1837) (hereafter *Fifth AR*), 7–8.

12. Howe, *Ninth Annual Report* (Boston, 1841) (hereafter *Ninth AR*), 8, 4–5; *Eighth AR,* 3.

13. George Combe to Howe, 24 March 1839, HPP.

14. *Eighth AR,* 16; Jeannette Howe to S. G. Howe, 14 Oct. 1843, HPP; Rogers, Teachers' Journals (hereafter TJ), 6 Dec. 1842, BPP.

15. TJ, 21 Jan. 1843, 16 March 1843.

16. Mary Swift Lamson, *Life and Education of Laura Bridgman* (Boston, 1881; New York, 1975), 70. Laura spent much of her time knitting purses, designed in the shape of pitchers. Her teacher noted that demand for them was "often in advance of the supply." Certainly one of the great selling points of these products was the fact that they were created by such novel workers, making the merchandise more valuable as a curiosity. There is some evidence to suggest that Laura's work, for this reason, was particularly of interest.

17. *Fifth AR,* 7.

18. Howe, *Annual Report* (Boston, 1834), 11; Sarah Wight to Howe, 7 Apr. 1851, HPP.

19. *Eighth AR,* 4.

20. Howe to L. M. Brown, 30 Dec. 1844, HPP; Howe to Charles Sumner, 7 Sept. 1850, Howe Family Papers, Houghton.

21. For a more complete discussion of these reforms, see Robert C. Fuller, *Alternative*

Medicine and American Religious Life (New York, 1989), chs. 1–3; James C. Whorton, *Crusaders for Fitness: The History of American Health Reformers* (Princeton, 1982), 3–92; Marshall Scott Legan, "Hydropathy, or the Water-Cure," in *Pseudo-Science and Society in Nineteenth-Century America,* ed. Arthur Wrobel (Lexington, KY, 1987), 74–99.

22. Fuller, *Alternative Medicine,* 30–33; Howe, *Discourse on Social Relations,* 37.

23. S. G. Howe to Horace Mann, 15 Aug. 1846, Mann Papers, MHS; E. E. Denniston to S. G. Howe, 26 Oct. 1847, Howe Papers, MHS.

24. Fuller, *Alternative Medicine,* 38–49; Howe, *Tenth Annual Report* (Boston, 1842) (hereafter *Tenth AR*), 24.

25. Orson Fowler cited in Whorton, *Crusaders for Fitness,* 6.

26. Howe, *Discourse on Social Relations,* 4.

27. In the area of sexual practices, there were some health reformers who clearly broke with conventional Christian morality, although they usually supported their innovations in religious terms. For example, John Humphrey Noyes's experiments with communal marriage at the Oneida colony must be considered part of the health reform movement, as were the "free love" ideas of Mary Gove Nichols, one of the nation's leading proponents of hydropathy. Whorton, *Crusaders for Fitness,* 121–123.

28. Ibid., 25.

29. Howe, *Discourse on Social Relations,* 28.

30. Philip Greven, *The Protestant Temperament* (Chicago, 1977), 65–73.

31. One ironic exception to this rule was Gall, the founder of phrenology. He believed that some of the organs of the brain which he located in his researches proved man's innate predisposition to sin. He drew a natural faculty for cruelty, for example, into his map of the human brain. His student, Spurzheim, revised the scheme, giving the faculties more morally neutral or positive descriptions, thus making the science more attractive to liberal Christians on both sides of the Atlantic. John D. Davies, *Phrenology, Fad and Science: A Nineteenth-Century Crusade* (New Haven, 1955) 7.

32. Howe, *Discourse on Social Relations,* 16. Howe was particularly incensed by the use of corsets, a "very absurd and unnatural attempt to set up a standard of beauty, in the outline of form, exactly the reverse of nature."

33. Ibid.; Howe to Horace Mann, 9 July 1840, Mann Papers, MHS.

34. Howe, *Discourse on Social Relations,* 39–40.

35. *Eighth AR,* 7; S. G. Howe, "Notes on Laura Bridgman," *Education of Laura Bridgman,* 209–210.

36. Howe, *Seventh Annual Report* (Boston, 1839) (hereafter *Seventh AR*), 5.

37. *Eighth AR,* 14.

38. Howe, *Tenth AR,* 20; Francis Lieber, "On the Vocal Sounds of Laura Bridgman," *Smithsonian Contributions to Knowledge,* 2, art. 2 (1850).

39. Ibid., 6; *Ninth AR,* 34; Lamson, *Life and Education,* 135–138.

40. TJ, 16 June 1841, 9 June 1841, 20 Aug. 1841, 27 July 1841.

41. Michael Katz, *The Irony of Early School Reform: Educational Innovation in Mid-*

Nineteenth Century Massachusetts (Cambridge, 1968), 131–138, discusses the reformers' interest in "object learning."

42. Swift, TJ, 26 July 1843.

43. Jeannette Howe to Samuel Gridley Howe, 14 Oct. 1843, Perkins; TJ, 12 Apr. 1842, 20 Aug. 1841, 28 June 1841.

44. *Eighth AR,* 15.

45. TJ, 31 Dec. 1841, 15 June 1841.

46. *Seventh AR,* 9.

47. *Tenth AR,* 19; *Ninth AR,* 39.

48. TJ, 5 Oct. 1841.

49. Swift, TJ, 11 Apr. 1844. In spite of Swift's misgivings about exposing Laura to historical examples of human cruelty, by July the child was reading a story about a battle between two African tribes which described "the Tuaricks killing the Tibbors." As Swift predicted, Laura "was horror-struck & did not seem to know what to say. She never before has heard that there is such a thing as man's killing man—in this world." Swift, TJ, 8 July. 1844.

50. Ibid., 22 March 1842.

51. Ibid., 23 Aug. 1843, 27 Aug. 1843, 27 Apr. 1842.

52. Ibid., 9 June 1843.

53. *Sixth AR,* 8; *Tenth AR,* 16.

54. George Combe, *Constitution of Man* (Boston, 1834; rpt., New York, 1974), 51–52; Harold Schwartz, "Samuel Gridley Howe as Phrenologist," *American Historical Review* (April 1952): 644–651. Howe despaired of ever reaching Laura's faculties of "Tune" and "Colouring," but he devised exercises to test and exercise her organ of "Time." He reported that the child could correctly maintain time when striking the keys of a piano, thus proving that "the capacity of perceiving and measuring the lapse of time is an innate and distinct faculty of the mind." *Eighth AR,* 18.

55. Whorton, *Crusaders for Fitness.* See also Bernard Wishy, *The Child and the Republic* (Philadelphia, 1968), ch. 4. Greven, *Protestant Temperament,* part 3, discusses the ideal of physical, mental and spiritual balance among those Greven calls "moderates."

56. *Fifth AR,* 8.

57. Combe, *Constitution of Man,* 54; *Seventh AR,* 3.

58. *Sixth AR,* 8; Lamson, *Life and Education,* 157.

59. *Ninth AR,* 7.

60. *Eighth AR,* 20; Lamson, *Life and Education,* 69.

61. *Ninth AR,* 12.

62. Horace Mann, "Laura Bridgman," *Common School Journal,* 16 May 1842, 145.

63. Jonathan Messerli, *Horace Mann: A Biography* (New York, 1972), 182; Horace Mann to Howe, 8 March 1838, HPP.

64. Messerli, *Horace Mann,* ch. 11; David Tyack and Elisabeth Hansot, *Managers of Virtue: Public School Leadership in America, 1820–1980* (New York, 1982), 58–59; Merle Curti, *The Social Ideas of American Educators* (New Jersey, 1978), 101–138;

Horace Mann, "Means and Objects of Common School Education (1837)," *Lectures on Education* (Boston, 1855: rpt. New York, 1969), 12.

65. Horace Mann, "Laura Bridgman," 146.

66. Ibid., 16 May 1842, 1 Feb. 1841.

67. Horace Mann, "Means and Objects of Common School Education," *Lectures on Education* (Boston, 1855; rpt. New York, 1969), 20.

68. Mann, "Means and Objects," 22.

69. Mann, "Laura Bridgman," 1 Feb. 1841.

70. Rogers, TJ, 29 June 1842.

71. Swift, TJ, 7 June 1843.

72. Drew, TJ, 19 August 1841.

73. TJ, 16 August 1843.

74. TJ, 6 Oct. 1841.

75. Howe to Dr. Julius, Hamburg, 30 March 1840, HPP.

5. The Instinct to Be Good

1. John Davies, *Phrenology, Fad and Science* (New Haven, 1955), ch. 1; George Combe to Howe, 15 March 1840, typescript copy in Howe Papers, Perkins (hereafter HPP); Neil Gerard McCluskey, *Public Schools and Moral Education: The Influence of Horace Mann, William Torrey Harris and John Dewey* (New York, 1958), 23–31; Harold Schwartz, "Samuel Gridley Howe as Phrenologist," *American Historical Review* (April 1952), 645–647. Schwartz describes Howe as "Combe's leading American interpreter."

2. Horace Mann to Mrs. James H. Mills, 7 and 6 Nov. 1838, Mann Papers, Massachusetts Historical Society (MHS).

3. George Combe, *Notes on the United States of North America during a Phrenological Visit in 1838–9–40* (Philadelphia, 1841), 204–205.

4. George Combe, *Notes*, 204–205; Howe, *Ninth Annual Report* (Boston, 1841) (hereafter *Ninth AR*), 32.

5. George Combe to Howe, 15 March 1840, typescript copy in HPP.

6. Howe to Horace Mann, 17 May 1841, Howe Papers, Houghton (hereafter HPH).

7. Harold Schwartz, *Samuel Gridley Howe: Social Reformer, 1801–1876* (Cambridge, 1956), 149. For a description of Howe's role in Brown's raid see pp. 217–246.

8. Howe to Horace Mann, 4 Aug. 184?, HPH; Howe, *Address Delivered at the Anniversary Celebration of the Boston Phrenological Society* (Boston, 1836), 22.

9. Howe, *Address*, 23.

10. Davies, *Phrenology, Fad and Science*, 153.

11. Howe to Horace Mann, 4 August 184?, HPH.

12. Daniel Walker Howe, *The Unitarian Conscience: Harvard Moral Philosophy, 1805–1861* (Middletown, CT, 1988), 49.

13. Ernest Tuveson, "The Origins of Moral Sense," *Huntington Library Quarterly*, May 1948, 241–242.

14. Basil Willey, *The Eighteenth Century Background: Studies on the Idea of Nature in the Thought of the Period* (Boston, 1961), 57–60.

15. E. Brooks Holifield, *The Gentlemen Theologians: American Theology in Southern Culture, 1795–1860* (Durham, NC, 1978), 130–131.

16. Andrew Delbanco, *William Ellery Channing: An Essay on the Liberal Spirit in America* (Cambridge, 1981), 23–24.

17. William Ellery Channing, "Likeness to God (1828)," *The Works of William Ellery Channing* (Boston, 1900), 299; Delbanco, *William Ellery Channing*, 23–24; Daniel Walker Howe, *Unitarian Conscience*, 45–49. Daniel Walker Howe suggests that Boston's Unitarians had two distinctive moral sense theories to choose from. The "sentimentalist" tradition of Shaftesbury defined the conscience as an emotional attraction to the good; a competing school of thought, "rational intuitionism," also held that we have an intuitive attraction to the good but suggested that this begins as an *intellectual* understanding rather than an emotional attraction to moral truth. Daniel Walker Howe suggests that this more rationalistic version of the moral sense was preferred by most of Boston's most influential Unitarian moralists on the Harvard faculty and was supported by the writings of the Scottish philosopher Thomas Reid.

    While the rationalists believed that an understanding of right and wrong begins as an intellectual insight, they agreed that an emotional response to moral issues was also needed to provide the motivation to act. Because both versions of moral sense ultimately stress the reliability of moral intuition and the importance of emotions, the distinction between them is subtle and does not seem to have concerned Samuel Gridley Howe, who alternately described Laura's moral reasoning as an intellectual and an emotional activity.

18. Howe, *Sixth Annual Report* (Boston, 1838) (hereafter *Sixth AR*), 6–7.

19. Ibid., 6–7.

20. Howe, *Seventh Annual Report* (Boston, 1839)(hereafter *Seventh AR*), 10.

21. *Ninth AR*, 41.

22. Ibid., 42.

23. Howe, *Eleventh Annual Report* (Boston, 1843) (hereafter *Eleventh AR*), 7; S. G. Howe, *A Discourse on the Social Relations of Man; Delivered before the Boston Phrenological Society, at the Close of Their Course of Lectures* (Boston, 1837), 5.

24. *Ninth AR*, 39; Combe, *Constitution of Man*, 52.

25. *Ninth AR*, 39.

26. Ibid., 23.

27. Howe, *Thirteenth Annual Report* (Boston, 1845) (hereafter *Thirteenth AR*), 49.

28. *Ninth AR*, 38.

29. Ibid., 39.

30. Ibid., 38; *Eleventh AR*, 36.

31. *Ninth AR*, 37; *Eleventh AR*, 34. For a discussion of American culture's interest in returning to "organic conventions," see R. W. B. Lewis, *The American Adam: Innocence, Tragedy, and Tradition in the Nineteenth Century* (Chicago, 1955), ch. 1.

32. *Ninth AR*, 37–38; *Tenth AR*, 28–29; Charles Dickens, *American Notes* (1842; rpt. New York, 1961), 57.

33. *Tenth AR*, 28; Teachers' Journals (hereafter TJ), 10 Sept. 1841, 9 Jan. 1843, 18 March 1842, Laura Bridgman Papers, Perkins.

34. Mary Swift, TJ, 9 Jan. 1843.

35. *Tenth AR*, 28.

36. *Ninth AR*, 38.

37. Lewis, *American Adam*, 5.

38. Horace Mann, *Common School Journal*, 6 May 1842, 148.

39. Ibid., [Date?] 1842, 148.

40. Ibid., 15 May 1843.

41. *Eleventh AR*, 24.

42. Howe, *Fourteenth Annual Report* (Cambridge, 1846) (hereafter *Fourteenth AR*), 39.

43. Swift, TJ, 26 Oct. 1843.

44. TJ, 9–10 March 1842, 23 May 1842, 4 March 1843, 1 Nov. 1843.

45. *Tenth AR*, 24; TJ, 7 Dec. 1842.

46. TJ, 15 Feb. 1842, 6 Jan. 1843, 30 March 1842.

47. Rogers, TJ, 16 March 1842.

48. Ibid., 10 March 1842.

49. *Tenth AR*, 29.

50. Howe to Dr. Julius, 30 Aug. 1841, HPP.

51. Ibid.; *Tenth AR*, 29.

6. Punishing Thoughts

1. Edwards cited in Philip Greven, *The Protestant Temperament* (Chicago, 1977), 31. Timothy Dwight cited in Peter Gregg Slater, *Children in the New England Mind in Death and in Life* (Hamden, CT, 1977), 105. My discussion of Calvinist child-rearing practices draws on Slater, 102–114, and Greven, 21–61.

2. Howe, "Boston Grammar and Writing Schools," *Common School Journal*, 1 and 15 Oct. 1845. Greven suggests that, while evangelical families often used "the rod" to impose discipline, most orthodox parents preferred to break the wills of their children through other means. Ideally, the use of stern emotional coercion, balanced by a frequent appeal to parental love and affection, made the rod unnecessary. Greven, *Protestant Temperament*, 49–55. Greven's comments are based on research into *parental* discipline, not school discipline.

3. Laura Richards, *Samuel Gridley Howe* (New York, 1935), 2–4.

4. Mann to Howe, 11 May 1845, Mann Papers, Massachusetts Historical Society (MHS).

5. Harold Schwartz, *Samuel Gridley Howe: Social Reformer, 1801–1876* (Cambridge, 1956), 43–44; Richards, *Samuel Gridley Howe*, 58–60, 201–203, 249–250; S. G. Howe, *A Discourse on the Social Relations of Man; Delivered before the Boston Phrenological Society, at the Close of Their Course of Lectures* (Boston, 1837), 7, 39; Ar-

thur Wrobel, "Phrenology as Political Science," in *Pseudo-Science and Society in Nineteenth Century America*, ed. Arthur Wrobel (Lexington, KY, 1987), 129.

6. Howe, *Discourse on Social Relations*, 26–28, 39–40.

7. Carl Kaestle, *Pillars of the Republic: Common Schools and American Society, 1780–1860* (New York, 1983), 95–103.

8. Howe, *Discourse on Social Relations*, 25; Howe, "Boston Grammar and Writing Schools," 319.

9. Howe, "Boston Grammar and Writing Schools," 313.

10. Bernard Wishy, *The Child and The Republic: The Dawn of Modern American Child Nurture* (Philadelphia, 1968); Robert Wiebe, *The Opening of American Society* (New York, 1984), 265–269.

11. Howe, *Ninth Annual Report* (Boston, 1841) (hereafter *Ninth AR*), 12; Howe to Mr. Sturtevant, 6 Aug. 1845, Howe Papers, Perkins (hereafter HPP).

12. Mrs. L. Minot, "Art. V.—Review of Eighth Annual Report of the Trustees of the Perkins Institution and Massachusetts Asylum for the Blind," *Christian Examiner,* July 1840, 364–365.

13. *Ninth AR*, 35.

14. Rodney Hessinger, "Lancaster System," *Historical Dictionary of American Education* (Westport, 1999), 208–209.

15. Howe, *Eleventh Annual Report* (Boston, 1843) (hereafter *Eleventh AR*), 23.

16. Ibid., 23.

17. Ibid., 35.

18. Ibid., 35.

19. For an interesting discussion of orthodox approaches to child punishment, see William McLoughlin, "Evangelical Childrearing in the Age of Jackson: Francis Wayland's Views on When and How To Subdue the Willfulness of Children," *Journal of Social History* 9 (1975): 20–39; *Eleventh AR*, 35.

20. Howe to Mr. Bartlett, 13 Sept. 1841, HPP; Maude Howe Elliott and Florence Howe Hall, *Laura Bridgman: Dr. Howe's Famous Pupil and What He Taught Her* (Boston, 1904), 130.

21. Rogers, Teachers' Journals (hereafter TJ), 8 Sept. 1842, Laura Bridgman Papers, Perkins; *Eleventh AR*, 36.

22. *Eleventh AR*, 36.

23. Ibid., 36.

24. TJ, 9 Feb. 1846, 16 March 1842, 4 March 1843, 30 March 1842.

25. TJ, 23–4 May 1842.

26. Swift, TJ, 31 March 1843.

27. Ibid., 7 June 1843, 13 March 1843, 12 Dec. 1843.

28. Sarah Wight, TJ, 4 Nov. 1845; Mary Swift Lamson, *Life and Education of Laura Bridgman* (Boston, 1881; New York, 1975), 235.

29. Rogers, TJ, 14 Feb. 1842.

30. Swift, TJ, 1 Nov. 1843.

31. Ibid., 3 June 1844.

32. Howe, *Thirteenth Annual Report* (Boston, 1845), 41.

33. Swift, TJ, 15 March 1844.

7. Sensing God

1. "Some Account of Laura Bridgman," *Youths' Magazine; or Evangelical Miscellany*, June 1841, 208.

2. William Ellery Channing, "Unitarian Christianity," *Three Prophets of Religious liberalism*, ed. Conrad Wright (Boston, 1964). For a discussion of the Unitarian controversy, see Conrad Wright's introduction to this volume.

3. Channing, *Three Prophets*, 50.

4. Ibid., 63.

5. Ibid., 50–56, 69.

6. Ironically, Channing's plea for tolerance included the partisan boast that liberal Christians had always considered that virtue "more highly and justly than many of our brethren." Ibid, 83. Not surprisingly, the orthodox felt more antagonized than tolerated by Channing's remarks.

7. S. G. Howe to Horace Mann, undated, Horace Mann Papers, Massachusetts Historical Society (MHS). This letter was probably written in 1841, as it discusses Channing's "The Present Age: An Address Delivered before the Mercantile Library Company of Philadelphia, May 11, 1841." See William Ellery Channing, *The Works of William E. Channing, D.D.* (Boston, 1900), 159–172; S. G. Howe to Elijah J. Hamlin, 26 Aug. 1820, typescript copy, Howe Papers, Perkins (hereafter HPP).

8. Daniel Walker Howe, *The Unitarian Conscience: Harvard Moral Philosophy, 1805–1861* (Middletown, CT, 1988), 156.

9. S. G. Howe to Horace Mann, 4 Aug. 184?, Howe Papers, Houghton; S. G. Howe, *Address Delivered at the Anniversary Celebration of the Boston Phrenological Society* (Boston, 1836), 26–27; John Davies, *Phrenology, Fad and Science: A Nineteenth-Century Crusade* (New Haven, 1955), 153.

10. Horace Mann, Journal, 24 May 1841, Mann Papers, MHS.

11. Horace Mann, *The Common School Controversy; Consisting of Three Letters of the Secretary of the Board of Education of the State of Massachusetts, in Reply to Charges Preferred against the Board, by the Editor of the Christian Witness* (Boston, 1844), 25, 10.

12. David Tyack and Elisabeth Hansot, *Managers of Virtue: Public School Leadership in America, 1820–1980* (New York, 1982), 28–31, 58; Carl Kaestle, *Pillars of the Republic: Common Schools and American Society, 1780–1860* (New York, 1983), chs. 6–7; Michael Katz, *The Irony of Early School Reform: Educational Innovation in Mid-Nineteenth Century Massachusetts* (Cambridge, 1968), part 1.

13. Raymond Culver, *Horace Mann and Religion in the Massachusetts Public Schools* (New Haven, 1929); Tyack and Hansot, *Managers of Virtue*, 59–62; Neil Gerard McCluskey, *Public Schools and Moral Education: The Influence of Horace Mann, William Torrey Harris and John Dewey* (New York, 1958), 15–16, 54–98.

14. Howe to D. Hardwell, 18 Feb.1839, HPP.

15. Maude Howe Elliott and Florence Howe Hall, *Laura Bridgman: Dr. Howe's Famous Pupil and What He Taught Her* (Boston, 1904), 150; Howe, *Eleventh Annual Report* (Boston, 1843) (hereafter *Eleventh AR*), 17. Howe was interested in printing portions of the Bible, but his choice of literature was also closely determined by his patrons. Most of the financial support he received for printing raised letter books came from religious organizations such as the Bible Society. Howe sometimes objected to the printing of "sectarian" books, arguing that, since books for the blind were so scarce, those produced should aim to serve the widest possible audience. S. G. Howe to Rev. Thayer, 26 December 1844, HPP. In private correspondence, he made it clear that he did not care for the sectarian tracts which some religious societies paid him to print, but he believed that any literature was better than none and was glad to make any addition to his library for the blind.

16. Howe to Robert Sedgewick, 9 Feb. 1837, HPP.

17. Howe, *Annual Report of the Trustees of the New England Institution for the Education of the Blind* (Boston, 1834), 10.

18. S. G. Howe to Mr. Ford, Granville, Vermont, 20 June 1841, HPP. In fairness to Howe, it should be noted that he was careful to get parental permission when one of his students wished to hear the preaching of Theodore Parker. Parker was a controversial Unitarian minister, shunned by most of his fellow Unitarian clergymen for his transcendental heresies. In the 1840s he ministered to an eclectic congregation—the city's largest—assembled in the Music Hall. Howe, who met Parker while honeymooning in Rome in 1844, regularly attended Parker's meetings upon his return, and became an intimate friend. But he was careful not to allow his sympathies for Parker to eclipse his obligation to remain religiously neutral. In 1847, for example, he told the parents of a boy who wanted to attend Parker's services, "I am the more particular about [receiving permission] because I like Mr. Parker's preaching very much myself & I often go to hear him; but I know that there is a very strong prejudice against him & that many parents would suppose their children were going to destruction by sitting under his teachings." Howe to J. B. Drew, 11 June 1847, HPP.

19. Howe to Mr. Dewitt, 9 Oct. (no year), HPP.

20. Channing, "Remarks on Associations," *Works*, 144.

21. Anne C. Rose, *Voices of the Marketplace: American Thought and Culture, 1830–1860* (New York, 1995), 2–8. Samuel Gridley Howe, *A Discourse on the Social Relations of Man; Delivered before the Boston Phrenological Society* (Boston, 1837), 35–36. Historians of American religion suggest that by the mid-1830s fervent piety, a religion of the heart, had replaced theological reasoning, the religion of the head, as the medium of religious knowledge and the standard of church membership for most Protestant denominations. While the early nineteenth century was an era of intense competition between denominations, historians such as Sidney Mead have argued that, beneath the great diversity of Protestant faiths promoted in America's new free marketplace of religion, most Protestant Americans shared a consensus, usu-

ally summarized by the term "evangelical." Seen in historical perspective, even Boston's liberal Unitarians played a role in this evangelical movement and had much in common with their more orthodox neighbors. Unitarians, no less than the orthodox, downplayed the importance of formal theology in favor of a new emphasis on sentiment and emotion as a guide to the religious life; both shared a faith in human free will and the potential to escape from sin; orthodox evangelicals were often as eager as Unitarians to claim that their faith was rational and perfectly in accord with the latest findings of inductive science; and both Unitarians and evangelicals often felt inspired to incarnate their new views in a variety of social reform movements. While a historical perspective may reveal these similarities between Unitarians and orthodox evangelicals, Howe was clearly far more attuned to the differences between the two groups.

22. Howe, *Discourse on Social Relations*, 29.

23. *New England Puritan*, 7 Aug. 1845; "Infant Conversions," *New England Puritan*, 29 April 1847; "Religious Instruction," *New England Puritan*, 20 May 1847; "Character Formed in Early Life," *New England Puritan*, July 13 1845. For a discussion of orthodox views on child conversion, see Bernard Wishy, *The Child and The Republic: The Dawn of Modern American Child Nurture*, (Philadelphia, 1968), ch. 2. While the sincere concern these writers felt for the eternal fate of their children should not be discounted, the orthodox had an additional reason to promote infant conversion. Since the start of the Unitarian controversy, liberals had used the doctrine of infant damnation as one of their most powerful arguments against Calvinism. According to orthodox theology, all children are born guilty of Adam's sin, and those who die without receiving God's saving grace are destined for Hell. Such a conclusion was unavoidable for those prepared to carry the logic of Calvinism to its conclusion. But, in the early nineteenth century, an increasing number of Christians found this notion abhorrent. Some orthodox writers, trying to hold to the belief that conversion was a prerequisite for salvation, urged parents to try to induce "infant conversions." Others, influenced by the new romantic literature about child nurture, adopted the view that early religious education was an essential foundation of "character" building. The goal of this "Christian nurture" was not necessarily childhood conversion but an attempt to "fix" the character of children during this period of great malleability, ensuring that they would grow up to be good Christians.

24. Howe to Mr. Bartlett, 13 Sept. 1841, HPP.

25. Howe, *Ninth Annual Report* (Boston, 1841) (hereafter *Ninth AR*), 40; *Eleventh AR*, 39–40; *Tenth Annual Report* (Boston, 1842) (hereafter *Tenth AR*), 31.

26. *Tenth AR*, 27; Rogers, Teachers' Journals (hereafter TJ), 7 Dec. 1842, Laura Bridgman Papers, Perkins.

27. S. G. Howe to S. Vaughan, 26 Sept. 1836, HPP; *Ninth AR*, 41.

28. Following the logic of common sense realism's faculty psychology, Unitarians claimed that the soul's innate desire to know God actually proved God's existence. Just as the structure of the eye implied the reality of an external world to be seen,

the presence of spiritual faculties in the human mind implied the reality of a Higher Being which was the proper object of this innate religious faculty. Howe often used this argument, claiming that "the internal evidence of his own nature" not only led humans to seek God but provided "incontrovertible evidence" of God's very existence. *Ninth AR,* 41.

29. George Combe, *Notes on the United States of North America during a Phrenological Visit in 1838–9–40* (Philadelphia, 1841), 26, 49–50.

30. *Ninth AR,* 40; Howe, *Address,* 21.

31. *Eleventh AR,* 10. Howe rejected the suggestion that blind children are more religious because they have "a greater sense of dependence." Calling this feeling of dependence "an intellectual perception," he claimed that blind children exhibit a yearning for religion prior to realizing their unusual state of dependence on others. He did not offer a better explanation for his observation that blind children are more religious than their sighted counterparts.

32. *Ninth AR,* 40.

33. James Turner, *Without God, Without Creed: The Origins of Unbelief in America* (Baltimore, 1985), passim; Daniel Walker Howe, *Unitarian Concience,* ch. 3.

34. S. G. Howe, cited in *The Education of Laura Bridgman,* ed. Julia Ward Howe (Boston, 189?), 175.

35. *Tenth AR,* 30; *Thirteenth AR,* 29; Daniel Walker Howe, *Unitarian Conscience,* 78–81.

36. *Tenth AR,* 31.

37. Howe to D. Hardwell, 18 Feb. 1839, HPP; Daniel Walker Howe, *Unitarian Conscience,* 97. Phrenologists, as heirs of the same moderate enlightenment tradition which shaped Unitarianism, effected a similar compromise between head and heart religion. While they claimed that humans first experience religion through the promptings of the various religious sentiments, they added that the Creator intended that the intellectual faculties should ultimately guide those emotional urges to their proper destination.

38. *Ninth AR,* 41.

39. Howe, *Discourse on Social Relations,* 24; Anne C. Rose, *Transcendentalism as a Social Movement, 1830–1850* (New Haven, 1981), 80–83.

40. *Eleventh AR,* 40; S. G. Howe, "Transcendentalism," *Education of Laura Bridgman,* 217–218.

41. Howe, *Address,* 26–27. As part of their declaration of intellectual independence, the transcendentalists rejected New England's predominant philosophical tradition, the psychological empiricism of Locke, Bacon, and the Scottish Enlightenment. Nature, they proclaimed, could not be understood as a mechanism; the soul could not be studied as a *natural* object; God would not be confined within human reason; and close scientific scrutiny of the material world would never yield the most important discoveries, because the senses only obscured the higher, transcendent truths beyond.

While Howe shared some of the transcendentalists' interest in intuition and radical social change, he remained committed to the research program and educational theories of the moderate Enlightenment. Though he sometimes disparaged some of Locke's heirs as cold materialists, he accepted the Lockean view that the body, mind, and soul could be studied through inductive science, since human nature, no less than any other branch of nature, was endowed by its Creator with rational, discernable laws. The transcendentalists, in his view, did little more than "envelop this matter in mysteries."

Howe's attempt to educate Laura's natural instincts in accord with the principles of the Scottish Enlightenment perhaps accounts for the lack of interest that the transcendentalists took in Howe's experiment. In the view of Emerson, Howe, no less than his colleague Horace Mann, was pursuing "the gloomy democratical" approach to education, based on an attempt to control and direct the natural appetites rather than to elicit each child's natural genius. See Howe, "Transcendentalists," 218. For a good example of Mann's similar views, see Horace Mann, "What God Does, and What He Leaves for Man to Do," *Lectures and Annual Reports on Education* (Boston, 1872).

42. *Tenth AR*, 28; Lamson, *Life and Education*, 97–98.

43. Howe, *Eighth Annual Report* (Boston, 1840) (hereafter *Eighth AR*), 16; *Tenth AR*, 27–28.

44. *Eleventh AR*, 39.

45. Lamson, *Life and Education*, 119–120.

46. Wishy, *The Child and the Republic*, 30.

47. Howe to Mr. Dewitt, 9 October 1837(?), HPP.

48. Lamson, *Life and Education*, 183, 101.

49. Drew, TJ, 9 Aug. 1841, 11 Aug. 1841.

50. Rogers, TJ, 14 Aug. 1842.

51. Elliott and Hall, *Laura Bridgman*, 149.

52. *Eleventh AR*, 37.

53. Ibid., 37–38.

54. *Ninth AR*, 42.

55. Ibid., 40.

56. *Eleventh AR*, 97–98.

57. Ibid., 37–38.

58. Horace Mann, *Common School Journal*, 15 May 1843.

59. Ibid., 146–147.

60. At times, even Howe found his friend's pronouncements about Laura Bridgman to be excessive. "Such minds as his," he wrote after reading one of Mann's articles on Laura, "seem to have an intensive tendency to buy and sell and manage ton weights, but cannot or will not handle a single pound." Jonathan Messerli, *Horace Mann: A Biography* (New York, 1972), 342.

8. Crisis

1. Harold Schwartz, *Samuel Gridley Howe: Social Reformer, 1801–1876* (Cambridge, 1956), 103–104; Julia Ward Howe, *Reminiscences, 1818–1899* (Boston, 1900), 81–83.

2. Mary Swift Lamson, *Life and Education of Laura Bridgman* (Boston, 1881; New York, 1975), 106; Drew, Teachers' Journals (hereafter TJ), 10 Sept. 1841, Laura Bridgman Papers, Perkins (hereafter BPP). Further evidence of Daniel Bridgman's uncommunicative approach to his children comes from a letter Laura wrote to one of her teachers in Boston, during a stay in Hanover in 1842. Laura was concerned about her younger sister Ellen, a young child who was evidently "annoying" her mother by constantly clinging to her. Laura explained that the problem was made worse by her father: "My father never likes to caress or pacify [Ellen]. He does not like to go near my little birdie Ellen & she never approaches him when he comes in to the house." Laura thoughtfully requested that her teacher send some toys for the child, hoping that this might amuse the child and relieve her mother. Laura promised to "pay for the things as soon as it is convenient." Laura Bridgman to Mary Swift (Lamson), 12 Dec. 1842, Lamson Papers, Massachusetts Historical Society (MHS).

3. Laura Bridgman, Journals, August 1841, BPP; Maude Howe Elliott and Florence Howe Hall, *Laura Bridgman: Dr. Howe's Famous Pupil and What He Taught Her* (Boston, 1904), 108.

4. Lamson, *Life and Education*, 171; Elliott and Hall, *Laura Bridgman*, 135.

5. Lamson, *Life and Education*, 213.

6. Ibid., 169.

7. Ibid., 245.

8. Howe, *Eleventh Annual Report* (Boston, 1843) (hereafter *Eleventh AR*), 38.

9. Ibid., 37. There is no evidence that Howe was conscious of the discrepancy between his public account of Laura's religious questions and the facts as recorded by her teacher. His distortion of the record may be explained, in part, by his long absences from the Perkins school during his courtship with Julia Ward, during the two years when Laura's interest in religion was steadily growing. Howe may have been less familiar with the development of her mind than he claimed to be in his reports. But a more convincing explanation would seem to be that his confidence in phrenology led him to ignore evidence which contradicted his expectations. He believed that, according to phrenological laws, Laura should not be ready and able to understand religious truths. Believing that the mind, if allowed its freedom, will seek only those truths it is prepared to absorb, Howe assumed that Laura's religious questions were "artificial," induced by outside influence. Here, as elsewhere, he ignored the emotional need that Laura Bridgman clearly felt to "see God." Assuming that the only religious knowledge worthy of the name was derived through the rational study of nature, Howe failed to appreciate the fact that Laura's religious experience was rooted in her very different experience of the world.

10. Rogers, TJ, 25 Feb. 1842.

11. Mary Swift, TJ, 26 Apr. 1843, 13 Jan. 1844.

12. Ibid., 8 May 1843, 12 May 1843, 20 Dec. 1843.

13. TJ, 7 Jan. 1843, 10 Jan. 1843.

14. Swift, TJ, 31 Aug. 1843, 29 Dec. 1843.

15. Ibid., 16 Sept. 1843.

16. Lamson, *Life and Education*, 241.

17. Swift, TJ, 12 Jan. 1844. This discussion of Laura's religious nature, in particular the role played by her unique feelings of dependence, is in some ways similar to an analysis of Laura made by G. Stanley Hall, the late nineteenth-century psychologist. As the last scientist to observe Laura first-hand, Hall wrote several accounts. In one of them he made this relevant, though somewhat condescending, observation: "When one takes the trouble to enumerate the facts of the New Testament and the cardinal Christian doctrines with their standard forms of illustration, of which she can have even no childish conception, it is seen how minimal the intellectual element of faith may be; while if, on the other hand, with Schleirmacher, we consider the essence of Christianity to be the formulation of the instinct of dependence so unprecedentedly strong both by nature and education in her, we shall possibly wonder less that so many of her friends have found edification in her numerous conversations and letters concerning her religious experience and belief." G. Stanley Hall, "Laura Bridgman," *Mind: A Quarterly Review of Psychology and Philosophy* (April 1879): 171–172.

18. Howe to Charles Sumner, 29 March 1843, Howe Papers, Houghton (hereafter HPH); Schwartz, *Samuel Gridley Howe*, 113.

19. Edward Everett to Charles Sumner, 11 Aug. 1843, Everett Papers, 46:514–516, MHS, cited in Schwartz, *Samuel Gridley Howe*, 113; Thomas Sargeant, Devon, England, to Howe, 14 Feb. 1844, Howe Papers, Perkins (hereafter HPP); Harriet Martineau to Howe, 17 June 1843, HPP.

20. Jane Welsh Carlyle to Jeannie Welsh, 1843, *Collected Letters of Thomas & Jane Welsh Carlyle* (Durham, 1987), 16:183–185; Julia Ward Howe, *Reminiscences, 1819–1899*, 96–97; Julia Ward Howe to Eliza Ward Francis, 13 June 1843, HPH, cited in Schwartz, *Samuel Gridley Howe*, 114; Julia Ward Howe, *Memoir* (Boston, 1876), 26–28.

21. Howe to Charles Sumner, 18 June 1843, HPH.

22. Ibid., 30 June 1844, HPH. The work Howe refers to is R. Fowler, *Some Observations on the Mental State of the Blind, and Deaf, and Dumb, Suggested by the Case of Jane Sullivan, Both Blind, Deaf, Dumb, and Uneducated* (Salisbury, 1843).

23. Howe to Charles Sumner, 30 June 1844, HPH.

24. Schwartz, *Samuel Gridley Howe*, 115–117; Lamson, *Life and Education*, 258.

25. Howe to Charles Sumner, 24 March 1844, HPH; Julia Ward Howe, *Memoir*, 29; George Combe to Howe, 13 July 1845, HPH.

26. Lamson, *Life and Education*, 228–229. Writing years later, Mary Swift (Lamson) confirmed that Laura spent several months "anxiously waiting" for Howe's reply to her letter.

27. Lamson, *Life and Education*, 203–205, 233–234.

28. Swift, TJ, 2 and 3 Feb. 1844.

29. Lamson, *Life and Education*, 231–232.

30. Ibid., 233.

31. Swift, TJ, 24 Jan. 1844, 4 March 1844.

32. Lamson, *Life and Education,* 250–253.

33. Ibid.

34. Ibid., 253, 277.

35. Swift, TJ, 16 Jan. 1844.

36. Lamson, *Life and Education,* 275–276.

37. Swift, TJ, 10 July 1844.

38. Lamson, *Life and Education,* 276–277.

39. Mary Swift later wrote: "Could Dr. Howe have anticipated her mental development during his absence, he would doubtless have left her under the charge of some person who sympathized with his views and who could have satisfied her questionings; but it was my privilege only to give the intellectual training which should prepare the way for my more favored successor." Lamson, *Life and Education,* 277.

40. Elliott and Hall, *Laura Bridgman,* 150; Howe quoted in G. Stanley Hall, "Laura Bridgman," 171; Howe, *Thirteenth Annual Report* (Boston, 1845) (hereafter *Thirteenth AR*), 32–33. In his next annual report Howe specifically exonerated Mary Swift of responsibility for Laura's unauthorized religious instruction, saying she was "faithful and industrious. Had all others been as discreet and wise as she, we should not have to regret some impressions the child has received."

41. Howe to Horace Mann, n.d., Mann Papers, MHS; C. C. Felton to Howe, n.d., HPP; *Thirteenth AR,* 33.

42. *Thirteenth AR,* 32.

43. Ibid., 31.

44. "The Deaf, Dumb and Blind," *Littel's Living Age* (Boston, 1844), 765, rpt. from *Christian Observer,* undated clipping in BPP.

45. Dr. George Cheever, D. D., "Dr. Howe's Report on the Blind," *New York Evangelist,* 10 April 1845.

46. John D. Rupp, New York, to S. G. Howe, S. Boston, 6 May 1845, HPP; "Perkins Institution for the Blind," *New England Puritan,* 18 April 1845.

47. "Perkins Institution for the Blind," *New England Puritan,* 18 April 1845.

48. *Christian Watchman,* 1 May 1846.

49. Neil Gerard McCluskey, *Public Schools and Moral Education: The Influence of Horace Mann, William Torrey Harris and John Dewey* (New York, 1958), 76–78.

50. Schwartz, *Samuel Gridley Howe,* 122–136.

51. McCluskey, *Public Schools,* 59–61.

52. Dr. Heman Humphrey ("Watchman"), *New England Puritan,* 29 Oct. 1846. As a supporter of common school reform and a member of the State Board, Humphrey may have found it politically convenient to criticize Mann's sectarian excesses anonymously, and indirectly, by attacking Howe's sentiments rather than Mann's. Humphrey may have had an additional incentive for taking aim at Howe. In 1837 Howe publicly criticized "the President of Amherst College" for promoting evangelical revivals on his campus. Before the Boston Phrenological Society, Howe scolded Humphrey for "the fanatical excitement, the terror, the agony, the intense cerebral action which he was exciting in youths committed to his care." S. G. Howe,

A Discourse on the Social Relations of Man; Delivered before the Boston Phrenological Society, at the Close of Their Course of Lectures (Boston, 1837), 34.

53. Dr. Heman Humphrey ("Watchman"), *New England Puritan,* 29 Oct. 1846.

54. Horace Mann to Howe, 4 June 1846, Mann Papers, MHS.

55. Horace Mann, "Note by the Editor," *Common School Journal,* 1 Feb. 1847, 48.

56. The Rev. Matthew Hale Smith, "The Ark of God on a New Cart," *Boston Recorder,* 15 Oct. 1846, 166.

57. "Causes of the Increase of Public Wickedness," *New England Puritan,* 10 Dec. 1846.

58. "Moral Condition of Boston," *Boston Recorder,* 15 Oct. 1846. The sermon, delivered by Matthew Hale Smith, was later published as *The Ark of God on a New Cart* (Boston, 1846).

59. Merle Curti, for example, described Mann's enemies as "bigots" who acted "without justification." Merle Curti, *The Social Ideas of American Educators* (Totowa, NJ, 1978), 109. Such a view may tell us more about the historians' own biases than it does about the very difficult dilemma faced by anyone attempting to establish a common ground of religious values for use in a democratic educational system. Calvinist critics quite rightly suggested that, if Mann had successfully removed all traces of orthodox "sectarianism" from the curriculum, the remainder would look remarkably like Mann's own liberal Unitarian beliefs. For a more evenhanded view of the issue, see Jonathan Messerli, *Horace Mann: A Biography* (New York, 1972), 315.

60. Raymond Culver, *Horace Mann and Religion in the Massachusetts Public Schools* (New Haven, 1929), 198. While Culver blames the entire controversy on the "religious prejudice" of some orthodox men, he compiles abundant evidence against Mann's claim that there was an extensive conspiracy against his reforms. Culver believes Mann's opposition was "comparatively isolated, instigated and carried through by a small group of individuals."

61. Horace Mann, *The Common School Controversy: Consisting of Three Letters of the Secretary of the Board of Education of the State of Massachusetts, in Reply to Charges Preferred against the Board, by the Editor of the Christian Witness* (Boston, 1844), 10.

62. Even such staunch Calvinist journals as the *New England Puritan* promoted the new doctrine of environmentalism. While they clung to the concept of pre-destination, they held the contradictory notion that "it is utterly impossible to prevent your children from being moulded in exact conformity to the bias and impressions you give them. These will govern, they will be masters. If you imprint the lovely image of virtue, and the sweeter and lovelier impress of piety in childhood, so as to give the balancing power to character, you will see the same image, bold, beautiful, distinct, in the man." "Character Formed in Early Life," *New England Puritan,* 13 July 1845. The most important work of the orthodox nurture movement was Horace Bushnell, *Views of Christian Nurture* (Hartford, 1847). See also Dr. Heman Humphrey, *Domestic Education* (Amherst, 1840). For a review of orthodox and liberal theories of child nurture, see Bernard Wishy, *The Child and the Republic: The Dawn of Modern American Child Nurture* (Philadelphia, 1968), 11–66.

63. Myra C. Glenn, *Campaigns against Corporal Punishment: Prisoners, Sailors, Women and Children in Antebellum America* (Albany, NY, 1984), 145–146; Carl Kaestle, *Pillars of the Republic: Common Schools and American Society, 1780–1860* (New York, 1983), 87–88, 180; Michael Katz, *The Irony of Early School Reform: Educational Innovation in Mid-Nineteenth Century Massachusetts* (Cambridge, 1968), 152–153; Wishy, *The Child and the Republic*, 22–23; Daniel Walker Howe, "The Decline of Calvinism: An Approach to Its Study," *Comparative Studies in Society and History* 14 (1972): 306–327; Daniel Walker Howe, *The Unitarian Conscience: Harvard Moral Philosophy, 1805–1861* (Cambridge, 1970), 100–106. Given the common ground shared by liberals and many orthodox, some historians have concluded that the epic struggle which Howe and Mann felt they were waging against the foes of progress was largely a product of their own imaginations. Mann's biographer, Jonathan Messerli, suggests that Mann suffered from a "conspiracy complex" which led him to exaggerate the extent of his opposition in order to feed his self-image as a martyr to the cause of educational Truth. If, as Messerli suggests, Mann's belief that he was hounded by an orthodox conspiracy was largely self-delusion, then this was a delusion fully shared by Howe and reinforced by his friendship. Messerli, *Horace Mann*, 274, 332–334.

64. Writing at the beginning of the next century, Thomas Wentworth Higginson, a contemporary of Howe and Mann's, noted the fact that this circle of reformers was battling a form of Calvinism that was already well on its way to extinction. Higginson was speaking of Howe's friend, Theodore Parker, but his comments apply to Howe and Mann as well. Writing about Parker's powerful attacks on the revivals of the Second Great Awakening, Higginson wrote that "the difficulty was that they were just such discourses as he would have preached in the time of Edwards and the [First] 'Great Awakening;' and the point which many thought the one astonishing feature of the new excitement, its almost entire omission of the 'terrors of the Lord,'—the far gentler and more winning type of religion it displayed, and from which it confessedly drew much of its power,—this was entirely ignored in Mr. Parker's sermons. He was too hard at work in combating the evangelical orthodoxy to recognize its altered phases. Forging lightning-rods against the tempest, he did not see that the height of the storm had passed by." Thomas Wentworth Higginson, *Contemporaries* (Boston, 1899), 52.

65. "The Heresy of Love," *Christian Observatory*, Sept. 1847, 393.

66. Rev. A. W. McClure, "Laura Bridgman," *Christian Observatory* (March 1847): 180–189.

67. William B. Fowle to Horace Mann, 6 February 1847, Mann Papers, MHS; *Eleventh AR*, 35; McClure, "Laura Bridgman."

68. McClure, "Laura Bridgman."

69. *Christian Register*, 27 March 1847; "The Asylum for the Blind," *North American Review* (April 1845): 499–500.

70. *Thirteenth AR*. While the state of Massachusetts had agreed to pay the tuition for twenty blind students, Howe refused to reject any for mere monetary reasons and

had allowed almost twice that many Massachusetts students (37) to attend. At the same time, state funds were reduced because funds designated for education of the blind were pooled with similar funds to pay tuition for the state's deaf students to attend the American Asylum at Hartford. The American Asylum's decision to allow deaf students to attend there at a younger age meant that Perkins no longer enjoyed the use of an annual surplus in this fund. While a study of the economics of the Perkins school is beyond the scope of this work, there is ample circumstantial evidence to suggest that Howe's loose management style may have also added to the school's financial difficulties. Howe found it degrading to have to worry about pragmatic concerns like money when his cause was righteous. And when his cause was not just but simply personal, he displayed a similar difficulty in managing his money.

71. Howe, *Fifteenth Annual Report* (Cambridge, 1847), 29.
72. Ibid.
73. Ibid.
74. Ibid., 31.

9. Disillusionment

1. Wight, Teachers' Journals (hereafter TJ), 29 Aug. 1845, Laura Bridgman Papers, Perkins (hereafter BPP).
2. Julia Ward Howe, *Reminiscences* (Boston, 1900), 151; Gary Williams, *Hungry Heart: The Literary Emergence of Julia Ward Howe* (Amherst, 1999), 78.
3. Lamson, *Life and Education*, 278.
4. Howe to Lieber, 17 April 45, Lieber Papers, Huntington.
5. Harriet Martineau to Howe, 15 August 1845, Howe Papers, Perkins (hereafter HPP).
6. Sarah Wight, TJ, 28 September 1845; Rogers to Howe, 26 May 1845, HPP.
7. Howe to Lieber, 17 April 45, Lieber Papers, Huntington.
8. Wight, TJ, 15 September 1845.
9. Howe, *Fifteenth Annual Report* (Boston, 1847) (hereafter *Fifteenth AR*), 27.
10. Ibid.
11. Wight, TJ, 29 Aug. 1845, 15 Nov. 1845, 12 Dec. 1845.
12. Lamson, *Life and Education*, 323.
13. Wight, TJ, 9 Feb. 1846, 23 Dec. 1845, 24 Oct. 1845, 4 Nov. 1845.
14. Wight, TJ, 2 Apr.1847, 10 March 1846.
15. Elliott and Hall, *Laura Bridgman*, 176; Wight, TJ, Sept. 1846.
16. Laura Bridgman to Mary Thayer, 20 Nov. 1845, BPP; Elliott and Hall, *Laura Bridgman*, 223.
17. Howe, *Fourteenth Annual Report* (Cambridge, 1846) (hereafter *Fourteenth AR*), 30; Wight, TJ, 9 Feb. 1846, 7 Jan. 46, 13 Dec. 1845; Lamson, *Life and Education*, 304, 311, 317; Elliott and Hall, *Laura Bridgman*, 200.
18. Sarah Wight, TJ, 7 Jan. 1847.

19. *Fifteenth AR*, 33; Wight, TJ, 13 Dec. 1845, 16 Feb. 1847.

20. Lamson, *Life and Education*, 322–323; "Laura Bridgman on the Massachusetts Volunteers," *Emancipator*, 17 March 1847.

21. Howe, *Eighteenth Annual Report* (Cambridge, 1850) (hereafter *Eighteenth AR*), 52.

22. Ibid.

23. Wight, TJ, June 1846; *Eighteenth AR*, 68.

24. *Eighteenth AR*, 58.

25. Lamson, *Life and Education*, 330–331.

26. *Eighteenth AR*, 59; Lamson, *Life and Education*, 320.

27. *Fifteenth AR*, 31.

28. George Combe to Howe, 13 July 1845, Howe Papers, Houghton (hereafter HPH).

29. Maria Edgeworth to Howe, 1 May 1845, typescript copy, HPP.

30. Harriet Martineau to Howe, 15 Aug. 1845, HPP.

31. Wight, TJ, 8 Feb. 1847.

32. Wight, TJ, 1 Jan. 1846; Lamson, *Life and Education*, 280.

33. *Fifteenth AR*, 23–24; Howe to Sarah Wight, 17 June 1846, HPP.

34. Elliott and Hall, *Laura Bridgman*, 218.

35. Wight, TJ, 7 Aug. 1847, 16 Feb. 1847.

36. Ibid., 24 Dec. 1845.

37. Ibid., 24 Dec. 1845, 4 April 1847.

38. Ibid., 24 Dec. 1845, 13 July 1847.

39. Lamson, *Life and Education*, 318.

40. Ibid.

41. Wight, TJ, 24 Dec. 1845.

42. Ibid., 1 May 1847.

43. Ibid., 11 July 1847.

44. Ibid., 12 July 1847.

45. *Zion Herald and Wesleyan Journal*, 15 March 1848.

46. *Eighteenth AR*, 47.

47. Harold Schwartz, *Samuel Gridley Howe* (Cambridge, 1956), chs. 11–12.

48. G. A. Rupell to Howe, 16 March 1849, HPP.

49. *Eighteenth AR*, 63.

50. Ibid., 65.

51. Ibid., 64–66.

52. Lamson, *Life and Education*, 290.

53. Wight, TJ, 10 Sept. 1846; Elliott and Hall, *Laura Bridgman*, 197.

54. *Eighteenth AR*, 85.

10. A New Theory of Human Nature

1. John Davies, *Phrenology, Fad and Science: A Nineteenth-Century Crusade* (New Haven, 1955), ch. 1; Mary Ellen Bogin, "The Meaning of Heredity in American Medi-

cine and Popular Health Advice: 1771–1860" (Ph.D. diss, Cornell University, 1990), 176–177.

2. S. G. Howe, *Address Delivered at the Anniversary Celebration of the Boston Phrenological Society* (Boston, 1836), 23.

3. Howe, *Sixteenth Annual Report* (Cambridge, 1848) (hereafter *Sixteenth AR*), 7–10.

4. Howe, *Fifteenth Annual Report* (Cambridge, 1847) (hereafter *Fifteenth AR*), 16.

5. Ibid., 16, 10.

6. Jacob Doughty to Howe, 28 May 1840, Howe Papers, Perkins (hereafter HPP); Maria Brackett to Howe, 5 July 1847, HPP.

7. Howe, *Fourteenth Annual Report* (Cambridge, 1846) (hereafter *Fourteenth AR*), 12.

8. Ibid., 14–15.

9. Ronald Walters, *American Reformers 1815–1860* (New York, 1997), 219–222; David Rothman, *The Discovery of the Asylum* (Boston, 1990), ch. 10; Philip M. Ferguson, *Abandoned to Their Fate: Social Policy and Practice toward Severely Retarded People in America, 1820–1920* (Philadelphia, 1994), 45–81.

10. Maria S. Brackett to Howe, 5 July 1847, HPP.

11. James Harris to Howe, 18 Feb. 1837, HPP.

12. *Fifteenth AR, 4–6.*

13. Some of the students placed under Howe's care in those years not only were blind but also were what he described as "feeble-minded" or "idiotic." He soon concluded that these children did not belong in a school like Perkins; but since there was no other institution available for them, he did his best to help them. He found that, under the school's regimen of orderly routine, personal hygiene, and education, most of these children made small improvements. Inspired by his success, he began a successful campaign to create the nation's first school for the mentally handicapped. In 1848 the school opened on the grounds of the Perkins Institution, with Howe serving as its first director. Harold Schwartz, *Samuel Gridley Howe: Social Reformer, 1801–1876* (Cambridge, 1956), ch. 10; *Sixteenth AR, 4.*

14. Ibid., 36–37.

15. Ibid., 37.

16. Ibid., 9.

17. Ibid., 9–10, 44.

18. Charles E. Rosenberg, "Bitter Fruit," *No Other Gods,* (Baltimore, 1961); Bogin, "Meaning of Heredity," ch. 2.

19. *Sixteenth AR, 50.*

20. Ibid., 46–47.

21. Ibid., 50.

22. Howe, *Seventeenth Annual Report* (Cambridge, 1849) (hereafter *Seventeenth AR*), 24.

23. Howe, "Cause and Prevention of Idiocy," *Massachusetts Quarterly Review,* June 1848, 331.

24. *Fourteenth AR, 37.*

25. Ibid., 37; Howe, "Laura Bridgman," *Barnard's American Journal of Education* (De-

cember 1857): 383. The Bridgman family's objections to Howe's "small brain" remarks are in Lina Simmons to Florence Howe Hall, 13 Sept. 1889, Laura Bridgman Papers, Perkins.

26. Howe, *Thirteenth Annual Report* (Boston, 1845), 48.

27. Ibid., 83.

28. Howe, *Eighteenth Annual Report* (Cambridge, 1850), 82–85.

29. Ibid., 85.

11. My Sunny Home

1. Howe, *Eighteenth Annual Report* (Cambridge, 1850) (hereafter *Eighteenth AR*), 47; Francis Lieber to Dorothea Dix, n.d 1851?, Lieber Papers, Huntington Library. Lieber's article is in Smithsonian Contributions to Knowledge, vol. 2, Art. 2, 1851.

2. Laura Bridgman to Sarah Wight, 29 Dec. 1850, Laura Bridgman Papers, Perkins (hereafter BPP).

3. Laura Bridgman to Sarah Wight, 10 Feb. 1851, BPP.

4. Laura Bridgman to Sarah Wight Bond, 8 May 1853, BPP. Letters between Laura and Mary Swift Lamson can be found in the Lamson Papers, Massachusetts Historical Society (hereafter LP).

5. Maud Howe Elliott and Florence Howe Hall, *Laura Bridgman: Dr. Howe's Famous Pupil and What He Taught Her* (Boston, 1904), 278.

6. Laura Bridgman to Sarah Wight Bond, 6 Nov. 185?, BPP.

7. Howe to J. W. Brown, 30 Nov. 1852, Howe Papers, Perkins (hereafter HPP); *Eighteenth AR*, 88.

8. *Eighteenth AR*, 14–27.

9. While this proposal failed, Howe eventually succeeded in creating a "cottage system" at the Perkins School. Rather than living in a centralized building, children lived in smaller houses on the school grounds, each supervised by a "house mother." Howe believed that this innovation would, to some extent, recreate the experience of family living and counteract some of the harmful effects of institutional life.

10. Howe to Harmony Bridgman, 23 Oct. 1852; Howe to Laura Bridgman, 6 Dec. 1852, HPP.

11. Laura Bridgman to Mary Swift Lamson, 12 Dec. 1852, LP.

12. Laura Bridgman to Mary Swift Lamson, 12 Dec. 1852, LP; Harmony Bridgman to Howe, 27 Dec. 1852, BPP.

13. Mary Swift Lamson, *Life and Education of Laura Bridgman* (Boston, 1881; New York, 1975), 341; Elliott and Hall, *Laura Bridgman*, 262–264.

14. Howe to Dorothea Dix, 5 Nov. 1853, HPP.

15. Julie Burnham, "Reminiscences of Laura Dewey Bridgman" (typescript copy, BPP, 1937).

16. E. C. Sanford, "The Writings of Laura Bridgman," *Overland Monthly*, 1887; Laura Bridgman's Journals, 2 January, 1850, BPP.

17. H. W. Bond, *Transcript*, 29 November 1881, clipping in LP; Reminiscence of Louise Reed Steward in *Valley News*, undated clipping in Rauner Library, Dartmouth.

18. Lamson, *Life and Education*, 352, 350.

19. Mrs. Herrick to Miss Wood, 26 June 1878, BPP.

20. Lamson, *Life and Work*, 355–356.

21. Laura Bridgman to Howe, 26 Oct. 1862, BPP.

22. Elliott and Hall, *Laura Bridgman*, 286.

23. Harold Schwartz, *Samuel Gridley Howe: Social Reformer, 1801–1876* (Cambridge, 1956), 275, ch. 18.

24. Elliott and Hall, *Laura Bridgman*, 310.

25. Laura Bridgman to Mary Swift Lamson, 30 Jan. 1876, LP.

26. G. Stanley Hall, "Laura Bridgman," *Mind: A Quarterly Review of Psychology and Philosophy* 14 (April 1879): 151.

27. Ibid., 156–167.

28. Robert M. Young, *Mind, Brain and Adaptation in the Nineteenth Century* (Oxford, 1970), passim.

29. See, for example, Charles Darwin, *The Expression of the Emotions in Man and Animals* (New York, 1896), 267; Hall, "Laura Bridgman," *The Nation*, 24 Oct. 1878, 259.

30. Lamson, *Life and Education*, 367. This poem was published at the time and widely admired, more for its sentiment and its novelty than for its poetic value.

12. Legacy

1. "Anatomical Observations on the Brain and Several Sense Organs of the Blind Deaf-Mute, Laura Dewey Bridgman," *American Journal of Psychology* 3, no.3 (1890).

2. "Laura Bridgman's Funeral," *Boston Daily Advertiser*, 27 May 1889.

3. Sophia Shaler, *Masters of Fate: The Power of the Will* (New York, 1921), 22. Shaler explains that Sullivan did not simply adopt Howe's method but improved it. One of her significant innovations was a new method of spelling. Rather than spelling out separate words, she taught Keller "such flow of sentences as might fall upon a normal child's ears, believing that, as a baby learns to pick out and recognize sounds, so Helen would gradually distinguish words and phrases and comprehend them." Shaler speculates that this may account for Keller's "rich vocabulary and sweep of imagery." Conversely, Laura's experience of words as discrete entities, rather than elements of longer phrases, may account, in part, for her unique but often wooden writing style. See also Frances Koestler, *The Unseen Minority: A Social History of Blindness in America* (New York, 1976), 455.

4. Michael Anagnos, "Helen Keller: A Second Laura Bridgman," *56th Annual Report of the Perkins Institution* (Boston, 1888), 10.

5. Helen Keller, *Midstream: My Later Life* (New York, 1929), 245–246.

6. William James, "Laura Bridgman," *Atlantic*, 1904, 98, 96.

7. Ibid., 95–96, 98.

8. Helen Keller to Dr. Farrell, 6 Oct. 1937, typescript copy, Dartmouth.

9. Dorothy Herrmann, *Helen Keller: A Life* (New York, 1998), passim; Koestler, *Unseen Minority*, 451–457, 463–464.

10. Margaret A. Winzer, *The History of Special Education: From Isolation to Integration* (Washington, DC, 1933), 211; David Warren, *Blindness and Early Childhood Development* (New York, 1977), 174; Koestler, *Unseen Minority*, 466, 474–476.

11. Few of those now classified as deaf-blind are entirely devoid of both sight and hearing, as Laura Bridgman was. Because the label of deaf-blindness covers a wide range of conditions, estimates of the number of people afflicted with a double sensory handicap vary widely; some researchers estimate that more than 35,000 deaf-blind adults and 11,000 deaf-blind children live in the United States today. *Eighteenth Annual Report U.S. Department of Education* (1996), cited in *Educating One and All: Students with Disabilities and Standards-Based Reform* (Washington, D.C., 1997), 93. For a discussion of deaf-blind people in the twentieth century, see Herrmann, *Helen Keller*, 337–343; Koestler, *Unseen Minority*, 469–470.

12. Russ Rymer, *Genie: A Scientific Tragedy* (New York, 1994); Oliver Sacks, "To See and Not See," in *An Anthropologist on Mars: Seven Paradoxical Tales* (New York, 1995); Susan Schaller, *A Man without Words* (Berkeley, 1991).

13. Paul K. Longmore, "Uncovering the Hidden History of People with Disabilities," *Reviews in American History* 15, no.3 (September), 357; Benedicte Ingstad and Susan Reynolds Whyte, eds., *Disability and Culture* (Berkeley, 1995); Joseph Shapiro, *No Pity: People with Disabilities Forging a New Civil Rights Movement* (New York, 1993); Winzer, *History of Special Education*, 380–381.

Acknowledgments

I live and teach in a small New Hampshire town just a short drive from Laura Bridgman's birthplace and the secluded hilltop graveyard where she and her family are buried. But, oddly enough, I first came across this quintessential New England story in the stacks of the Emory University library in Atlanta, in a two-sentence reference in a text on American ideas about human nature. I was drawn immediately to Laura's plight and Howe's curious experiment, and further investigations grew into my doctoral dissertation at Emory. This work has been greatly enriched by the thoughtful readings I received at that early stage from Patrick Allitt, E. Brooks Holifield, and Jean-Christophe Agnew. I am particularly grateful to Jonathan Prude for his probing questions and his friendship and encouragement as this manuscript took shape.

The Spencer Foundation was instrumental in supporting the research and writing of this book, providing me with a dissertation grant to complete the first draft and a postdoctoral grant that allowed me to make final revisions. Research for this book was done at a number of libraries and schools for the blind. The Massachusetts Historical Society, the Library Company of Philadelphia, and the American Antiquarian Society each provided excellent library services and helpful counsel, as well as the financial support of Mellon Research grants. Thanks also to the staffs at Harvard's Houghton Library and the Rauner Library at Dartmouth College. I particularly want to acknowledge the help of Kenneth Stuckey, research librarian at the Perkins School for the Blind, who shared his insights into the history of Perkins and provided me with a congenial place to work and ready access to the school's rich archive.

My colleagues in the Humanities Department at Colby-Sawyer College in New Hampshire generously encouraged me as I completed this project. Thanks especially to Olivia Storey for her thoughtful editorial advice and to Don Coonley for adjusting his own busy teaching schedule to allow me the time to make final revisions. A number of other friends and colleagues read some or all of this manuscript and contributed useful suggestions: Marcia Carlisle, Carl Dimow, Bruce Freeberg, Anne Page Stecker, Charles Strickland, Conrad E. Wright, and Harvard University Press's anonymous reviewers. I also benefited from the excellent editorial guidance of Joyce Seltzer, David Lobenstine, and Susan Wallace Boehmer at HUP.

Finally, I want to thank my family for their steadfast support during the research and writing of this book. My children, Charlie and Emma, pulled me back from the nineteenth century when I needed it. The lessons I learned while watching them grow up have enriched my understanding of Laura Bridgman's childhood, and the experience of being their father and teacher helped me to think about Laura's guardians with greater insight and humility. My own parents supported this work in a variety of ways, most of all by teaching me the value of ideas. Finally, I want to thank my wife, Lauren Bray, to whom this book is dedicated—for listening to this story again and again as it has evolved in my mind, for sharing her own insights about education and childhood, and for giving me her loving encouragement at every step along the way.

E.F.

Andover, NH

Index